Statistical Analysis of Employment Data in Discrimination Lawsuits and EEO Audits

A statistical guide for attorneys, human resource professionals and EEO compliance personnel

Dwight D. Steward, Ph.D.

Econometrics Publishing

Palo Alto, California

Boston, Massachusetts

The opinions expressed in this manuscript are solely the opinions of the author and do not represent the opinions or thoughts of the publisher.

STATISTICAL ANALYSIS OF EMPLOYMENT DATA IN DISCRIMINATION LAWSUITS AND EEO AUDITS

A statistical guide for attorneys, human resource professionals and EEO compliance personnel

Econometrics Publishing

Palo Alto, California

Boston, Massachusetts

ISBN-10: 0615340504

ISBN-13: 978-0-615-34050-0

To my wife, Michelle, and daughters, Kelli and Kasi, and my parents for their inspiration

I would like to thank my friends and colleagues, Scott Angelius, Jeannie Elliott, Stephanie Botello, Doug Berg, Brandy Brookshier, Amy Raub, and Laura Howard for their invaluable assistance in writing this manuscript.

I would also like to thank the many economists, statisticians, attorneys and friends who have reviewed this manuscript and whose professional relationships have contributed so much to this book.

Table of Contents

Introduction

Statistical analysis can play a pivotal role in both avoiding and settling employment disputes. Major employers routinely use relatively sophisticated statistical analyses to audit their decisions concerning hiring, promotions, and compensation. Similarly, it is common in large employment disputes to use statistical data to either prove or disprove allegations of discrimination. The way in which employment data is analyzed can have a significant impact on how the decision-makers, the judge, or the jury interpret the statistical findings.

I began writing this book about twelve years ago to help these individuals better understand the statistical methodologies used in employment analyses. My primary goal is to provide human resource professionals, attorneys, and Equal Employment Opportunity (EEO) officials with a textbook on these methodologies that is comprehensive but understandable.

While this book focuses on the statistics used in employment discrimination cases, it is not a statistics cookbook of magic mathematical formulas. Instead, I provide the reader with the conceptual framework that is based on tried-and-true statistical principles, current labor and employment research, and my professional experiences as a researcher, teacher, and expert witness.

Hopefully, through the many revisions that have been made during the past 12 years while drafting this manuscript, I will be able to reach these individuals in a meaningful way.

The book is organized into four main sections. In the **first section**, I provide a general introduction to how statistics are used in employment discrimination lawsuits. I discuss the typical research objectives of statistical analyses in employment discrimination cases with claims involving disparate impact and disparate treatment. This section also includes a discussion of the employment data that is routinely included in a statistical analysis of employment discrimination.

There is a description of the typical fact and expert witnesses who are called in these types of employment cases. This section concludes with a discussion of the special concerns that arise in class certification hearings and the implications of Daubert and related cases on statistical evidence. The information in this section is particularly useful for attorneys who are not very familiar with class action employment discrimination cases. The section on electronic discovery will be useful to more seasoned employment attorneys as well.

In the first section, I also discuss the techniques that are used to describe employment data, including techniques used to create descriptive statistics for employment data. Finally, part of this section discusses the use of Excel spreadsheets to calculate descriptive statistics.

In the **second section** of the book, I provide a concise, non-mathematical discussion of the statistical foundations that underlie employment discrimination analyses. The objective of this section is to provide the reader with enough of a background in statistics to allow him or her to develop a deeper understanding of the statistical methodologies used in employment cases. The statistics discussion in this section of the book requires that readers have an understanding of only basic arithmetic. The formulas may be skipped without losing the underlying theme.

The discussion develops the concept of statistical hypothesis testing. I also explore how research questions are turned into testable statistical hypotheses and how these tests are performed in practice. The section closes with a discussion on how some courts have handled statistical evidence and defined 'statistical significance' in employment discrimination cases.

The **third section** contains chapters devoted to the analysis of hiring, salary, promotion, and termination discrimination claims. In these chapters, I discuss the economics and procedures underlying these employment issues. Using the statistical concepts developed in the second section, I present examples that provide the reader with insights into the statistical methodologies used in hiring, promotion, and salary discrimination cases. The chapters in this section are non-mathematical in nature.

Economics and statistics are not spectator sports. The **fourth section**, titled 'Employment Statistics in Action', provides additional examples, case references, and an employment and labor research bibliography that readers can use to further their understanding of the concepts presented in the text. This section includes an extensive dictionary of the statistical and economic terms that arise in employment analyses of discrimination. Many of the entries for statistics terms include completed examples. There is also a list of legal employment cases that have used statistical evidence, a research bibliography, and standard statistical tables for the reader.

Section I

Background on EEO Litigation

Employment Statistics in the Courts

Employment statistics can be the centerpiece in employment litigation and EEO audits and investigations. The objective of this chapter is to give the reader a basic understanding of how statistics are used in employment cases and to provide insights into the discrimination allegations surrounding a company's employment decisions.

This chapter begins by providing an introduction to the role of labor economists and statisticians in class-action and pattern-and-practice employment discrimination lawsuits. We also discuss major equal opportunity legislation. Following the introduction to class-action employment discrimination lawsuits, there is a discussion of how the testimony of fact and expert witnesses impacts the statistical analysis of employment discrimination claims. There is a special emphasis in this section on how the testimony of company representatives and human resource professionals helps (or hinders) the statistical analysis of employment discrimination claims. This section concludes with a discussion of the special research issues that arise in class certification hearings. This section also explores the implications of Daubert and related cases on the presentation of statistical evidence in the courts.

Background

Since the 1960s, legislators have taken a number of steps to ensure that employees are not discriminated against on the basis of their age, race, gender, national origin, or disability. The major laws and executive orders include the Equal Pay Act of 1963, the Civil Right Act of 1964, the Age Discrimination in Employment Act of 1967, the American with Disabilities Act of 1990, and the Civil Rights Act of 1991. Other legislation has addressed issues concerning the rights of Vietnam-era veterans and family and medical leave issues. Executive Orders 11246 and 1141 have explicitly forbidden employment discrimination by federal contractors.

Charges of Employment Discrimination

Many federal and state agencies have been created to administer and enforce the various equal employment opportunity laws. The agencies include the Equal Employment Opportunity Commission (EEOC), the Office of Federal Contract Compliance Programs (OFCCP), and the Department of Labor's Wage and Hour division. The EEOC, the most widely known federal anti-discrimination agency, administers Title VII, the Age Discrimination in Employment Act, the Equal Pay Act, and the American with Disabilities Act. In addition, most states have enacted fair employment practice laws and created state agencies to handle individual complaints.

The procedures for suing for employment discrimination vary. However, cases involving Title VII claims, which comprise the largest percentage of cases, follow a consistent procedure. First, the charging party must file a charge with the EEOC or a suitable state agency within a specified period after the allegation of discrimination. This period ranges from 180 days to 300 days, depending on the jurisdiction and the type of case. Following the initial filing, the responsible agency investigates the discrimination charge by interviewing witnesses and, if warranted, performs an initial employment data probe.

After investigating the charge and drawing up the preliminary findings, the agency typically takes one of three actions: (1) ends the investigation, (2) issues a right-to-sue letter, or (3) sues on behalf of the charging party. The EEOC sues on behalf of the charging party relatively infrequently. If the EEOC does not sue on behalf of the charging party, the charging party will drop the issue, retain an attorney or represent himself or herself as a *pro se*.

Historical Data on EEOC Charges

The table on the following page shows that the EEOC processed between 75,428 and 82,792 charges of discrimination each year between 2000 and 2007. For comparison, there are approximately 130 million workers in the U.S.

As the table shows, discrimination on the basis of race, gender and age are the most common EEOC charges. In most years, race, gender, and age charges make up approximately 35%, 30% and 20%, respectively, of the total discrimination charges received by the EEOC. In recent years, age and retaliation charges have increased. Charges of discrimination based on national origin, particularly after the 9/11 terrorist attacks, have also increased. National origin charges now comprise 11% of all EEOC discrimination charges.

EEOC Discrimination Charge Statistics, Fiscal Years 2000 through 2007

	FY 2000	FY 2001	FY 2002	FY 2003	FY 2004	FY 2005	FY 2006	FY 2007
Total Charges	79,896	80,840	84,442	81,293	79,432	75,428	75,768	82,792
Race	28,945	28,912	29,910	28,526	27,696	26,740	27,238	30,510
	36.2%	35.8%	35.4%	35.1%	34.9%	35.5%	35.9%	37.0%
Sex	25,194	25,140	25,536	24,362	24,249	23,094	23,247	24,826
	31.5%	31.1%	30.2%	30.0%	30.5%	30.6%	30.7%	30.1%
National Origin	7,792	8,025	9,046	8,450	8,361	8,035	8,327	9,396
	9.8%	9.9%	10.7%	10.4%	10.5%	10.7%	11.0%	11.4%
Religion	1,939	2,127	2,572	2,532	2,466	2,340	2,541	2,880
	2.4%	2.6%	3.0%	3.1%	3.1%	3.1%	3.4%	3.5%
Retaliation - All Statutes	21,613	22,257	22,768	22,690	22,740	22,278	22,555	26,663
	27.1%	27.5%	27.0%	27.9%	28.6%	29.5%	29.8%	32.3%
Retaliation - Title VII only	19,753	20,407	20,814	20,615	20,240	19,429	19,560	23,371
	24.7%	25.2%	24.6%	25.4%	25.5%	25.8%	25.8%	28.3%
Age	16,008	17,405	19,921	19,124	17,837	16,585	16,548	19,103
	20.0%	21.5%	23.6%	23.5%	22.5%	22.0%	21.8%	23.2%
Disability	15,864	16,470	15,964	15,377	15,376	14,893	15,575	17,734
	19.9%	20.4%	18.9%	18.9%	19.4%	19.7%	20.6%	21.4%
Equal Pay Act	1,270	1,251	1,256	1,167	1,011	970	861	818
	1.6%	1.5%	1.5%	1.4%	1.3%	1.3%	1.1%	1.0%

Note that the number of total charges for any given year is lower than the sum of charges shown in this table. This is because individuals may cite more than one type of discrimination in a single charge. For instance, an older female employee may allege both age and gender discrimination in a single charge.
Source: www.eeoc.gov/stats/charges.html.

EEOC Discrimination Charges and the Economy

The relationship between the economy and the number of EEOC charges is particularly interesting. Conventional wisdom suggests a number of potential linkages. It is commonly believed that when the economy slows, the number of discrimination charges and employment discrimination lawsuits increases.

In a slow economy, all other factors being equal, employers tend to reduce their workforces. As an employer's workforce contracts, the likelihood of an employment discrimination charge is thought to increase, because some of the terminated employees will belong to protected classes and believe that their termination was the result of discrimination. Additionally, there are fewer salary increases and promotional opportunities in a slow economic environment, which further increases the possibility of employment disputes regarding the employer's motivations.

Conversely, when the economy is growing and jobs are being created, employment discrimination charges are thought to decrease. A growing economy with expanding job opportunities decreases the likelihood that any given employer will have to lay off workers. Employees are also more likely to have multiple employment opportunities and will be more likely to seek other employment if they feel that they are being treated unfairly. Increased employer profitability during good economic times also generally increases employees' opportunities for promotions and salary increases.

Historical EEOC charge data generally exhibits a pattern that is consistent with the conventional wisdom. The figure on the following page plots the percentage growth in the number of EEOC charges and the annual change in U.S. gross domestic product (GDP). GDP is a measure of the U.S. economy that shows the total market value of goods and services produced by workers and capital within the U.S. borders during a given period of time.

As the figure shows, between 1994 and 2007, economic growth was generally correlated with a decrease in the number of EEOC discrimination charges.

This trend is particularly evident over the last five years. For instance, in 2003, the number of charges decreased 3.73% from 2002. In that same time period, the U.S. experienced an increase in GDP growth from 3.57% in 2002 to 5.93% in 2003. Additionally, in 2007, following three consecutive years of decreasing GDP growth rates, the number of EEOC discrimination charges increased 9.27% from the previous year.

EEOC Discrimination Charges and Economic Conditions are Correlated

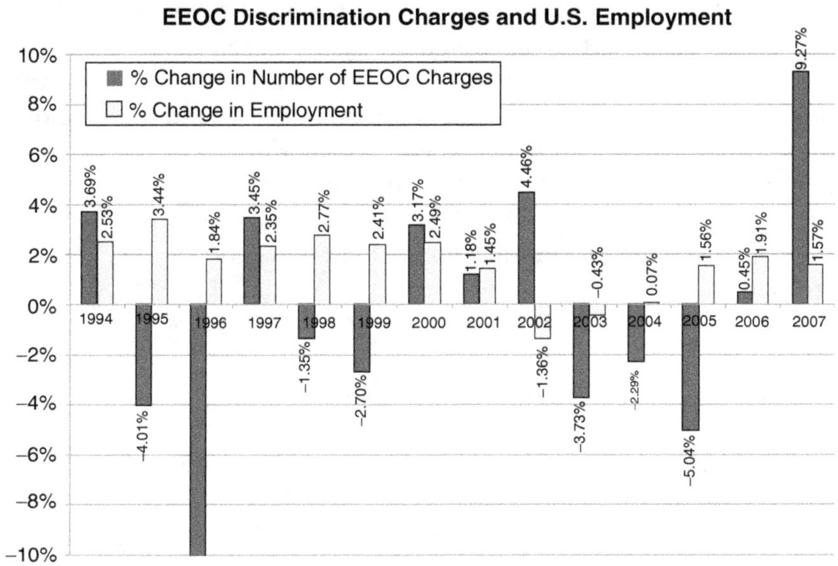

This figure plots the percentage growth in the number of EEOC charges and the annual change in U.S. gross domestic product (GDP). The percentage change in EEOC charges is the percentage change in the number of EEOC charges filed from the previous year.

Source: www.eeoc.gov/stats/charges.html

The percentage change in GDP is the change in GDP from the previous year. GDP is the total market value of goods and services produced by workers and capital within the U.S. borders during a given period of time.

Source: research.stlouisfed.org/fred2/series/GDP

Disparate Treatment and Disparate Impact

Many discrimination cases involve claims of disparate treatment by an employer and/or through the employer's employment practices. Disparate treatment is intuitively straightforward. In disparate treatment cases, employers allegedly treat certain individuals less favorably because of their race, religion, sex, age, disability or national origin. Proof in these types of discrimination cases typically hinges on the charging party, or plaintiff, being able to show that the employer's conduct was intentionally discriminatory.

In disparate impact cases, employers allegedly use a selection process that disproportionately affects protected group members. The disparate impact paradigm, which is derived from the landmark *Griggs v. Duke Power Co.*, 401 U.S. 424 (1971) U.S. Supreme Court decision, is used to prove discrimination and makes it illegal to employ a selection procedure that disproportionately affects protected group members even if the employer did not intend to discriminate. The proof in these types of discrimination cases typically hinges on the charging party's ability to demonstrate that the employment-related selection process produced a disparate impact on the protected group and that the selection process was not job-related.

Class-Action Employment Lawsuits

A class-action employment discrimination lawsuit is brought by an individual or several individuals on behalf of a larger group of employees. In class-action employment lawsuits, it is argued that it would be impractical or impossible for individual employees to bring individual lawsuits. Instead, the named plaintiff or plaintiffs in the employment discrimination class-action lawsuit represents the interests of the absent class members. For a class to be certified and for an action to be brought by the representatives of the employee class against the employer, the composition of the class must meet certain requirements. Most of the class-action employment discrimination lawsuits that have been certified since the 1970s have involved racial, gender, or age discrimination.

Although the number of class-action discrimination lawsuits has fallen since the 1970s, the importance of class-action employment discrimination lawsuits in the business environment has increased significantly. For instance, more than 1,000 class-action employment discrimination lawsuits were filed in the U.S. in 1976, whereas fewer than 100 were filed in 2000. However, in 2000 the average settlement received by the plaintiffs was more than 100 times that received in 1976, even after accounting for inflation.

In addition, the explicit and implicit costs of litigating an employment discrimination lawsuit have increased dramatically in recent decades. For example, the high-profile, class-action employment discrimination lawsuits filed against Coca Cola and Texaco took more than two years to get through the legal system and incurred significant costs for attorneys, litigation support professionals, and expert witnesses. The implicit cost of dealing with a class-action employment discrimination lawsuit has increased substantially as well. Some notable class-action lawsuits are listed in the figure below.

Notable Employment Discrimination Lawsuits	
Paige v. California	Alleged that the California Highway Patrol's promotional process discriminated against non-whites.
Bryant v. Bell Atlantic Maryland	Alleged that white males were treated more favorably with respect to mandatory overtime.
Dukes et al. v. Wal-Mart Stores, Inc.	Alleged that gender discrimination was present in pay and promotions.
Tyler v. Union Oil Co. of California	Alleged that there was age discrimination in the redeployment pool.
Allison v. Citgo Petrol. Corp.	Alleged that there was racial discrimination with respect to hiring, promotion, compensation, and training policies.
Robinson v. Metro-North Commuter	Alleged that there was a disparate impact on African-American employees with respect to employment decisions related to discipline and promotion.
Ingram v. Coca-Cola	Alleged that race discrimination was present in pay, promotions, and evaluations.

In many class-action employment discrimination lawsuits, the testimony of economists and statisticians is crucial and often takes center stage. Generally, economists and, to a lesser extent, statisticians provide expert witness testimony on the statistical significance of an employment disparity between protected and non-protected employees. A typical statistical analysis of employment discrimination in a class-action lawsuit could involve showing the likelihood that the observed employment-related shortfall could have been generated in the absence of discrimination, analyzing statistics related to the employer-defendant's defenses, or a critique of the reliability of the statistical evidence in the case. In many instances, the statistical analysis and related expert witness testimony include analyses that address all three of these issues. It often confounds people to learn that two experts can draw vastly different conclusions from the same set of data.

Role of Economists

Economists perform many different roles in employment cases.

- Provide testimony on the statistical and practical significance of an employment disparity between protected and non-protected employees.
- Construct damage models that can be used to compensate class members.
- Construct sampling models to help the court estimate class damages.

In practice, the statistical analysis of employment discrimination allegations in class-action lawsuits is quite involved. Depending on the complexity of the data and, more importantly, the complexity of the employer's employment processes, producing a reliable statistical study can take a significant amount of time. As will be discussed in detail in the following chapters, a statistical analysis requires the labor economist to construct an analysis database from the employer-defendant's employment data, closely study the employer-defendant's employment processes, and set up and estimate reliable statistical models of the employment processes in question.

Economists are also called upon to help construct damage models that, in theory, can be used to compensate class members. Many times the same expert used in the liability or class certification phase constructs a mathematical model that shows in terms of dollars how much the class members have collectively suffered as a result of the employment discrimination. For instance, statistical salary models of similarly situated employees have been used to estimate back- and front-pay losses in class-action cases.

In some cases, economists and statisticians have constructed sampling models to help the court estimate class damages. For instance, a personal injury class action, *Cimino v. Raymark Industries*, involved a sampling of the personal injury claims of more than 2,000 asbestos victims. In this case, the court extrapolated the damages for the remaining non-sampled class members from 160 individual cases.

Economists also often play an important role in pattern-and-practice employment lawsuits. Like class-action lawsuits, pattern-and-practice employment lawsuits allege that the employer-defendant has some type of employment practice that discriminates against members of a protected class. The major difference is that pattern-and-practice lawsuits involve a single or multiple plaintiffs who are suing on their own behalf rather than representing a class of employees. Statistical evidence is typically introduced in these types of employment cases to support or rebut the existence of a discriminatory employer practice or a pattern of discrimination. The discrimination allegations in these lawsuits may involve promotion, salary, employee discipline, employment conditions, and job ratings.

Economists in Pattern-and-Practice Employment Lawsuits

Salary Discrimination	In *Cullen v. Indiana Board of Trustees,* regression analyses were used to support a claim of gender-based discrimination in salaries.
Promotion Discrimination	In *Munoz v. Orr,* statisticians attempted to demonstrate promotion discrimination against Hispanic males. However, the expert ignored factors affecting promotion and failed to use regression analysis.
Termination Discrimination	In *Kadas v. MCI Systemhouse Corp,* statisticians attempted to demonstrate age-related discrimination in terminations. The evidence supported the defendant's case.
Lost Wages	In *Cummings v. Standard Register Co.*, the economist forecasted lost earnings due to discrimination

The analysis in pattern-and-practice employment discrimination cases tends to involve claims of disparate treatment. In disparate treatment cases, economists test statistical hypotheses that employers treat the protected employees less favorably than the way in which they treat members of the non-protected groups. Lawsuits involving discriminatory job assignments and biased employee discipline policies tend to involve claims of disparate treatment.

In disparate impact cases, economists are called upon to test statistical hypotheses concerning the effect of a particular employment practice on members of a protected group. Economists and statisticians are also frequently called in to investigate the validity of selection procedures. Discrimination lawsuits involving pre-hiring requirements and job testing are examples of cases that tend to involve claims of disparate impact.

In both disparate treatment and disparate impact, economists are required to identify the appropriate employee population, construct summary statistics from the data, and develop and test the appropriate statistical hypothesis. The statistical methods described in this manuscript are used in both types of litigation. The following chapters present many examples detailing how statistics are used in pattern-and-practice lawsuits.

Other Witnesses in Employment Cases

Unlike academic research, the employment discrimination research and analyses of labor economists and statisticians are impacted significantly by the work of related expert witnesses, the testimony of other witnesses, and the rules of the court. For instance, labor economists typically rely heavily on interviews and the deposition testimony of company representatives to learn about the employer-defendant's employment practices.

Employment Witness Roll Call

In employment discrimination class-action and pattern-and-practice cases, there are certain witnesses, in addition to the plaintiffs, who have an impact on the statistical analysis performed by the labor economist or statistician. Generally, these witnesses include the company's human resources representative, compensation representative, and industrial psychologist. An economist or statistician performing a statistical employment analysis uses the testimony of these individuals to learn about the company's contended employment practice.

Industrial psychologists who are retained in discrimination cases provide another important resource for the labor economist or statistician. The industrial psychologist tends to be the expert witness who provides the plaintiff or defendants with insights on the inner workings of the employment practice or employment selection process being challenged. For example, these experts provide testimony on checks and balances and the fairness of a company's job-performance rating system.

Witnesses Who Impact the Formulation of Statistical Employment Discrimination Models

Human Resources Representative	Testimonies and interviews help determine which factors the company views as being relevant for the employment policy at issue.
Compensation Representative	Testimonies and interviews provide an understanding of the company's compensation policies.
Industrial Psychologist	Testimonies and interviews provide insights on the inner workings of the employment practice or employment selection process at issue.

Legal Analysis in Employment Discrimination Litigation

In most employment discrimination cases there are a number of legal issues that the court must rule on prior to the case proceeding to trial. These issues or "matters of law" are argued either through legal briefs or in front of a judge. The issues, which are typically laid out in a party's motion for summary judgment or class certification brief, generally involve determining whether there is sufficient evidence to proceed to trial. If the judge rules that there is not sufficient evidence to proceed to trial, or to meet class certification requirements, then he or she will grant the defendant's motion for summary judgment or, in class-action lawsuits, deny the plaintiff's motion for class certification. If the judge grants the defendant's summary judgment motion or fails to certify the class, then the case is essentially completed pending an appeal by the plaintiffs.

As discussed above, employment discrimination cases involve claims of either disparate impact or disparate treatment by the employer. In the pre-trial phase, the court considers a number of factors when determining whether there is sufficient evidence for the case to continue. For instance, in disparate treatment cases, the courts use a burden-shifting approach to determine whether there is sufficient evidence to take the case to a jury. In this paradigm, the onus initially is on the plaintiff to show that there is at least a minimal amount of evidence that can be used to infer that discrimination could have taken place. The burden then shifts to the defendant to show that there were legitimate reasons for the employment actions that were taken. If the employer successfully justifies the employment actions, the burden then shifts back to the plaintiff to show that the employment actions were a pretext for the discrimination. Statistical evidence is frequently used by plaintiffs to show pretext. The burden-shifting approach is illustrated in the example below.

As described above, these claims may be brought on behalf of a single plaintiff, multiple plaintiffs or a class of employees. The claims in the employment discrimination case generally are the same regardless of whether the case was filed on behalf of a single plaintiff or a class of employees. However, if the employment discrimination case is filed on behalf of a class of employees, then the plaintiff has the additional burden of meeting the requirements for a class. The work of economists and statisticians frequently takes center stage in the class-action certification portion of the lawsuit.

Burden Shifting in an Employment Discrimination Case

In an employment discrimination case, the burden begins with the plaintiff establishing a *prima facie* case of race discrimination (see, for example, McDonnell Douglas Corp v. Green, 411 U.S. 792 (1973); West v. Nabors Drilling USA, Inc. 330 F. 3d 379, 384 (5th Cir. 2003)).

Plaintiffs must show that they:

- Were a member of a protected class
- Were qualified for the position in question
- Suffered from an adverse employment action
- Were replaced by someone who is not a member of the protected class to which the plaintiff belongs or were treated less favorably than similarly situated employees of a different race

The requirements may vary with the issue in question. Promotions, for example, may be more specific than other types of employment issues (see Haynes v. Pennzoil Co., 207 F. 3d 296, 300 (5th Cir. 2000)).

If the plaintiff succeeds in establishing a *prima facie* case, then the burden shifts to the defense, who then needs to demonstrate a legitimate, nondiscriminatory reason for the employment action. The defendant commonly uses existing employee handbooks and the testimony of company representatives to provide rationale for the selections that were made.

Assuming that the defendant successfully demonstrates a legitimate, nondiscriminatory reason for the selection, the presumption of discrimination dissolves and the burden shifts back to the plaintiff. The plaintiff then must prove that the reasons given by the plaintiff are a pretext for discriminatory employment action. At this point, the plaintiff may rely on testimony from fact witness and may present statistical evidence of gross statistical disparities resulting from the employment action.

In many companies, the human resources representative is a mid- to high-level executive who oversees the hiring, promotion, pay, job performance, and termination policies. The discrimination analyst uses the testimony of and/or interviews with the human resources representative to identify which factors the company views as being relevant to the contended employment policy. For example, in a case involving allegations of discrimination in promotions, the analyst uses the information and testimony of the human resources representative to determine the relative importance that different promotion factors, such as job performance and time in grade, have in the decision to promote an individual employee. Like the human resources executive, the compensation representative is a mid- to high-level executive who oversees issues involving pay, job assignments within pay grades, and the monitoring of market pay trends.

Daubert and Statistical Evidence

The court's gatekeeper role that has developed as a result of the Daubert decision often influences the statistical analyses that are performed in employment discrimination cases. In the Daubert case, the U.S. Supreme Court set forth a threshold for admissibility of expert's testimony. Generally, Daubert requires the court to consider several factors when determining whether a scientific analysis is admissible. These factors include whether the theories and techniques used by the expert have been tested and subjected to peer review and publication. In addition, the court considers whether the expert's methods have a known error rate and whether the techniques are widely accepted.

Some observers believe that Daubert and similar state-level cases that govern the admissibility of scientific evidence in the courts have caused researchers to shift away from the standard scientific method. That is, researchers who provide research for litigation tend to rely on standard techniques and the developed body of statistical research instead of trying to break new ground or perform trailblazing research. It is rare to see a statistical study employ techniques that are much more advanced than those taught in an undergraduate statistics course.

The major benefit of the current approach to providing scientific evidence in the courts is that if the researcher does in fact adhere to the established literature, then the results concerning discrimination should be more reliable. The basic statistics and tests used in salary discrimination analyses are relatively routine and well established in many courts across the country. All else being equal, more reliable and robust statistical analyses permit the evidence to provide more useful insights to the court and the jury.

The downside to the current research setting is that, in some cases, there is no literature for reference. In these employment discrimination cases, the introduction of statistical evidence, even if it is potentially relevant, may be hampered. For instance, the statistics that are most familiar to the courts do not always use newer statistical techniques that could potentially provide probative information to the court concerning the alleged discrimination.

Conclusions and Summary

Employment statistics can be the centerpiece of employment litigation and EEO audits and investigations. This chapter provided an introduction to the role of economists and statisticians in employment discrimination lawsuits. Following the introduction to class-action employment discrimination lawsuits, there was a discussion of how the testimony of fact and other expert witnesses impacts the statistical analysis of employment discrimination claims. The implication of Daubert and related decisions on the presentation of statistical evidence in the courts was also explored.

Employment Data

In this section, we dive into the employment data that is used to analyze employment discrimination claims. Employment data comes from many different sources. To produce a meaningful and reliable analysis, the researcher must have a solid understanding of these sources and understand how the company collects and maintains this data.

We begin by providing a description of the general classes of employment data that are required to perform a statistical employment analysis. As will be discussed, the employment data, which usually is provided to the expert during the discovery phase of the employment lawsuit, comes from many different sources.

To produce a meaningful and reliable analysis, the researcher must have a solid understanding of these sources and understand how the company collects and maintains this data. This section discusses these issues in more detail and introduces the reader to the basic terminology of electronic employment databases.

Employer-Defendant Personnel Records

In larger companies, personnel records are administrated by the human resources department and maintained by the information technology department. Since the 1980s, the human resources function has been increasingly outsourced to third parties that specialize in human resource management. The employment information maintained by the in-house or outsourced entity includes data covering hiring, pay, and promotions. It is common for one department or section of human resources to be responsible for pay-related activities, while another department or section is responsible for insurance, benefits, and exit interviews. The human resources department, which can vary from a single part-time employee to hundreds of individuals, is usually responsible for collecting data, maintaining hardcopy files, and entering employment data into sophisticated electronic databases.

Employment personnel databases, many of which are modules of a complete, firm-wide data software system produced by companies such as PEOPLESOFT, ORACLE, and SAP, generally provide a menu-driven user interface that allows the human resources personnel to manage changes in job title, salary, family status, and other considerations. In most cases, obtaining electronic data files requires discussions with the human resources department. The electronic data produced in a case is usually provided by the firm's information technology department, while the hardcopy files are generally obtained from the human resources department. In cases where some or all of the human resource functions are outsourced to a third party, obtaining the data may be more difficult since multiple entities are involved in the data collection process.

In most employment cases, primarily the discrimination analyst is interested in the employer-defendant's application, hiring, personnel, and compensation databases. The specific data needs and statistical concerns for each type of case are discussed in more detail in the following chapters.

Types of Employer-Defendant Personnel Records

Application Data	Files and applications of individuals who responded to a company's job announcement. Usually the most incomplete and varied dataset.
Hiring Data	Contains hardcopy and electronic information and outcomes for the different phases of the hiring process. Typically very well-documented and more complete than application data.
Personnel Data	Includes employee demographics and other employment–related, non-compensation information.
Compensation-Job Data	Contains information about how the company's employees are paid and the jobs they perform. Updated when a new transaction, such as a promotion or other compensation-related event, occurs.

Application Data

The application data contains the files and applications of individuals who responded to a company's job announcement. Depending on how the company received the employment application, the application data may contain resumes and/or standardized application data. Most companies use multiple recruiting sources, such as on-campus recruiting, newspaper and trade magazine want-ads, online job search databases, media ads, and word of mouth. Consequently, the applications from one source may be standardized, such as those received online, and include the same set of information for all applicants; applications from other recruiting sources may only result in a resume being sent in by the applicant. Application data of government and public entities tends to be more uniform than that of private companies, since the former usually require a common application form.

Regardless of the institution, application data is the most incomplete and varied type of employment data that typical employment attorneys and discrimination analysts encounter. It is not uncommon for companies to meet only the minimum requirements or suggestions of the EEOC or other government agencies when deciding which files to retain. This practice is commonplace and makes perfect business sense, because most of a firm's application data concerns information on individuals who were not qualified for the position or showed only a passing interest in the job and were not otherwise qualified for employment at the company. For instance, Microsoft receives over 6,000 applications per day. Most of the applications received by the company are from individuals who do not meet even the basic qualifications for employment with the company.

The major complication associated with the varied nature of application data is that employment discrimination cases involving allegations of discrimination in hiring require that the attorney assemble a wide range of data for the experts to analyze. Much of the information in employment discrimination cases involving allegations of discrimination in hiring or recruitment are hardcopy documents that must be converted into an electronic format before they can be analyzed. It is also important to note that the information is usually significantly less detailed and less complete for applicants who were not hired. For instance, at the time of application, the individual may not have provided a complete work history with dates and a description of his/her experience. Often this type of information is provided during subsequent phases of the employment and hiring process. These data limitations should be considered when articulating the questions to be addressed in the analysis.

More importantly, each application source (e.g., want ads, online job databases) presents a special set of issues for the economist or statistician who is examining allegations of employment discrimination. For instance, the applicant pool for a job position that is advertised primarily through online job databases is significantly different than that for a job that is advertised primarily through on-campus recruiting. These issues are especially important for companies that use a variety of methods to recruit employees and will be examined in more detail in the later chapter that analyzes allegations of hiring discrimination.

Hiring Data

An employer-defendant's hiring data contains hardcopy and electronic information and outcomes for the different phases of the hiring process. This data is distinctly different from application data and often is maintained outside of the application database. Hiring data typically informs the analyst about pre-employment job-related test scores, which employees were interviewed and their interview scores, and which employees opted out at some point during the hiring process.

Generally, the employment attorney seeks data that is typical of a hiring process, such as: basic qualifications, initial application screening, phone interview, testing, interview, job offer and, ultimately, the hiring phase. These phases will be discussed in more detail in subsequent chapters.

Hiring data is generally very well documented and substantially more complete than application data. Firms tend to keep a more complete set of hiring data because, among other reasons, they frequently use pre-hiring data to assess their employee selection process. However, it is not uncommon for hiring data to be a mix of electronic data, such as spreadsheets, and hardcopy documents, such as written tests. For example, firms who use the *Achiever* pre-employment test may frequently check the scores on the *Achiever* test against factors such as first-year job performance and employee attrition rates. It is also common for firms to use the information to measure performance later in employees' career with the company.

Like application data, each set of hiring data presents issues that should be considered before collecting data. Perhaps the greatest concern is ensuring that all the data concerning the job applicant's relevant qualifications is collected and included in the hiring data. For instance, if there is a basic education requirement for the job(s) in question, then the data needs to include education information. In many instances, even if there are no allegations of recruiting bias in the employment discrimination case, applicant data must be collected in order to make the hiring data useful in the analysis.

Personnel Data

An employer-defendant's personnel data includes employee demographics and other employment-related, non-compensation information. This information includes marital status, family status, and vacations. Like application and hiring data, personnel data is usually maintained in a separate database and administrated by human resource employees. For larger companies, employee identification items and similar basic information is almost always available electronically.

With the exception of demographic information, the importance of collecting personnel data is frequently underrated. Information in the personnel database can provide important insights into the working life of an employee. When incorporated appropriately in the analysis, an employee's sick leave, vacation frequency, and participation in company-sponsored courses can provide useful insights into the employee's level of job-specific, on-the-job training and soft skills development. Job-specific training and soft skills such as one's ability to work on a team are difficult to measure empirically, but are often important determinants of an individual's salary.

Compensation-Job Data

An employer-defendant's compensation-job data includes information about how the company's employees are paid and the jobs they perform. This includes an employee's base salary, commissions, and performance bonuses, as well as detailed information about the employee's job. This type of data is almost always available electronically.

Compensation is the most commonly outsourced human resource function and compensation data is typically kept in a separate database that is updated when changes are made to employees' compensation. Compensation databases are commonly referred to as transactional databases, because they are updated when a new transaction, such as a promotion or other compensation related-event, occurs. In practice, a firm's compensation database may include several spreadsheet-like tables that contain a common identifier, such as employees' social security number. Databases with data tables that are related by a unique identifier are referred to as relational databases.

Each of the data tables contains specific types of information concerning the employee's compensation history. For instance, most popular human resource software packages contain a table with employees' complete salary history. The pieces of information in the data tables are commonly referred to as data fields. The data fields are columns within the data table that contain information on a certain characteristic, such as the employee's salary, date of birth and company-specific identification number. A data record is a row of data field entries that are specific to a particular employee transaction. In each data table, a new compensation data record is created each time a new compensation transaction occurs in the employee's work history.

Job-related information for each employee is also usually included in the compensation data tables. Job-related tables have information such as the job title, supervisor's name and position, and related information. Job-related tables are typically linked to compensation tables through a company-provided identifier or the employee's social security number. Job-related information is constructed in the same way as the compensation data, using data tables, data fields, and data records. In many tables, the job and occupational titles are coded numerically, so deciphering this information requires referring to additional documents, such as a data dictionary.

A company may 'lease' some or all of its employees from companies and/or employ independent contractors. In day-to-day terms, a leased employee or an independent contractor may perform many of the same job functions as do other employees, but their future job opportunities and other employment factors may be substantially different from those of a regular employee. In any event, it is important to keep the specific employment arrangement of the company's workforce in mind as the data is collected for the statistical analysis.

Conclusions and Summary

In this chapter, we dove into the employment data that is used to analyze employment discrimination claims. We began by providing a description of the general classes of employment data that are required to perform a statistical employment analysis. We also introduced the reader to the basic terminology of electronic employment databases.

Describing Employer Personnel Data

In this chapter, we discuss how basic statistics, such as salary means and salary quartiles, are used to describe a company's employment processes in discrimination cases.

The fundamental insights provided by these methods form the foundation of the more advanced statistical discrimination analyses that we will discuss in subsequent chapters. We begin with a sample case study to motivate the discussion.

Situation

A software company's general counsel and human resources department asked the defense counsel to review a letter sent by the attorney who represents several of its employees. The letter states that the salary data for the company's sales force shows that African-American salespersons are paid less than similarly situated salespeople of other races at the same company for performing the same work. The employees also allege that the promotion rate of African-American salespersons to the position of sales manager is lower than that of other employees. The letter suggests that the company's assignment of territories is to blame for this salary disparity.

At this point, no lawsuit has been filed and the attorney and the represented employees are simply requesting a meeting to explore ways to resolve the issue. The attorney's letter, which has an attachment showing the salaries of each of the employees in the sales group, suggests that the average salary for African-American salespersons is \$55,556 while the average salary for other salespersons is \$61,500. The letter further states that the promotion rate to sales manager for African-American salespersons was 11.1%, while other employees have had a promotion rate of 30.6% over the past four years.

After reviewing the letter and discussing the listed employees with the human resources department, the defense attorney agrees that the salespeople are similarly situated in all relevant ways. The base salary for the North Ridge Division's salespersons is shown in the table on the following page. The table includes the annual base salary (pre-commission and bonuses) for the nine African-American and the employees of other races. At this point, for simplicity, the two sides in the dispute have agreed to divide the salary analysis into two groups (African-American and all others) for the purposes of the settlement talks. It is understood that if the issues go forward, further analysis of the various subgroups of employees will be needed.

Base Salary Data for Software Sales Employees - North Ridge Division

African-American		**All Other Races**	
Employee ID Number	Salary	Employee ID Number	Salary
234	$35,000	190	$30,000
710	$40,000	235	$40,000
791'	$45,000	907	$50,000
984	$55,000	475	$55,000
156	$60,000	189	$55,000
690	$60,000	654	$60,000
131	$60,000	124	$65,000
858	$65,000	892	$70,000
965	$80,000	334	$90,000
		444	$100,000

Background
At this point, no lawsuit has been filed and the attorney and the represented employees are simply requesting a meeting to explore ways to resolve the issue.

The attorney's letter, which has an attachment showing the salaries of each of the employees in the sales group, suggests that the average salary for African-American software salespersons is $55,556, while the average salary for other salespersons is $61,500. The letter further states that the promotion rate to sales manager for African-American salespersons was 11.1%, while other employees have had a promotion rate of 30.6% over the past four years.

Research Question

Do the plaintiff's attorney's salary calculations accurately describe the salary opportunities of African-American and other salespersons at the company?

The case study above illustrates a typical situation in employment discrimination cases. At the very onset of a statistical analysis, the analyst must provide an accurate description of the company's employment process or employment selection outcomes. The task is not to determine whether the plaintiff's allegations are true or false. At this initial stage, the task is simply to describe the employment outcomes accurately. Hypothesis testing concerning the validity of the discrimination allegations occurs later.

Generally, when describing employment data or any other type of data, the researcher is interested in two types of descriptions. First, the researcher wants to describe the employment process for the average or representative employee. Employment discrimination cases usually require describing the representative employment experiences for protected and non-protected employees separately. While the statistical average is perhaps the most widely known statistic, it may not be the most accurate way of depicting this aspect of the data.

Second, the analyst wants to show the natural dispersion in the employment outcomes. The analyst must describe not only the average, but also the natural expected deviation around that average. Although the concepts of dispersion and variance can be somewhat difficult to grasp, it is important to understand that the description of the employment outcome dispersion is as important as the average outcome. In some instances, the dispersion provides more insights into the employment process than does the average outcome.

For example, according to the U.S. BLS, the average salary of a person employed as a computer programmer and as a software salesperson is nearly the same. However, upon closer inspection, the natural dispersions in salary outcomes are dramatically different for the two occupations. The range of salary outcomes for the 'average salesperson' is substantially greater than that of the 'average computer programmer'. It is common for software salespeople to receive significant commissions and performance-based bonuses while computer programmers are more likely to be paid a salary. Looking at only the average salary outcomes of the two occupations mistakenly suggests that employment opportunities for the two occupations are similar, when in fact they are very dissimilar.

Describing the Average Employment Outcome

An employment attorney or researcher can rely upon many different statistics to describe the average employment outcome. As discussed above, statistics other than the average outcome may best describe the data. These statistical methods, which include the trimmed mean, median, quartiles, and frequency distributions, are presented in the following sections.

Statistics Used to Describe the Average Employment Outcome	
Mean	The average value; the sum of the observations divided by the number of observations.
Trimmed Mean	The mean with the highest and lowest observations excluded.
Median	The middle value of the dataset.
Quartiles	The middle values of the four sections of the dataset.
Frequency Distribution	A table of salary category frequencies.

Mean

The mean is simply the average value of a dataset. In the case of employment, the mean tells us the salary of the average worker. By taking the mean salary for two groups of workers, one can observe any differences in salary for the average employee in each group.

The mean, or average value, is calculated by summing the observations and dividing by the number of observations.

Formally, the sample mean is calculated as:

$$\bar{x} = \frac{1}{n}\sum_{i=1}^{n} x_i$$

where n is the number of individuals in the sample and $\sum$ is the symbol for the summation. $\sum_{i=1}^{n} x_i$ is equal to $x_1 + x_2 + \ldots + x_n$. In words, take the first number, x_1, add it to the second number, x_2, add that to the third number, x_3, and continue doing that until reaching the last number, x_n.

Example

In this case, the attorney has already calculated the mean salary for African-American salespersons and all other salespersons. The mean salary for African-American salespersons is derived by adding the salaries of all African-American salespersons and dividing by the total number of African-American salespersons:

$$mean(African - American) = \frac{1}{9}(35,000 + 40,000 + 45,000 + \cdots + 60,000$$
$$+65,000 + 80,000) = \frac{1}{9}(500,000)$$

Thus, the average salary for African-American salespersons is $55,556. Similarly, the mean salary for all other salespersons is calculated by adding the salaries of all other salespersons and dividing by the total number of salespersons who are not African-American:

$$mean\ (all\ other) = \frac{1}{10}(30,000 + 40,000 + 50,000 + \ldots + 70,000$$
$$+90,000 + 100,000) = \frac{1}{10}(615,000)$$

Thus, the average salary for all other salespersons is $61,500.

Trimmed Mean

If the employment data contains an extremely small or extremely large number of data observations, the arithmetic mean may not provide the best measure of the data's average value. Removing the largest and smallest outlying data observations and then calculating the mean may produce a more accurate depiction of the average employment outcome.

This recalculated mean is called the trimmed mean. Formally, the trimmed mean is calculated as follows:

$$\frac{1}{n - 2k}\sum_{i=k+1}^{n-k} x_i$$

where n is the number of individuals in the sample and k is the number of observations removed at the high and low ends of the sample. For example, if only the highest and lowest observations are removed, then k is equal to one.

$$\sum_{i=k+1}^{n-k} x_i \text{ is equal to } x_{k+1} + x_{k+2} + \ldots + x_{n-k},$$

where the x_i values are listed in order of increasing salary.

In this case, we will remove the highest and lowest salary observations for African-American salespersons and all other salespersons. The trimmed mean salary for African-American salespersons is calculated by adding all of their salaries excluding the highest and lowest observations and dividing by the total number of African-American salespersons minus two:

$$\begin{aligned} \textit{trimmed mean}(\textit{African} - \textit{American}) &= \frac{1}{7}(40,000 + \cdots + 65,000) \\ &= \frac{1}{7}(385,000) \end{aligned}$$

Thus, the trimmed mean salary for African-American salespersons is \$55,000. Similarly, for all other salespersons, remove the highest and lowest observations and divide by the total number of salespersons of other races minus two:

$$\textit{trimmed mean (all other)} = \frac{1}{8}(40,000 + \cdots + 90,000) = \frac{1}{8}(485,000)$$

The trimmed mean salary for all other salespersons is \$60,625.

Median

The median is another way to describe the center value of a dataset. It is equal to the value of whatever observation lies in the middle of the observation set. In terms of salaries, half of the people in the dataset will have salaries above the median and half will have salaries below the median.

The median is equal to the value of the dataset's middle observation. Half of the dataset's observations will be greater than or equal to the median. The other half of the dataset's observations will be less than or equal to the median. Formally, the median is defined by two equations:

$$\Pr(X \le m) \ge 1/2$$

$$\Pr(X \ge m) > 1/2$$

where X is any value in the dataset and m is the median of the dataset.

Example

In the case study, there are an odd number of African-American salespersons. The median salary is simply equal to the middle salary value when salaries are arranged by increasing value. In this case, the median salary for African-American salespersons is the middle value of $60,000.

There is an even number of all other salespersons. Consequently, there are two middle salary values. The median salary for all other salespersons is equal to the average of the two middle salary values. In this case, the median is

$$median = \frac{1}{2}(55,000 + 60,000) = \$57,000$$

Note that although the mean salary is greater for all other salespersons than for African-American salespersons, the median salary is smaller!

Generally, the median is less sensitive than the mean to outliers in the dataset. Consider a case where nine employees earn $30,000 and one employee earns $900,000. The median salary is $30,000; however, the mean salary is $117,000.

Quartiles

Quartiles expand on the insights provided by the median by providing two additional "medians" for the upper and lower halves of the data. Quartiles also show the spread of the data. Quartiles give an upper and lower bound for 50% of the observed data. In other words, 50% of the observed salaries will fall somewhere between the upper and lower quartiles.

Quartiles divide the dataset into four sections. First, recall that the median divides the data into two halves. The first quartile is the value of the middle of the lower half created by the median. Twenty-five percent of the dataset has values lower than the first quartile, denoted Q_1, and 75% of the dataset has values higher than Q_1. The second quartile is the median, m. The third, quartile denoted Q_3, is the value of the middle of the upper half created by the median. Seventy-five percent of the dataset has values lower than the third quartile, and 25% of the dataset has values higher than Q_3.

Example

The median divides the dataset into two halves. To find the first quartile, rank order the data (i.e., sort from highest to lowest values) and then take the median of the lower half. For African-American workers, it is the median of ($35,000, $40,000, $45,000, $55,000) or $\frac{1}{2}(40,000 + 45,000)$.

The lower quartile, or Q1, is $42,500. To find the third quartile, take the median of the upper half. For African-American salespersons, it is the median of ($60,000, $60,000, $65,000, $80,000), or $\frac{1}{2}(60,000 + 65,000)$. The third quartile, or Q3, is $62,500.

For all other workers, the first quartile is the median of ($30,000, $40,000, $50,000, $55,000, $55,000), or $50,000. The third quartile for all other workers is the median of ($60,000, $65,000, $70,000, $90,000, $100,000), or $70,000.

Frequency Distribution

A frequency distribution table is a simple way to organize data. Salary data can be grouped into x-dollar intervals. The number of people in each salary group is then tallied. Salary intervals are generally selected at the researcher's discretion. As a rule of thumb you want to select enough interval groups to permit the identification of trends, but not so many groups that there are only a few people in each one.

Example

To construct a frequency distribution table, group salaries in $20,000 intervals.

Salary Interval Example

Salary Intervals	Frequency for African-American Workers	Frequency for All Other Workers
$30,000–$49,999	3	2
$50,000–$69,999	5	5
$70,000–$89,999	1	1
$90,000–$109,999	0	2

Describing Dispersion in Employment Outcomes

As discussed earlier, examining only the average employment outcomes without considering the natural variation in the underling employment process can result in an inaccurate description of the employer-defendant's data in some instances. Researchers can construct many basic statistics to describe the natural variation of a given employment outcome. These statistics, which include the range, inter-quartile range, frequency distributions, and the variance, are described in the following sections.

Tests to Describe Dispersion in Employment Outcomes	
Range	The difference between the highest and lowest observations.
Inter-quartile Range	The difference between the first and third quartiles.
Frequency Distributions	The relative frequency of salaries in different ranges.
Variance	The average of the squared deviation of each observation from the mean value.

Range

The range of a dataset is equal to the difference between the highest observation value and the lowest observation value. In employment salary data, it is the difference between the highest observed salary and the lowest observed salary. Range, denoted Y, is equal to:

$$Y = x_n - x_1$$

where x_n is the largest observed value and x_1 is the smallest observed value.

Example

In our example, the range tells us the difference in salary between the highest-paid worker and the lowest-paid worker.

The range of salaries for African-American salespersons is $\$80,000 - \$35,000 = \$45,000$. The range of salaries for all other persons is $\$100,000 - \$30,000 = \$70,000$.

Inter-Quartile Range

The inter-quartile range measures the spread of the dataset, ignoring outlier effects. It is the range of the middle 50% of the dataset. In employment data, it is the difference between the first and third quartile salaries. The inter-quartile range is:

$$IR = Q_3 - Q_1$$

where Q_3 is the third quartile and Q_1 is the first quartile.

The inter-quartile range for African-American workers is $62,500 − $42,500 = $20,000. The inter-quartile range for all other workers is $70,000 − $50,000 = $20,000.

Frequency Distributions

Frequency distribution tables can also be used to examine the dispersion of data. Relatively low frequencies in each category indicate a highly dispersed dataset. For instance, having relatively few individuals in each salary group for a given employer suggests that individuals earn differing amounts and that relatively little similarity in salary outcomes could be expected from the pay process.

Variance

Variance measures the spread of a dataset. It is the average of the squared standard deviation of each observation from the dataset's mean. Formally, variance, denoted σ_x^2, is:

$$\sigma^2 = \frac{1}{n}\sum_{i=1}^{n}(x_i - \bar{x})^2$$

where $\bar{x}$ is the mean of the dataset. Written out, the variance is:

$$\sigma^2 = \frac{1}{n}\left[(x_1 - \bar{x})^2 + (x_2 - \bar{x})^2 + \ldots + (x_n - \bar{x})^2\right]$$

To calculate the variance, subtract the mean salary from each observed salary. Then square the difference. Sum the differences and then divide by the total number of observations.

For clarity, the calculations for African-American workers are shown in the table below.

Standard Deviation Calculation Example

Employee	Salary	Salary Minus the Mean $(x_i - \bar{x})$	$(x_i - \bar{x})^2$
1	$35,000	−$20,556	422,549,136
2	$40,000	−$15,556	241,989,136
3	$45,000	−$10,556	111,429,136
4	$55,000	−$556	309,136
5	$60,000	$4,444	19,749,136
6	$60,000	$4,444	19,749,136
7	$60,000	$4,444	19,749,136
8	$65,000	$9,444	89,189,136
9	$80,000	$24,444	597,509,136

Now, take the average of the last column of numbers to compute the variance. This number is quite large (169,135,802.70) and has little intuitive appeal.

Instead of reporting variance, statisticians often report the **standard deviation**. The standard deviation is the square root of the variance.

The standard deviation (the square root of 169,135,802.70) for African-American employees' salaries is $13,005.22.

The same calculation can be made for all other salespersons' salaries. The variance for all other salespersons is 405,250,000. The standard deviation for all other salespersons' salaries is $20,131. Thus, salaries for all other employees are more disperse than are the salaries for African-American employees.

Describing the Relationship Between Employment Factors

Sometimes an issue involves the relationship between two employment factors. For instance, how do wages and the employee's age vary? Cross tabulations and correlation coefficients can be used to compare two aspects of a dataset. In employment cases, cross tabulations can be used to compare race and promotion rates.

To illustrate, consider the promotion outcomes for a given company. The table below presents the number of people promoted and not promoted by race. The table is referred to as **cross-tabulation** of race and promotion outcome.

	Employee's Race	
Promotion Outcome	Number of White Employee Promotions	Number of African-American Employee Promotions
Employee Promoted	3	1
Employee Not Promoted	7	8

Correlation Coefficients

Correlation coefficients measure the extent to which two variables are related. The correlation coefficient is a number that is calculated from the data and has a value between 1 and −1. The closer the correlation coefficient number is to 1 or −1, the stronger the association between the two variables.

A correlation coefficient of zero means there is no correlation between the two variables. A negative correlation coefficient means that as one variable grows larger, the other variable grows smaller. Similarly, a positive correlation coefficient implies that as one variable grows larger, the other variable also increases.

The correlation coefficient, defined as $\rho(X, Y)$, is equal to:

$$Corr = \frac{Cov(X, Y)}{\sigma_X \sigma_Y}$$

where Cov(X,Y) is the covariance between variable X and Y and

σ_X, σ_Y are the standard deviations (the square root of variance) for X and Y, respectively.

Algebraically, this equation is equivalent to:

$$Corr = \frac{\frac{1}{n}\sum_{i=1}^{n}(x_i - \bar{x})(y_i - \bar{y})}{\sqrt{\frac{1}{n}\sum_{i=1}^{n}(x_i - \bar{x})^2} \cdot \sqrt{\frac{1}{n}\sum_{i=1}^{n}(y_i - \bar{y})^2}}$$

Using Microsoft Excel to Describe Employment Data

Excel is great tool for exploring basic relationships within an employment dataset. Below we provide a very brief introduction to some of the formulas that can be found in the Excel software package. Excel also has a data analysis add-in package that contains additional tools for data summary and description.

Mean

The Excel command for calculating the mean is

AVERAGE(number1, number2, . . .)

For adjacent cells, such as A1 through A19, type: "=AVERAGE(A1:A9)". The colon tells Excel to include all cells between A1 and A9. Similarly, typing A1:E1 would include all cells in the horizontal row between A1 and E1.

You can also select all the desired cells by clicking the first one and holding down the mouse button while dragging across all the cells you wish to select. Another method is to select the first cell, then hold down shift and select the ending cell. For nonadjacent cells, such as B2, C5, and D12, type: "=AVERAGE(B2,C5,D12)". You can also select these cells by clicking on the first cell you wish to include, then holding down control while selecting the other cells you wish to include.

Trimmed Mean

To manually compute a trimmed mean, sort the salary data. Then you can exclude the highest and lowest observations and compute the average. For example, if the data was sorted, instead of using "=AVERAGE(A1:A9)", you might use "=AVERAGE(A2:A8)".

Excel also contains a trimmed mean command:

TRIMMEAN(array, percent)"

The first term tells Excel over which data to calculate the mean. In our example above, the array would be A1:A9. Note that all the data must be in adjacent cells. The second term tells Excel what percentage of the data to exclude. Excel rounds this term so that the trimmed mean excludes two observations – one high and one low. To exclude 25% of the data contained in cells A1 through A9, type "=TRIMMEAN(A1:A9, 0.25)".

Median

The Excel command for calculating the median is

MEDIAN(number1, number2, . . .)

For instructions on selecting cells, refer to the section on the mean.

Quartiles

The Excel command for quartiles is **"QUARTILE(array, quart)".** The first term tells Excel over which data to calculate the quartile. In our example above, the array would be A1:A9. Note that all the data must be in adjacent cells. The second term tells Excel which quartile value to return. If *quart* equals zero, Excel returns the minimum value. If quart equals one, Excel returns the first quartile. If *quart* equals two, Excel returns the median value. If quart equals three, Excel returns the third quartile. If *quart* equals four, Excel returns the maximum value. For example, if we wanted to compute the first quartile (or 25th percentile), we would type "=QUARTILE(A1:A9, 1)".

Frequency Distribution

The Excel command for frequency distributions is

FREQUENCY(data_array, bins_array)

The data array is the same array that we have been using to calculate the mean, median, and quartiles. The bin array tells Excel how to slice the data. In adjacent cells, type the values you want to include in the salary intervals. For example, assume that you are working with the data in the following table.

Sample Excel Data Excerpt

A Person Number	B Salary	C Bins
1	$35,000	$30,000
2	$40,000	$50,000
3	$45,000	$70,000
4	$55,000	$90,000
5	$60,000	
6	$60,000	
7	$60,000	
8	$65,000	
9	$80,000	

The first column is the data array of salaries and the second column is the bin array. Using this bin array, Excel would calculate the number of salaries observed that are less than $30,000, between $30,000 and $49,999, between $50,000 and $69,999, between $70,000 and $89,999, and greater than or equal to $90,000.

Entering the formula for the frequency distribution is a bit more complicated, because it returns an array instead of a single number. To enter the formula, first select a number of adjacent cells equal to the number of intervals for which you are calculating the frequency. In this case, there are five intervals (less than $30,000, between $30,000 and $49,999, between $50,000 and $69,999, between $70,000 and $89,999, and greater than or equal to $90,000), so select five cells by clicking and dragging. Next, type "=FREQUENCY(B1:B9, C1:C4)". Instead of hitting enter, press and hold control-shift-enter at the same time. Five numbers should appear. If you click on one of the cells, the formula is "{=FREQUENCY(B1:B9, C1:C4)}".

Range

The range can be calculated by using the commands for minimum and maximum. To compute the range, find the difference between the maximum and minimum by typing

=MAX(number1, number2, . . .) – MIN(number1, number2, . . .)

For instructions on selecting cells, refer to the section on the mean.

Inter-Quartile Range

The inter-quartile range can be calculated by using the quartile command. To computer the inter-quartile range, find the difference between the first quartile and third quartile by typing

=QUARTILE(array, 3) – QUARTILE(array, 1)

Note that all the data must be in adjacent cells.

Section II

Statistical Concepts

Probability and Employment Discrimination

The vast majority of human resource professionals and attorneys are not mathematicians. Fortunately, employment statistics are not really about math.

While more than a few HR professionals and attorneys will quickly and proudly describe themselves as mathematically challenged, the average person in these fields tends to be well versed in liberal arts and the art of crafting, understanding and dissecting complex arguments. Contrary to what many may believe, these individuals actually are better equipped than many other professionals to understand concepts in statistics, because they have a background in understanding and conceptualizing complex ideas.

Attorneys and other professionals with similar training possess this advantage because the heart of a statistical analysis is not actually rooted in arcane mathematics or complicated calculations. Instead a simple but elegant plain-English argument lies at the center of every statistical analysis. In fact, the argument is the same in nearly every statistical employment analysis. Mathematics and the data manipulations are simply the tools that researchers use to address the core argument in the analysis.

In this chapter, we will look at the key question that underlies statistical analyses of employment discrimination. In addition, we will discuss in a general way how the analyst conceptually addresses this fundamental question.

The Underlying Question in Employment Discrimination Analyses

Statistical analyses of allegations of employment discrimination are generally predicated on one question.

The Underlying Question

If the employer were ***not*** *discriminating, what is the likelihood that the employment outcome would have been generated by sheer random chance?*

The simple question shown above encapsulates the essence of the statistical tests used to analyze allegations of employment discrimination. As will be discussed in more detail in later portions of this book, the actual calculations and analyses required to answer this question may be quite involved. However, the underlying concepts are straightforward and can be grasped quite easily.

The question above is built on the fundamental postulation that extreme deviations from the norm or the expected employment outcomes are unlikely to occur on a regular basis. Assuming that the analyst or observer has a solid understanding of the actual employment process in question, he or she can determine the expected range of employment outcomes that would result from a neutral and unbiased employment process. The 'answer' to the question involves comparing the actual employment outcomes to the expected employment outcomes.

Given the fundamental postulation that extreme deviations from the norm or expected outcome are unlikely to occur on a regular basis, large deviations are suggestive of a non-neutral employment process. In other words, it is unlikely, or there is a low probability, that a large deviation from the expected outcome will occur through sheer randomness.

Accordingly, if the numerical deviation between the actual employment outcome and the expected employment outcome is sufficiently large, then the deviation is said to be statistically important, or what is commonly referred to as statistically significant, to the observer. In essence, that is the basis of the statistical tests that are used in employment analyses.

Mathematical techniques come into play when we calculate the probability associated with a deviation from the expected outcome. In the simplest cases, we can calculate the probability through basic counting and arithmetic. In practice, however, we use published and generally accepted mathematical formulas called probability distribution functions to calculate the actual probabilities associated with the employment outcome in question.

The reasoning underlying statistical employment discrimination analyses is far from novel. It is rooted in ideas that are centuries old. Many of the concepts are based on calculating odds and probabilities in games of chance, such as rolling dice or playing cards.

The underlying statistical concepts in employment analyses can be compared to a person who is trying to figure out whether his or her poker-playing friends, who continually win, are cheating. In this situation, the person does not see the other person cheat, so he or she must try to calculate the odds associated with each of the winning hands. If you determine that it is unlikely that your buddy would have drawn these winning poker hands on such a regular basis simply by the luck of the draw, then that would lead you to suspect cheating. Conceptually, the only difference between the card example and, say, a statistical employment analysis is how we calculate the odds of the random occurrence (card hands vs. the number of protected individuals hired).

For an employment analysis of similarly situated individuals, we would evaluate the employment outcomes as follows.

The Underlying Answer

If it is determined that it is ***unlikely*** *that the employment outcome in question would have been generated by sheer random chance, then the outcome suggests an employer bias.*

Of course, the question and the answer assume that all the individuals are similarly situated, all appropriate employment factors were accounted for, and all statistical tests were performed correctly. For example, consider the allegations in a typical promotion case involving claims that female employees were promoted at a slower rate than similarly situated male employees at a company. To analyze the allegations of discriminatory promotion, the problem would be conceptually phrased as follows.

Conceptualizing a Gender Discrimination Promotion Case

The Underlying Question

What is the likelihood or probability that the slower promotion rate for women would have been generated by an unbiased and gender neutral promotion selection process?

The Underlying Answer

If it is determined that it is unlikely that the slower promotion rate of women could be the result of sheer random chance, then this finding suggests an employer bias.

The Concept of Statistical Significance

One question comes to mind at this point: How exactly do you determine what constitutes an "unlikely occurrence"? In other words, what constitutes a "statistically significant" employment outcome deviation from the expected or norm? The short answer is that we use the probability associated with the employment occurrence as our guide. If, after accounting for all the relevant factors, we find a small probability that an unbiased and neutral employment process could have generated the employment outcome in question, then it suggests an employer bias against the protected group in the case. As always, the answer and the question assume that all the individuals are similarly situated, all appropriate employment factors were accounted for, and all statistical tests were performed correctly.

To determine whether a given deviation is statistically significant, we first calculate the probability that the employment outcome could have been generated by sheer randomness. For instance, in a hiring case, all else equal, we would expect the individuals hired by an employer to reflect the underlying protected and non-protected distribution in the qualified and relevant applicant pool.

We can then determine the expected number of hired individuals from the protected and non-protected group members that would be obtained if, in fact, the selection process were unbiased and neutral. Based on the relevant applicant pool, we may find that we would expect ten individuals from the protected group to be hired, but only one was actually hired. Moreover, based on the applicant pool, we can calculate the probability that an unbiased and neutral selection process would have produced the actual hiring results. For instance, given the percentage of protected group members in the applicant pool, we may calculate that there is a 0.005 probability, or a likelihood of one in 200, that the observed employment outcome would have been generated by sheer random chance.

Second, after calculating the probability associated with our employment outcome, we compare it to a pre-determined critical probability point. The pre-determined critical probability point is simply the point at which a reasonable person would rule out random chance as the factor responsible for the employment outcome. For instance, we may select a critical point of 0.01, representing a 0.01 probability, or a likelihood of one in 100, that the employment outcome would have been generated by randomness.

Third, if the probability that the observed employment outcome would have occurred by sheer randomness is equal to or less than our predetermined critical point, then it suggests that something other than randomness has generated the employment outcome. As always, this assumes that all the individuals are similarly situated, all appropriate employment factors were accounted for, and all statistical tests were performed correctly. Although there is no consensus on this issue, social scientists routinely use critical probability points of 5%, 1%, 0.05% and lower as thresholds. As we will discuss in more detail in future chapters, it is routine and in many instances required that analysts use a higher threshold in litigation and related issues.

These three steps form the foundation of statistical significance and classical statistical testing.

Determining Statistical Significance in a Nutshell

1. **Calculate** the employment outcome for similarly situated protected and non-protected employee groups that would be expected if the employer were using an unbiased, protected, class-neutral selection process.
2. **Determine** the probability (p) that the observed deviation from the expected employment outcome would occur by sheer random chance in an unbiased and neutral employment process.
3. **Compare** the probability associated with the employment outcome deviation to the probability critical point (p_c), such as 0.01 or a 1% chance.
4. **Decide** the case by considering that if p is less than p_c, it suggests an employer bias against the protected group.

A Real-World Coin-Flipping Example

As you can see, the basic underpinnings of the statistical model are pretty straightforward, but it can be difficult to apply these concepts in practice. To drive home these concepts, let's focus on a simple real-world employment situation that mirrors a clearly unbiased process, such as flipping a coin. In later chapters we will discuss more complex examples, but for now let's focus on a simple coin-flipping exercise and a stylized employment situation that possesses similar characteristics.

Imagine a person flipping a coin to determine which team gets to go first at the beginning of a sporting event. Common sense suggests that the probability that a fair and unbiased coin turns up heads on any given coin flip is 0.50. The probability is the same for the coin turning up tails on any given flip. That is there is a 50% chance that the coin turns up heads and a 50% chance that the coin turns up tails.

Few real-world employment processes operate exactly in this manner, but the pre-application screening process used by some large employers offers a fairly good analogy. When large employers build large factories that will create a significant number of high-paying positions for relatively low-skilled workers, they typically receive tens of thousands of applications. This is especially true when the plant is in or near a major city. Many employers do not want to invest the time and resources needed to review and screen such a large number of very similar job applications.

Consequently, some employers hold a pre-application drawing. In the pre-application drawing, all interested individuals submit a simple, short pre-application form that is assigned a random number. Based on the number of job openings and past hiring patterns, the employer predetermines how many applications will be reviewed for the job openings. For instance, an employer may determine that it needs to review 5,000 applications to be able to fill 500 job openings. To obtain the desired number of applications, the employer will randomly select pre-application numbers. Individuals with a selected number are invited to submit a full job application. This process continues until the company receives the required number of job applications.

If the company follows this routine and does not solicit pre-application forms in a discriminatory manner, then the employment process will not be biased against any protected group. The employer's application pool will reflect the underlying proportion of protected and non-protected group members who submitted pre-applications. There may be factors, such as differing application rates among protected groups, but the underlying selection process is clearly random.

The outcomes from the pre-application drawing selection process in this example can be compared to outcomes of the process of an individual who is flipping a coin and recording the heads or tails outcome. In the employment situation, the coin flip is replaced by the employer's computer selecting the pre-application numbers. Instead of recording a heads or tails outcome, the employer's computer unknowingly selects a member of either a protected class member or a non-protected class. The coin flips generate a series of heads/tails outcomes and the pre-application drawing generates a series of protected/non-protected class members who are invited to apply.

Using this simple construct allows us to conceptually determine when we would classify a given outcome as an unlikely event that is statistically significant. The line of reasoning is as follows. If a coin were not weighted so that it were more likely to land on heads or tails, then sheer randomness would produce an equal number of outcomes that turned up heads and those that turned up tails. After a sufficiently large number of coin flips, if there were significantly more tails outcomes than expected, or if all the outcomes were tails, then we could reasonably assume that something is wrong with the coin (or the coin flipper). In this situation, it is reasonable to conclude that something is wrong, because there is a very low probability that a fair coin will produce only tails outcomes if it is flipped a large number of times.

Analogously, looking at the outcomes from the random employment process gives us a way to determine whether an outcome should be classified as an unlikely event that is statistically significant. If we assume that the potential applicant pool consisted of exactly 50% protected and 50% non-protected individuals, then the pre-application process will exactly mirror that of the coin flips. As with the coin-flipping example, it is reasonable to conclude that something is wrong if, after a sufficient number of pre-application draws, significantly fewer protected class members are invited to apply than expected.

In fact, by using only basic counting we can figure out the probability associated with any given set of employment application outcomes in the same manner as the one we would use for coin flips. Again, to keep things simple and tractable, let's assume we are going to conduct a preliminary investigation based on the distribution of protected and non-protected class members of the first five pre-application selections made by the employer. Of course, we would not do a real analysis on such a small sample, but the small numbers facilitate a conceptual understanding of the underlying statistical methodology. The underlying methodology will be the same for larger sample sizes, but the math will be more difficult. We will discuss more realistic examples in later chapters.

In our analysis of the five applications, a reasonable person would expect the percentage of protected group members who are invited to apply to equal that of protected group members in the pre-application pool. Given that 50% of the individuals in the pre-application pool were protected group members, a reasonable person would expect half of the five applications, or two or three of them (2.5 individuals to be exact), to be protected group members. Of course, since the person is reasonable, our he or she also recognizes that sheer random chance could generate an outcome that strayed from the expected number. Ignoring the small sample size, if the deviation from the expected is very large, then we would expect this to occur infrequently (or, as statisticians say, we would expect this to have a small probability of occurrence) and we would view the process with suspicion.

In our stylized example, what would be an unreasonable deviation for a reasonable person? In other words, what would constitute a statistically significant deviation? A reasonable person, who is assumed to be ignoring the small number of applications reviewed, would start to be somewhat suspicious if he or she saw no protected group members represented in the group of five applications. Why? The answer is discussed below.

As stated above, based on the pre-application drawing population, a reasonable person would expect two or three protected group members to be in the pool of five. There is a 0.31 probability or about a 1 in 3 chance, that two protected group members and three non-protected members would be in the pool of five applications. This probability can be calculated by simply counting up the possible outcomes from the pre-application process.

An Unlikely Flip of the Coin?

1. If a coin is flipped 5 times, 32 different heads/tails outcomes could occur through sheer random chance.
2. There is a **0.31** probability that exactly two of the five coin flips will turn up heads. This is because 10 of the 32 outcomes show two heads outcomes out of five coin flips.
3. There is a **0.1562** probability that only one of the five coin flips will turn up heads. This is because 5 of the 32 possible outcomes show one heads outcome out of five coin flips.
4. There is a **0.03125** probability that none of the five coin flips will turn up heads. This is because 1 of the 32 possible outcomes show no heads out of five coin flips.

Even if only one protected person were hired, we would most likely not become suspicious. This is because even though we expect two or three protected group members to be in the final application pool, a reasonable person understands that having only one protected class member in the group of five is an outcome that is reasonably likely to occur through random chance alone. In fact, just counting up the possible outcomes as before shows that there is about a one-in-six chance, or a 0.1562 probability, that only one protected class member would be in the pool of five. The person studying the process would simply say that random luck most likely caused the deviation from the expected outcome of two or three protected group members. This observer would view this deviation from the expected application outcome as being insignificant or unimportant.

However, if there is no protected class member in the final application pool of five, a reasonable person in our stylized example may become a little suspicious, because it is not likely that the outcome would have been generated by sheer random chance. Simply counting up the possible employment outcomes shows that there is less than a 1-in-25 chance (0.0312) that sheer randomness would have generated a result where no protected class members were in the application pool of five. Given this small probability, an observer could say that it is unlikely that randomness would have caused the deviation from the expected outcome. The observer could view this deviation or difference from the expected outcome as being significant or important. Of course, for the moment, we are still ignoring the small number of occurrences being studied.

Conclusion and Chapter Summary

This chapter discussed the conceptual foundations of each method of estimating the expected employment outcomes of an unbiased employment process. Like the other chapters in the book, the discussion did not use any advanced math; it requires only that the reader read and pay close attention.

The methodology discussed in this chapter underlies the statistical thinking that is employed in most employment discrimination analyses. In practice, this approach is used in situations like hiring, promotion and terminations that lend themselves to a dichotomous or at least a countable number of outcomes. For example, in hiring, an individual is either hired or not; in a termination case, the person is either fired or not. The countable nature allows the researcher in some, but definitely not all instances, to build a tractable mathematical representation of an unbiased employment process. In simpler situations, the mathematical representation of the employment process can be used in conjunction with centuries-old ideas to derive probabilities for the employment outcomes that are generally accepted and subject to little debate. In the next chapter, we will discuss in detail the types of statistical models that are used in employment analyses that fall into this general class of analytical models.

Sampling Distributions

The sampling distribution is the straw-person that allows us to test our discrimination hypotheses. If we find it unlikely that our straw-person distribution would have produced the employment outcome in question, this suggests that the outcome is consistent with discrimination.

In this chapter, we discuss sampling distributions. The sampling distribution numerically describes the potential outcomes that would be generated by a random and presumably nondiscriminatory employment process. In essence, the sampling distribution is the straw-person that allows us to test our discrimination hypotheses. If we find it unlikely that our straw-man distribution would have produced the employment outcome in question, this suggests that the outcome is consistent with discrimination.

The important concepts introduced in this chapter will be the backbone for hypothesis testing and other topics introduced in later chapters.

Thinking Like an Unbiased and Reasonable Person

As discussed in the last chapter, the ultimate goal of our statistical analysis is to determine the likelihood that our employment data was generated by an unbiased employment process. However, unlike in the last chapter, we are now interested in studying employment processes that have a large or possibly uncountable number of outcomes. For instance, unlike promotions or terminations outcomes, where a person is promoted (or not) or fired (or not), the range of salary outcomes is typically endless.

In a salary analysis, it would probably not surprise anyone if 100 different employees each had a different salary. If we select five people at random and calculate their average salary, we find (using counting rules), that there are 75,287,520 possible groups of five individuals that we can select for our average salary calculation. The underpinnings and the basic way in which we address the question will be the same as in the previous chapter. The only difference in this section is the underlying methodology, and specifically the formulas that we use to calculate probabilities.

Fortunately, the science of statistics tells us that if we can observe the actions of our unbiased and reasonable straw-person a sufficiently large number of times, their actions become very predictable. Statistical science tells us that no matter how the true and possibly unknown employment process works, the statistical measures we are concerned with will be distributed so that they follow a bell curve if we observe the employment process a sufficiently large number of times. Employment data statistics that are distributed like a bell curve are **normally distributed**. The **normal distribution function** is the mathematical formula that describes the probabilities associated with different ranges of employment data that is generated in this manner.

Like the concepts discussed in the previous chapter, concepts related to the normal distribution are far from novel and are generally accepted without controversy. The normal distribution has been used to describe not only economic-related issues such as salary outcomes, but also issues throughout the hard and soft sciences.

The figure below illustrates a normal distribution describing a hypothetical salary process. It shows the probability that a person will earn a salary within a particular salary range from a particular employer. In this figure, the range of salaries is shown on the bottom x-axis.

It is important to note that the area under the curve over a particular salary range (e.g., $45,000 to $55,000) – not the y-axis – shows the probability of observing a particular range of outcomes. This is because the probability for the normal distribution depends on both the height of the curve and the length of the range being studied. Standard tables, spreadsheets, and statistical programs can easily calculate probabilities for the normal distribution. See the abridged normal-distribution tables at the back of this book.

Important Features of the Normal Distribution

A normal distribution has many notable features that relate to employment topics. First, a normally distributed employment factor or employment statistic tends to produce values that are close to the mean of the employment factor. Conceptually, the normal curve for a normally

Normal Distribution Example

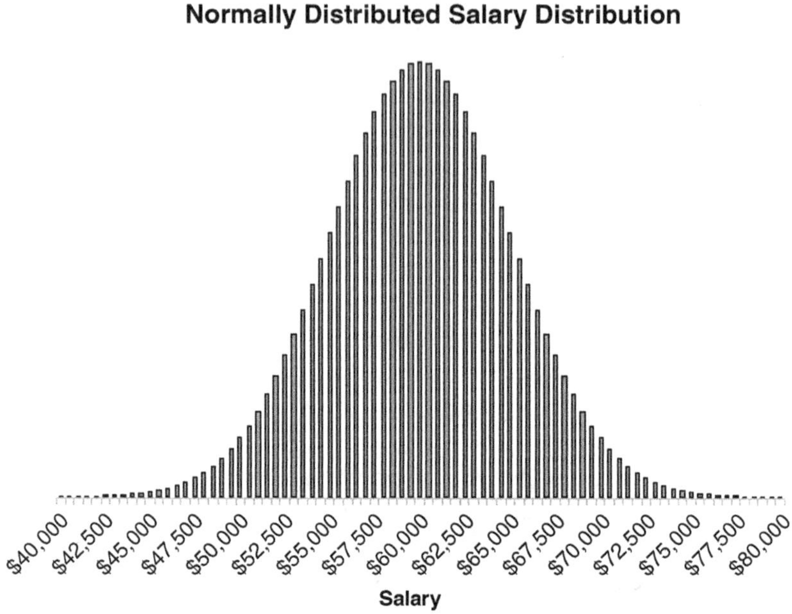

(Mean = $60,000; Standard Deviation = $5,000)

For any given normal distribution, **68%** of the data observations can be expected to be within one standard deviation of the mean. In this figure, 68% percent of the probability mass is between plus or minus one standard deviation, or within $5,000 of the mean salary of $60,000. That is, we would expect 95% of the salary observations to fall between $55,000 and $65,000.

Additionally, **95%** of the data observations will be within two standard deviations of the mean. In the figure, this means that 95% of the probability mass is within $10,000 of the mean. That is, we would expect 95% of the salary observations to fall between $50,000 and $70,000.

Nearly all of the data observations, or **99.7%** of the observations, will be within three standard deviations of the mean. That is, we would expect 99.7% of the salary observations to fall between $45,000 and $75,000.

distributed employment factor looks like a bell that is centered or balanced on the mean of the data. In the preceding figure, the mean of the salary observations is $60,000. For a normally distributed employment factor, extremely small or large values are not as likely as numbers near the mean of the data. Remember that the likelihood of observing a given range of values is shown by the area underneath the normal distribution curve.

For example, most people at our hypothetical company are predicted to earn between $55,000 and $65,000. This can be seen by visually inspecting the area under the curve from $55,000 to $65,000. Most of the probability mass of the curve is found in this region. Only a small amount of the probability mass lies to the left of $55,000 and to the right of $65,000.

Second, the width or girth of the conceptual bell curve is determined by a parameter called the **standard deviation**. The standard deviation is simply a measure of the dispersion of the employment data observations. The standard deviation measures how far a particular observation or number is from the mean of the data. A greater standard deviation indicates more dispersion in the employment data.

In the preceding figure, the standard deviation is $5,000. We will discuss standard deviations in more detail in the following chapters. For now, simply note that the higher or greater the standard deviation parameter is, the wider or more spread out the normal distribution curve will be.

Third, employment factors that are distributed in this way behave very predictably. Specifically, for any given normal distribution, 68% of the data observations are expected to be within one standard deviation of the mean. As shown in the figure, 68% percent of the probability mass is between plus or minus one standard deviation, or within $5,000, of the mean salary of $60,000. We expect about 68% of the employees in any random sample to have a salary between $55,000 and $65,000.

Additionally, 95% of the data observations are within two standard deviations of the mean. In the figure, 95% of the probability mass is within plus or minus $10,000 of the mean. We expect about 95% or so of the employees in any random sample to have a salary between $50,000 and $70,000. Nearly all of the data observations, or 99.7% of the observations, are within three standard deviations of the mean. As discussed in detail below, knowing these facts helps us determine which employment decisions would have most likely been made by an unbiased and reasonable person.

Fourth, if we repeat a given employment selection or compensation process a sufficiently large number of times, the resulting outcomes will likely be normally distributed. This outcome is based on a well-established idea in statistical sciences know as the **Central Limit Theorem**.

This theorem has a number of implications for our statistical work in employment. Most importantly, it provides a way to analyze questions involving complicated employment processes. For instance, let's say we randomly survey a group of 100 individuals who work at a very large multinational company and ask them about their annual salary. Then based on these 100 responses, we then take an average of the employees' responses. For the sake of the example, let's say we repeat this process 1,000 times. That is, we repeatedly and randomly survey different groups of 100 employees and ask them what their annual salary is. Once the surveys are complied, we calculate and record the average salary for the group of employees. We continue this process 1,000 times.

The Central Limit Theorem lets us make valid conjectures about the range of average salaries that we would expect to see from our random experiment. In other words, we can use it to model the effect of randomness. In our example, the underlying distribution of mean salaries that we calculated will be normally distributed. It is important to note even though the underlying data may not be normally distributed we will find that the Central Limit Theorem still holds. While the proofs of these statements are outside of the scope of this discussion, it does work!

That final, somewhat arcane factoid concerning the normal distribution is the backbone of many of our statistical employment analyses. The importance of this feature of the normal distribution will become clear in the next few sections.

Sampling Distributions

Sampling distributions are at the heart of the questions that we are asked to examine. They are also one of the most difficult concepts to grasp, so it is worthwhile to take the time to really understand the concept.

The sampling distribution of a sample statistic tells us the probability associated with each possible theoretical set of employment outcomes. For instance, we can calculate a sampling distribution that describes the possible mean salary outcomes for a random sample of ten employees drawn from a large employer's pool of 50 employees. In this instance, the sampling distribution tells us the probability associated with each huge number of possible employee samples (10,272,278,170 samples to be exact) that could be drawn randomly. In practice, we use the sampling distribution to approximate the outcomes that our unbiased and reasonable straw-person would have obtained. Accordingly, we use the sampling distribution as our measuring stick to determine the probability that the employment outcome in question could have been generated by an unbiased and reasonable employment process.

To drive home the sampling distribution concept, consider an experiment whereby we draw three employees at random from a total population of six employees. In this experiment, we want to study the mean level of experience. The first table in the figure on the next page shows the experience level of each of the six employees in the population. For example, employee number 1 has ten years of experience with the company.

We will use this information to calculate the mean job experience sampling distribution. The job experience sampling distribution for the sample mean shows us all the possible mean job experience outcomes that could have been produced by sheer random chance. We can derive the sampling distribution in this setting in a straightforward manner, because we can count all the possible values for the mean job experience.

Specifically, listing out all the possible samples of three people yields a total of 20 possible employee samples. The 20 possible three-person samples are shown in the lower portion of the figure on the next page. The sample distribution for the mean is shown in table form in the shaded columns of the lower table. In practice, many of our sampling distributions will not be reducible to table format. However, the principles behind the sampling distribution are the same.

The sampling distribution in this example could be used to study different sub-groups within the employee population. For example, if we wanted to compare the average job experience of women to that of men, we could determine whether the deviation were significant by considering the likelihood that randomness would have generated the job experience outcome. As before, we can use the sampling distribution to determine the effect of luck, so to speak.

Formally, we can generalize the sampling distribution for the mean as follows.

> If the random variable,
> $X = \bar{x}_1, \bar{x}_2 \cdots \bar{x}$, where $\bar{x}_i$ is the sample mean for random sample i
> then
> $E(\overline{X}) = \mu$, where $E(\overline{X})$ is the mean of $\overline{X}$

In addition, we can look at the variance of the sampling distribution. The following formulas are for a population with a large, uncountable (infinite) number of individuals and a population with a countable (finite) number of individuals.

Example of Derivation of a Sampling Distribution of the Mean

Employee Population

Employee Number	Years of Job Experience
1	10
2	4
3	15
4	5
5	1
6	10

Average Years of Experience in the **Population: 7.5**

Repeatedly sampling three employees from the population of six employees produces the following sampling distribution.

Sample Number	Members	Job Exp.	Mean Exp.	Sample Number	Members	Job Exp.	Mean Exp.
1	3,2,1	10,4,15	9.67	11	5,3,2	4,15,1	6.67
2	4,2,1	10.4.5	6.33	12	6,3,2	4,15,10	9.67
3	5,2,1	10,4,1	5.00	13	5,4,3	15,5,1	7.00
4	6,2,1	10,4,10	8.00	14	6,4,3	15,5,10	10.00
5	4,3,1	10,15,15	10.00	15	6,5,3	15,1,10	8.67
6	5,3,1	10,15,1	8.67	16	6,5,4	5,1,10	5.33
7	6,3,1	10,15,10	11.67	17	6,5,1	10,1,10	7.00
8	5,4,1	10,5,1	5.33	18	5,4,2	4,5,1	3.33
9	6,4,1	10,5,10	8.33	19	6,4,2	4,5,10	6.33
10	4,3,2	4,15,5	8.00	20	6,5,2	4,1,10	5.00

Average years of experience across **all samples: 7.5**

In an infinite population,

$$Var(\overline{X}) = \frac{\sigma^2}{n} \quad \text{and} \quad SD(\overline{X}) = \frac{\sigma}{\sqrt{n}}$$

In a finite population,

$$Var(\overline{X}) = \frac{(N-n)}{N-1}\left(\frac{\sigma^2}{n}\right) \quad \text{and} \quad SD(\overline{X}) = \frac{(N-n)}{N-1}\left(\frac{\sigma}{\sqrt{n}}\right)$$

Major Implications from Sampling Distributions of Mean and Variance

1. The sample mean will, on average, equal the population mean.

As shown above, the expected value of the sample mean suggests that, on average, in sufficiently large samples, the sample mean will equal the population mean. This can be shown by looking at the mean job experience for the underlying population and the individual employee samples. As the tables show, both the mean of the individuals in the underlying population and the mean of the different three-person samples are equal to 7.5 years.

However, this does not imply that individual sample means will not differ from the population mean. An individual sample mean can be either higher or lower than the population mean. Our example illustrates this fact as well. But if a sufficiently large number of samples are drawn, the mean of the sample means will be equal to the population mean.

2. The variance of an employment sample will reflect the underlying employee population.

The formula (shown above) for the variance tells us several important things about the expected behavior of the sample mean. First, the natural dispersion of the mean is captured by the standard deviation of the sampling distribution of the mean. This dispersion is also referred to as the standard error of the mean. As we can see from the formula for the variance above, the natural dispersion around the mean of the sampling distribution of the sample mean is related to both the dispersion parameter (σ) and the size of the sample (n). Refer to points 3 and 4 below.

3. If there is a large amount of natural dispersion in the underlying employee population, then there will likely be a large amount of dispersion in the sample based on the employees that are selected.

4. With a larger sample size, we expect less dispersion around the sample mean.

This reflects the fact that a larger sample size reveals more information about the underlying population than a small sample size does.

Conclusions and Chapter Summary

In this chapter, we discussed sampling distributions. The sampling distribution numerically describes the potential outcomes that would be generated by a random and presumably nondiscriminatory employment process. In essence, the sampling distribution is the straw-person that allows us to test our discrimination hypotheses. If we find it unlikely that our straw-man distribution would have produced the employment outcome in question, this suggests that the outcome is consistent with discrimination.

The important concepts introduced in this chapter are the backbone for hypothesis testing and other topics introduced in later chapters.

Spotlight: Evaluating Statistical and Economic Significance

This chapter examines the concept of economic significance and its relevance to statistical evidence in employment discrimination cases.

Since the 1970s, employment attorneys and the courts have relied heavily on the mathematical and probability concept of statistical significance in assessing the underlying importance of statistical disparities in employment discrimination cases. Although the concept of statistical significance can be helpful for the courts and help labor economists and statisticians assist a jury in understanding the underlying context of a statistical employment disparity, overreliance on the statistical significance paradigm, especially when it occurs at the expense of economic significance, can potentially yield misleading inferences concerning employment discrimination. In recent years, courts have begun implicitly utilizing both significance paradigms when dealing with statistical evidence in employment cases. This chapter examines the concept of economic significance and its relevance to statistical evidence in employment discrimination cases.

Introduction and Background

In many employment discrimination lawsuits, both the employer-defendant and the plaintiff realize that there is a statistical disparity between the protected and non-protected employee groups represented in the case. The meaning of the statistical disparity is frequently the point of contention and is subject to differing interpretation by the employer and the plaintiff in discrimination lawsuits. Since the 1970s, employment attorneys and the courts have relied heavily on the mathematical and probability concept of statistical significance in assessing the underlying importance of an observed statistical disparity in employment conditions between different groups of employees. The concept of statistical significance, which in essence is a method that assesses the likelihood that random chance, and therefore not discrimination, produced a given employment disparity, is also routinely used by courts to assist them in determining whether the underlying statistical employment analysis meets the reliability requirements of *Daubert v. Merrell Dow Pharmaceuticals*, 509 US 579 (1993).

Although the concept of statistical significance can be helpful for the courts and help labor economists and statisticians assist juries in understanding the underlying context of a statistical employment disparity, an overreliance on the statistical significance paradigm, especially when it occurs at the expense of economic significance, can potentially produce misleading inferences concerning employment discrimination. Economic significance is a well-established concept that considers the magnitude and implications of the alleged disparity in employment conditions. When used in conjunction with the traditional concept of statistical significance, the inferences from a given statistical analysis can be quite probative and compelling. In recent years, courts have begun implicitly utilizing both significance paradigms when dealing with statistical evidence in employment cases.

In recent years, the importance of statistical analysis in employment discrimination cases has grown from an analytical tool that was used almost exclusively in class-action employment discrimination lawsuits to one that is used in many different types of employment cases, including pattern-and-practice lawsuits and cases involving a single plaintiff. Previously opaque statistical notions, such as the standardized measurement of statistical significance, are now becoming common concepts that attorneys and courts routinely contend with when handling statistical evidence in employment discrimination cases.

A substantial amount of case law has directly and indirectly contributed to the definition of statistical significance and the ways in which experts present statistical employment evidence in employment cases. Generally, when determining whether an employment disparity is statistically significant, the courts tend to reduce the assessment to a standard deviation. The number of standard deviations associated with a particular employment disparity tells the court, in terms that are uniform across different types of employment analyses, the statistical likelihood or probability that random chance would have produced a particular employment outcome in the absence of discrimination. Conceptually, the higher the number of standard deviations associated with a particular employment discrimination outcome, the less likely it is that a random and non-biased employment process would have generated the outcome in the absence of discrimination. The calculation of the number of standard deviations is performed using generally accepted mathematical formulas.

Statistical Significance Testing in Employment Discrimination Cases

Employment case law is replete with examples and discussions dealing with issues of statistical significance testing in employment discrimination cases. For many statistical experts in the employment area, the Supreme Court case *Castenda v. Partida*, 430 U.S. 482 (1977) provides one of the more definitive statements on statistical significance testing. In this case, which dealt with jury discrimination, the court stated that "as a general rule for such large samples, if the difference between the expected value and the observed number is greater than two or three standard deviations, then the hypothesis [concerning randomness] would be suspect to a social scientist, 430 U.S. at 496 n.17". Although the case specifically dealt only with a specific statistic test (the binomial test), labor economists and statisticians have adopted and applied this rule to other types of statistical tests in the employment area. Other courts have made clear statements concerning statistical significance testing in employment discrimination cases. For example, in *Lopez v. Laborers*, 987 F.2d 1210, 1214 (5th Cir. 1993), the Fifth Circuit held that the court should not reject chance as the underlying explanatory factor unless the differences are greater than three standard deviations.

Statistically significant employment disparities are not always economically significant.

The reliance on the statistical significance paradigm in the courts is, in some respects, at odds with the professional and academic literature in economics, statistics and social sciences. Many studies in the social sciences suggest that the importance of a particular statistical or empirical result should be viewed not only in terms of statistical significance, but also in terms of economic significance. Although there is no universal definition, economic significance is a well-established concept that suggests that the researcher take into account issues such as magnitude and the overall implications of the reported correlation or effects. In the context of an employment discrimination case, determining the economic significance of a particular analysis would generally involve assessing the magnitude and scope of the alleged disparity in employment conditions between the protected and non-protected employee groups, as well as determining the congruence of the statistical analysis with the case facts.

In essence, the fields of economics and statistics suggest that the most compelling and reliable statistical evidence in an employment discrimination case would use both statistical and economic significance paradigms when assessing the importance of the reported statistical disparities. Consider, for example, alleged discrimination in a reduction-in-force lawsuit. A typical analysis would begin by examining whether the disparity in job terminations among groups was statistically significant. As discussed above, statistical evidence of discrimination would arise if the observed number of terminations were statistically and significantly greater than the expected number of terminations. If the statistical analysis shows disparity, then the courts examine whether this disparity is economically significant. This would entail looking at factors such as the magnitude of the statistically significant disparity, whether the disparity reflects permissible business practice, and whether ambient economic conditions may have created the disparity. In recent years, courts have found this two-pronged approach particularly suitable to the evidentiary framework established by McDonnell Douglas. (e.g., *Smith v. Xerox Corp.*, 196 F. 3d 358, 364–65 (2d Cir. 1999)).

Using both the statistical and economic significance paradigms allows courts to further check the reliability of a statistical employment analysis and provides juries with a better way to understand complicated and often confounding statistical evidence. In its strictest form, the statistical significance model is silent on the effects and tradeoffs of relevant, but unmeasured employment factors, yet the concept of economic significance allows the courts and the jury to at least consider their potential effect on the alleged statistical disparity. A number of recent cases have shown that courts are increasingly considering more than statistical significance. In general, the courts in these cases evaluate the statistical significance (or lack thereof) as well as related factors such as the magnitude and scope of the employment-related disparity and the congruence of the expert's research findings with the undisputed facts in the case.

In *Meacham v. Knolls Atomic Power Lab.* 381F. 3d56 (2d Cir. 2004), the court weighed the magnitude of the statistical disparity found by the plaintiffs versus the explanatory factors offered by the employer in an age discrimination case that involved an employee reduction-in-force (RIF) action. The plaintiff's expert found a highly statistically significant difference between the termination rates of employees who were at least 40 years old and those who were less than 40 years old. The data showed that about 98% of the individuals terminated were in the protected age class, which comprised only about 60% of the population that was eligible for the RIF. According to the plaintiffs' expert, the difference was highly significant and would occur by random chance only one in 1,260 times. The court found that the size of the disparity overwhelmed the explanatory economic factors offered by the defendant-employer.

In *Morgan v. United Parcel Service of America, Inc.*, 143 F.Supp.2d 1143 (E.D.Mo. 2000), aff'd, 380 F.3d 459 (8th Cir. 2004), *cert. denied*, 544 U.S. 999 (2005), the court again weighed the existence of an alleged employment disparity versus the explanatory factors offered by the employer. In Morgan, the court found that the economic factors that the plaintiff did not include in the statistical model, which the court found to be flawed but admissible, outweighed the statistical disparity in pay and promotions that the plaintiffs' expert purported to find. These and other recent employment cases strongly suggest that courts are taking a more rigorous approach to evaluating statistical evidence in employment cases.

Conclusions and Implications for the Use of Statistics in Employment Discrimination Cases in the Future

As courts become increasingly sophisticated and knowledgeable about the statistical methods in employment discrimination cases, the more stringent two-prong approach of assessing the importance of statistical results, which is favored by professional and academic economists and empirical statisticians, will become increasingly common. The process of determining economic significance does not lend itself to the discussion of a single metric such as a standard deviation; employment attorneys should consider many issues when using statistical evidence in employment cases in the future.

First, implementing a more rigorous approach to evaluating statistical evidence will necessarily increase the level of scientific rigor embodied in statistical analyses of employment discrimination. Second, while from a modeling standpoint it may not be necessary to have all the intimate details of an employment process, future analysis will require an even more careful dissection of the underlying employment process. Third, the nature of determining economic significance will require the skills of experts who possess a good understanding of employment processes as well as discrimination concepts in general, and may involve a more multidisciplinary approach to produce the most reliable and compelling statistical evidence. Finally, the two-step paradigm of evaluating significance fits well into, and may actually reflect, the evidentiary framework of discrimination cases.

Hypothesis Testing

The goal of this chapter is to use the ideas that we developed in the previous chapters to build a framework for understanding the statistical analysis of employment discrimination.

In this chapter, we introduce the scientific method called hypothesis testing. In this chapter, we focus on which employment statements are statistically testable (and which are not). We also discuss in a conceptual way how those tests are generally performed and formulated.

Following the discussion on how to formulate a statistical hypothesis test concerning discrimination, we then examine the importance of recognizing the errors that could be made when performing a hypotheses test of employment discrimination. In particular, we focus on two types of errors, conveniently known as Type I and Type II errors. In this chapter, we also discuss how these errors are addressed within our statistical framework. We close the chapter with a general discussion of the limitations of hypothesis testing.

The Basic Concepts

The concept of statistical hypothesis testing is an old and generally accepted method of using empirical data to help the researcher make reliable and insightful inferences concerning a particular issue. For our purposes, the issue is the allegation of employment discrimination. Statistical hypothesis testing involves three main steps.

First, the researcher makes an initial conjecture or hypothesis concerning the employment process in question. At the beginning of the analysis, the initial conjecture is not supported by empirical data, so the initial research hypothesis is called the **null hypothesis**. As will be discussed in detail, in employment discrimination cases, the null hypothesis is that the employment data in question is consistent with unbiased and nondiscriminatory behavior of the employer.

After the null hypothesis is constructed, the researcher constructs the **alternative hypothesis**. The alternative hypothesis is the statement we believe to be true if we reject the null hypothesis. For our purposes, the alternative hypothesis is the statement concerning the employment data that we believe to be true if we reject the null hypothesis of nondiscrimination.

Finally, the researcher performs a statistical test using the employment data. The statistical test helps determine whether the data in the employment discrimination case is consistent with the null hypothesis or the alternative hypothesis. If the employment data is consistent with the null hypothesis, we say that 'we accept the null hypothesis'. The employment data is consistent with the null hypothesis of nondiscrimination if we find that there is sufficiently high probability that the result could have been generated by random chance.

Conversely, the employment data is inconsistent with the null hypothesis if there is a low probability that the result could have been generated by random chance. If the employment data is consistent with the alternative hypothesis we say that 'we reject the null hypothesis'.

As you can see, we have already covered many of the concepts of statistical testing. The information in this chapter uses those concepts to develop a unified method for statistically testing employment discrimination hypotheses. In the next few sections, we will discuss the concepts in more detail.

Overview of a Classical Hypothesis Test of Employment Discrimination
1. State the null and alternative employment discrimination hypotheses. 2. Select and conduct the appropriate statistical test. 3. Determine the significance level of the statistical test. 4. Make inferences.

Step 1: State the null and alternative employment discrimination hypotheses.

In employment discrimination cases, our initial conjecture or null hypothesis is that the employment data in question is consistent with unbiased and nondiscriminatory behavior of the employer. In other words, we assume the employer's policies or actions that generated the data in question were not motivated by racial, gender-related, or other types of animus. Our null hypothesis is similar to the presumption that the defendant is innocent until proven guilty in a criminal trial. However, in our analyses, the employment data decides the outcome instead of a jury or a judge.

After stating the null hypothesis, hypothesis testing involves specifying the alternative employment discrimination hypothesis. The alternative hypothesis is the statement we believe to be true if we reject the null hypothesis. For our purposes, the alternative hypothesis is the statement concerning the employment data that we believe to be true if we reject the null hypothesis that the employer's data is not consistent with nondiscriminatory behavior.

It is important to understand that even if we reject null hypothesis, we are not saying the firm discriminated against the protected group of employees. We can never make that statement based on the results of our statistical hypothesis test. The general construction of the null hypothesis, which is commonly called 'h-not' in statistics, and the alternative hypothesis are shown in the figure below

A Hypothesis Test Concerning Employment Discrimination
H_O: The employer data is consistent with unbiased and nondiscriminatory employer behavior.
H_A: The employer's data is not consistent with unbiased and nondiscriminatory employer behavior.

The underlying assumption of 'innocence' that permeates all classical statistical tests is perhaps the most unpalatable part of the entire framework for some consumers of statistical analyses. Some people find it frustrating that the standard analysis presumes that the employer is not guilty of the skullduggery that it is accused of in the complaint or by the employees. In reality, the assumption is not used to favor the employer. Instead, we make this assumption because it is the only way our statistical test works!

As we discussed in the previous chapters, our statistical employment analyses are analogous to trying to estimate the probability that a fair coin would turn up heads in, say, 45 out of 50 coin flips. The key is that we must assume that the coin is fair to be able to figure out the underlying probabilities associated with the outcomes we observe. The plan is not to favor the coin flipper or the coin maker. We simply want to calculate the probabilities that will allow us to determine whether the coin is most likely fair.

The same is true with our employment analyses. In fact, setting up the analysis in this way (i.e., giving the employer the benefit of the doubt) greatly increases the importance of a highly significant finding. For instance, in some employment cases, the finding that there is less than a one-in-5,000,000 chance that the employment outcome could have been generated by random chance can be quite powerful.

Based on the assumption and conjecture that the employer is not discriminating, the next step is to consider what the data and the employment related-statistics derived from those data would look like in the absence of discrimination or discriminatory behavior of the employer.

This partially involves determining whether it is appropriate to conduct a **one-sided hypothesis test** or a **two-sided hypothesis test**. A one-sided hypothesis test involves a parameter of interest, such as the average salary of women, that is equal to or greater than another parameter or statistic, such as the average salary of men. A two-sided hypothesis test involves a parameter of interest that is equal to another parameter.

On the surface, this determination may appear to be an unimportant academic distinction without a difference, but the structure of the null hypothesis can in practice have a big impact on the inferences made by the analyst.

To illustrate, consider a statistical analysis of disparate pay allegations in a gender discrimination lawsuit. The focus of these studies is typically on the difference in the average salary paid to men and women at the company. A one-sided employment discrimination analysis involving salary discrimination against female employees would be written as follows.

One-Sided Hypothesis Concerning Salary Discrimination
H_0: Women employee average salary $\geq$ Men employee average salary
H_A: Women employee average salary $\leq$ Men employee average salary

In words, the null hypothesis or the initial conjecture concerning the employer's compensation actions states that the employer, on average, pays women as much as or more than similarly situated men at the company. The alternative hypothesis is that the employer, on average, pays female employees less than male employees.

A two-sided hypothesis test concerning alleged salary discrimination is written as follows.

Two-Sided Hypothesis Concerning Employment Discrimination
H_0: Women employee average salary = Men employee average salary
H_A: Women employee average salary ≠ Men employee average salary

In words, the two-sided null hypothesis states that the employer pays similarly situated women and men the same on average. The alternative hypothesis in the two-sided version is that the employer pays women employees differently (i.e., more or less) on average than male employees.

The distinction between one-sided and two-sided hypotheses is subtle. However, there are two reasons why the two-sided hypothesis is more appropriate for most statistical analyses of employment discrimination. First, the two-sided hypothesis better approximates and models the employer's stated position of nondiscrimination against any group, regardless of whether it is protected. Second, the two-sided hypothesis test accounts for the possibility that the average salary of men could, in fact, be less than that of women. Remember that we are dealing with random luck: while not everything is probable, anything is possible.

The selection of a one-tailed test can have major implications on the inferences that are made concerning discrimination. As will become much clearer in the following sections, there are instances in which a one-sided hypothesis test can cause the researcher to reject the null hypothesis that the employer is not discriminating, while a two-sided hypothesis test would not reject the null. This is problematic, because there are instances where a one-sided test suggests discrimination by the employer while a two-sided test does not.

The two-sided test does not suffer from this problem. If a researcher rejects a two-sided test, the one-sided test of employment discrimination will also be rejected. Even if the researcher did not believe that the two-sided test was more appropriate, the additional certainty associated with the higher threshold of the two-sided hypothesis strongly suggests that a two-sided test is more appropriate for employment discrimination analyses.

Step 2: Select and conduct the appropriate statistical test.

The selection and adoption of the appropriate statistical test is one of the more straightforward parts of the analysis. Each set of data and facts is best suited to be analyzed by a particular statistical methodology. The selection is dictated by many factors that lie outside our objective of learning about the underlying concepts. The important thing to remember is that, regardless of the statistical technique that is employed, the underlying ideas are essentially the same.

Whichever statistical methodology is selected to test the employment hypothesis will produce a test statistic that is based on the employment data in question in the case or project. A test statistic is a number that is generated from the employment data, the relevant sampling distribution, and the mathematical formula dictated by the statistical methodology used to test the employment hypothesis. The test statistic is used to determine whether we should accept or reject the null hypothesis that the employer is not discriminating.

Step 3: Determine the significance level of the statistical test.

Regardless of the approach and statistical test that is actually used in the analysis, the next step is to set up the conceptual framework for analyzing the stated hypotheses with the empirical data. The analysis may involve straightforward analyses of the mean or be more involved and require the use of more advanced techniques that allow the researcher to look at many factors simultaneously. Ultimately, a determination must be made regarding at what point the null hypothesis of nondiscrimination will be rejected. In other words, we need to determine the level of statistical significance for our test.

To do this, we first determine what constitutes an unlikely occurrence in our analysis. At what low probability will we consider the null hypothesis of nondiscrimination by the employer to be implausible? Will a less-than-one-percent chance that the data could have been generated by a non-discriminating employer be enough? 0.5%? Or will the standard be set higher? Clearly the threshold should be set high. How high that threshold should be is debatable.

As a rule of thumb, a finding that there is less than a 1-in-200 chance (0.5% probability) that the data were generated randomly would be viewed as statistically significant. At this probability level, most researchers agree that the result is statistically significant and the null hypothesis should be rejected.

Step 4: Make inferences.

Based on the significance level, we can determine the regions where we will either accept or reject our null hypothesis of nondiscrimination. If the employment data falls within the acceptance region for our statistical test, then it is viewed as being consistent with the null hypothesis. If the results of the statistical test fall within the acceptance region then we say that 'we accept the null hypothesis'. As before, if the data is consistent with the null hypothesis of nondiscrimination, or falls within the acceptance region, we find that there is a sufficiently high probability that the result could have been generated by random chance.

On the other hand, if the results of our statistical test fall outside of the acceptance region and within the rejection region, the employer's data is viewed as being consistent with the alternative hypothesis. In this situation, we say that 'we reject the null hypothesis'. If the test statistic falls within the rejection region, there is a low probability that the employment outcomes (e.g., salary, numbers of hires) could have been generated by random chance.

Let's consider the following hypothetical example. Recall the salary gender discrimination case that we introduced in the first part of the chapter. Based on our data and the 'black box' formulas in our methodology, we calculate the test statistic that will be used to evaluate our hypothesis of employment discrimination.

Since our test statistic is based on the underlying employment data, under most conditions it will behave in a predictable manner. Like the sampling distributions that we discussed in the previous chapter, the test statistic for our data has a sampling distribution. That is, if certain requirements are met, we can generate a formula that will give us the probability associated with observing a particular range of outcomes.

What does this added complication get us? We use the sampling distribution of the test statistic, in conjunction with our desired level of statistical significance, to determine whether we should accept or reject the hypothesis that the employer is not discriminating against the protected group. To do so, we need to know only the formula and the distribution. Fortunately, many test statistics have distributions that follow the bell curve, or the normal distribution formula, that we discussed in the previous chapters.

Let's assume that our black box test statistic, denoted as (T), that we use to test our salary gender discrimination hypothesis does in fact follow a normal distribution. Using our desired level of statistical significance of 1%, we can define the acceptance and rejection salary regions for the one-sided and two-sided statistical tests.

Let's begin with the two-sided hypothesis test, where we are testing the null hypothesis that the average salary of women are equal to those of men versus the alternative hypothesis that average salaries are not equal for women and men. We will reject the null hypothesis if the average salary of women is so much less than that of men that it is unlikely that a random and unbiased salary determination process would have produced the outcome. We will also reject the null hypothesis and the implicit assumption that all groups are compensated equally for the same work if we find that the average salary of men is significantly more than that of women employed at the company.

We will have two rejection regions for our statistical test. The desired level of statistical significance will be split evenly between the regions. Practically speaking, this means that we are going to consider the probability that the average salary for women is either higher or lower than that of men. The figure below shows the acceptance and rejection regions for our test statistic.

This figure contains two normal distribution graphs. The upper graph represents the underlying sampling distribution for the employment data. It shows what the salary sampling distribution would look like if the average salary of male employees and female employees were equal. Using our graph we may then ask, 'if the average salary is equal to that of males, and the company is not discriminating, what is the likelihood that the process would have produced the average salary outcome that we observed for women? And of course, most importantly, by using our sampling distribution we can test our hypothesis concerning employment discrimination.

According to our statistical significance level of 1%, we will reject the null hypothesis of nondiscrimination if we observe an average salary for women that falls onto the dark areas of our graph. This area corresponds to a total probability of 1%, where one half of the total probability is contained in each of the tails of the normal distribution.

Likewise, we can talk about statistical significance in standardized terms. To standardize our normally distributed salary sampling distribution, we transform the underlying salary sampling distribution into the **standard normal distribution**. We transform the values in our salary sampling distribution by subtracting the mean of the underlying salary distribution from each salary value and then dividing by the standard deviation of the salary variables. The standard normal distribution has the same bell curve shape as the regular normal distribution, but because we standardize the underlying variable, it will always have a mean value equal to zero and a variance equal to one.

The advantage of using the standard normal test statistic is that it allows us to discuss the results in uniformly standard terms that apply across the statistical tests that we may perform. When we standardize the terms, we know that a higher number of deviations from the mean value indicates that the outcome would be less likely to occur randomly (see the figure below and the previous chapters for more detail). For instance,

Making Statistical Inferences – A Salary Discrimination Example

Our data revealed that, on average, women earned $33,000 and men earned $36,500. The plaintiffs allege that the difference between this figure and the average salary of men is the result of gender discrimination and not random chance. The salary sampling distribution shows how likely it is that a random, nondiscriminatory salary determination process would produce an outcome where, on average, women earned $33,000 and men earned $36,500.

If the average salary of women were equal to that of men ($36,500), then the sampling distribution for the average salary would be as follows.

Salary Sampling Distribution

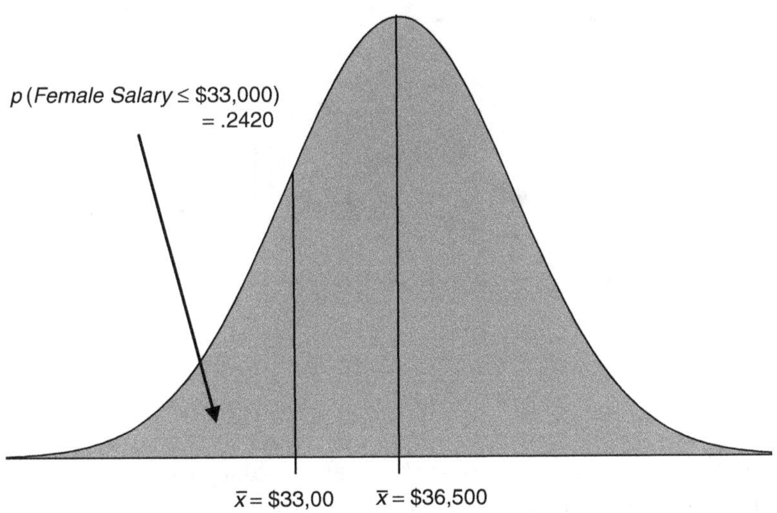

Using the normal distribution formula, we find that there is a 24.4% chance that the average salary outcome (or one where women earn less) could have been generated randomly by a nondiscriminatory salary determination process.

Alternatively we can use the standard normal distribution to calculate the probabilities (see the next figure).

Using the Standard Normal

Alternatively, we can use the standard normal distribution formula to calculate the probability. The advantage of using the standard normal test statistic is that it allows us to discuss the results in uniformly standard terms that apply across all statistical tests that we perform. When we standardize the terms, we know that a higher number of deviations from the mean value indicates that the outcome would be less likely to occur randomly.

To use the standard normal, we transform the underlying sampling distribution using the following formula.

$$z = \frac{x-\mu}{\sigma}$$

This transformation causes the mean of the normal to become zero and the standard deviation to be equal to one.

Salary Sampling Distribution

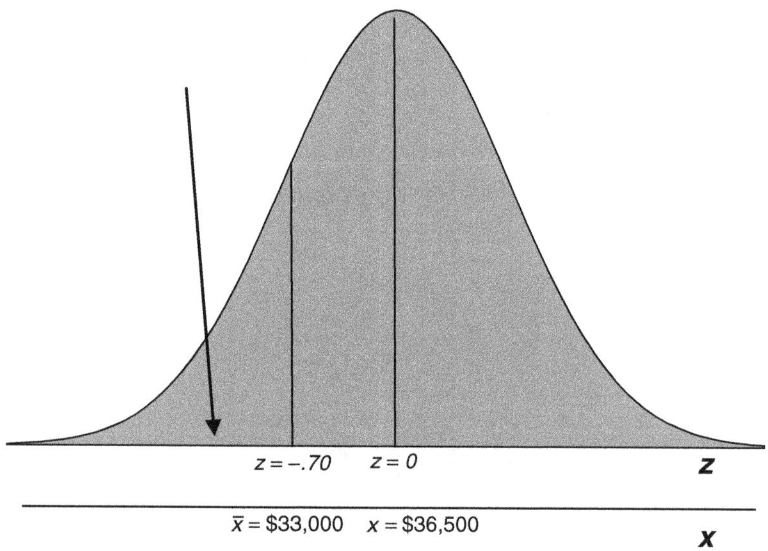

we may find in one analysis that the average salary for women is 'three standard deviations from the mean'. In another analysis we may find that the results suggest that the average salary for females is 'one-and-a-half standard deviations from the mean'. The finding in the first instance (three standard deviations) is less probable than the finding in the second analysis (one-and-half standard deviations). Using the standardized values allows us to make these types of comparisons across analyses.

Errors in Hypothesis Tests of Employment Discrimination

We have painstakingly developed the conceptual methodology to put our employment discrimination hypotheses to the test. However, the biggest chink in our armor is that even with the most sophisticated statistical models in the world, we still could make a mistake. Using our tests, we could incorrectly reject the null hypothesis that the employer is not discriminating when in fact that employer is not discriminating. Likewise, our test could fail to reject the null hypothesis and 'clear' an employer when in fact that employer is discriminating.

We must make every possible effort to avoid both of these mistakes. This section talks about the types of mistakes we can make when performing a statistical hypothesis test.

In the current setting, we could make two types of mistakes when testing a hypothesis concerning employment discrimination: Type I and Type II errors. The following two-by -two table illustrates these concepts.

Our Statistical Test Results	**Reality**	
	The employer is not discriminating (H_0 is true).	The employer is discriminating (H_0 is false).
Our test caused us to accept the null hypothesis (H_0) of nondiscrimination	$1 - \alpha$; GOOD (Significance level)	α; BAD – Type I Error
Our test caused us to reject the null hypothesis (H_0)of nondiscrimination	β; BAD – Type II Error	$1 - \beta$; GOOD (Power of the test)

The table above shows the possible outcomes of our statistical test concerning discrimination versus the actual behavior of the employer-defendant. Of course, we will never know the truth; the table assumes that we somehow were told the truth. The table and the outcomes shown above could be applied to the results of any statistical test of employment discrimination.

The upper left-hand corner of the table represents a situation where our statistical test, whatever it may be, produced the outcome where we 'accepted the null' hypothesis when, in fact, the employer was not discriminating against the protected group of employees. This outcome is desirable, because we want the statistical test of the employment discrimination hypothesis to accept the null hypothesis of nondiscrimination when it is true. This outcome is not an error.

Now look at the entry in the lower right-hand corner box of the table. The outcome of the statistical test concerning discrimination suggested that we should reject the null hypothesis of nondiscrimination, and it is correct. In this hypothetical situation, the employer was indeed discriminating against the protected group of employees. As before, the outcome of the statistical test in this situation is not an error. The value $1 - \beta$ is called the **power** of the test.

Type II Error: Falsely Rejecting the Employer's Claim of Nondiscrimination

Now look at the entry in the bottom row of the middle column. In this situation, our statistical test rejected the null hypothesis of nondiscrimination when, in fact, the employer was not discriminating. In other words, our statistical test wrongly suggested that the employer was discriminating when the employer was not. This type of outcome is not desirable. It is an error.

We call this situation a Type II error. Type II errors occur in hypothesis testing of employment discrimination when the statistical test rejects the null hypothesis of nondiscrimination when in fact the employer is not discriminating. Clearly we want to minimize the likelihood of committing a Type II error.

In an analysis of employment discrimination, to minimize the likelihood that the statistical test will falsely reject the null hypothesis of nondiscrimination, researchers commonly adopt a stringent and conservative definition of what constitutes a greater-than-expected deviation. In other words, the way to minimize Type II errors is to set a very high threshold for the level of what constitutes statistical significance and defines the associated rejection region. Researchers in employment discrimination cases frequently will not reject the null hypothesis unless there is less than a 0.5 percent chance (less than 1% in a two-tailed setting) that the employment outcome could have been generated naturally by a nondiscriminating employer. Researchers working on medical products may set an even higher level of significance. Choosing a high threshold for statistical significance produces a high threshold for what constitutes the associated rejection region for hypothesis tests.

Type I Error: Incorrectly Accepting the Employer's Claim of Nondiscrimination When in Fact the Employer is Discriminating

In contrast to Type II error, we could instead mistakenly accept the employer's claim of nondiscrimination when in fact the employer is discriminating against a protected group. In a Type I error, the plaintiffs' allegations are correct, but our statistical test suggests the opposite.

A Type I error is illustrated at the intersection of the third column and second row in our table of test outcomes. In this situation, our statistical test accepted the null hypothesis that the firm was not discriminating when, in fact, it was. In other words, our statistical test of employment discrimination found that the employer was not discriminating when it actually was discriminating against the protected group of employees. Like the Type II error discussed above, this outcome is not desirable and the likelihood of committing the error should be minimized.

Unfortunately, dealing with Type I errors in an employment setting is not as straightforward as dealing with Type II errors. This is partially due to the fact that the amount of a Type I error is usually related to the likelihood of a Type II error in the statistical test. Usually, as the likelihood of a Type II error decreases, the likelihood of a Type I error increases.

Expressed differently, as the researcher raises the threshold for rejecting the null hypothesis of nondiscrimination, the likelihood that the statistical test will wrongly accept the null hypothesis of nondiscrimination increases. As the likelihood of a Type II error decreases, the likelihood of a Type I error increases.

Conclusions and Chapter Summary

In this chapter, we introduced the scientific method called hypothesis testing. In this chapter, we focused on which employment statements are statistically testable (and which are not). Following the discussion on how to formulate statistical hypothesis tests concerning discrimination, we examined the importance of recognizing the errors that can be made when performing hypothesis tests of employment discrimination. In particular, we focused on two types of errors, conveniently known as Type I and Type II error.

Section III

Hiring, Paying and Promoting Employees

The Economics of Hiring Employees

In a hiring discrimination case or EEO audit, understanding the underlying decision-making process is critical.

Allegations of hiring discrimination can be particularly involved and difficult to analyze. The analysis of allegations of hiring discrimination tends to be complicated not because the statistics are more difficult than in other types of allegations, but because the underlying process of hiring an employee is quite involved. Moreover, hiring processes vary substantially among employers and even within different departments of the same employer. For some jobs, a given employer may use a formal, multi-staged, pre-employment screening process that includes an initial application screening by HR personnel, mandatory pre-employment testing and multiple employment interviews. The same employer may have a far less standardized hiring process for other jobs within the company.

The analysis of allegations of hiring discrimination is further complicated by the fact that it may involve any or all of the employer's hiring stages. Additionally, the job applicants considered at each stage could be either current employees or external candidates. Accordingly, a statistical analysis of hiring discrimination may involve the use of several different statistical techniques to perform a thorough review of all the claims made by the plaintiffs in an employment discrimination lawsuit. It is not uncommon for a hiring discrimination lawsuit to include allegations of discriminatory selection of employees for highly competitive job openings.

In this chapter, we provide a conceptual framework and understanding of a given employer's decision-making process in order to analyze allegations of hiring discrimination.

In the first part of the chapter, we describe and discuss the hiring process from the employer's perspective. In particular, we explore why an employer hires individuals, internal versus external hiring pools, and the stages of a typical hiring process. Becoming knowledgeable about a firm's hiring process generally involves first learning about the different internal and external applicant sources, or applicant pools, that the employer encounters when attempting to generate applications for a given job position. Depending on the type of job position that the company is attempting to fill, companies typically rely on internal and external application pools to fill job openings. Most hiring processes are also characterized by multiple stages or hurdles that the successful job candidates must navigate before being offered a job.

In the second section of this chapter, we talk about the hiring behavior of an employer from a labor-market perspective. We discuss the factors that employers consider when making hiring decisions.

Finally, we close the chapter up by putting all the pieces together and talking about their implications on the hiring analysis at the level of the employer and the labor market.

The Hiring Process

Companies hire people because they have a particular unfulfilled need. What is not always clear at first glance, however, is why an employer made a particular hiring decision. The first step to understanding an employer's hiring decision is to examine the pools that the employer is drawing from in its hiring process. Assessing the potential candidates can tell us a lot about the individual who is ultimately hired. Employers attempt to fill job positions with potential employees who do not currently work at the organization as well as individuals who are currently employed in other positions. These groups are typically referred to as external and internal applicant pools, respectively.

External Applicant Pools

External applicant pools comprise individuals who apply for a given position and who are not currently employed by the employer. Applications that a company receives from an external applicant source can result from advertisements that the employer places in the local newspaper, internet job database, or the classified ad section of a trade magazine. Applications from outside of the company may also be generated through word of mouth from the employer's current employees or from focused recruiting efforts such as interviews on college campuses. Citywide and regional job fairs, which are commonly organized by employers with similar, usually specialized, staffing needs such as telecommunication or technology companies, also generate external applications for some employers.

Although most of us are familiar with external applicant pools, they present several complications for the researcher conducting a statistical analysis of hiring discrimination.

First, from the employer or analyst perspective, it is not always clear what constitutes an application. In the age of the internet, employers receive a large number of inquiries for every job opening. The researcher finds that only some of these inquiries should be considered to be applications. At the onset of the analysis, it is critical that the concept of an application be defined and used consistently throughout the analysis. The definition of what constitutes an actual applicant can produce radically different estimates of the employer's pool of job candidates.

More specifically, some of the job inquiries that a typical employer receives are general form letters sent to many different employers simultaneously. Some of these form letters are nothing more than an attempt to determine whether job opportunities exist with a particular employer. In the analysis, these types of inquiries should most likely not be included as applications, or at least not as of the date when the general inquiry was sent. The employer and researcher may also find that, in a significant number of instances, individuals may have submitted the inquiry or application for a particular job opening without meeting even the minimal qualifications. In these instances, it is not always clear from an analytical standpoint whether inquiries or even formal applications received from these types of individuals should be included. Generally speaking, these types of applications should be included if the employer formally considered them at some point in the hiring process. Clearly defining the application pool is particularly important when dealing with employers that do not require a formal application for the position in question.

Second, even if there were no issues in determining what constitutes an application, it is typically difficult for employers to fully identify and benchmark the external pool from which the applications were generated. In some instances, individuals, or even particular groups, who submit an initial application, may voluntarily withdraw their application unbeknownst to the employer. In other instances, individuals may lose interest in a given position upon learning more about the working conditions. This type of self elimination from the hiring pool has been shown to be an important factor in discrimination cases and EEO audits involving physically demanding jobs. Determining the demographic composition of the potential applicant pool or of an employer's application data flow is difficult and potentially inexact.

The potentially inexact nature of the application source generally means that the analyst and the employer will have to perform multiple analyses and consider multiple factors to reliably evaluate an employer's application flow data and the underlying allegations of discrimination. Because the applications are derived from more varied applicant pools, the related analytical problems and complications tend to be more acute when analyzing application flow data that is generated by relatively unfocused recruiting methods, such as newspaper advertisements. The research complications are somewhat less acute when dealing with external applications from more focused recruiting sources, such as on-campus interviews.

Internal Applicant Pools

Internal applicant pools comprise individuals who apply for a given position and who are currently employed by the company. In general, an employer uses more limited recruiting methods to generate internal applications for a job opening. Employers who generate applications from internal sources are more likely to use intra-office and inter-office job postings and bulletin board notices placed within the company's offices.

In other instances, internal applications may be generated or triggered by employees reviewing and responding to an external ad placed in a newspaper classified ads section or by word-of-mouth. Even in these instances, it is still important, for reasons to be discussed in more detail later, to identify which applications are internal and which are external.

Those of us who do not work for a large employer are less familiar with the workings of an internal applicant pool. As with applications received from external sources, it is important to understand the special implications and data issues that arise when reviewing internal applications. As with external applications, it is not always clear from the employer or analyst perspective what constitutes an actual application. The manager responsible for handling the firm's internal applications typically receives a number of applications from current employees who are not even minimally qualified for the internal job posting. For instance, some people may apply for a management position without having the required supervisory experience. As stated earlier, if the employer considers the applications of non-qualified applicants in the decision process, then the analyst should incorporate them in the analysis in some way.

It tends to be easier to identify legitimate applications when dealing with internal applicant pools, but determining the appropriate benchmark for the demographic comparison may still present issues that must be addressed in the analysis. In some instances, there may still be problems related to self selection. For example, even if the job position were posted only on internal job listings available to current employees, not all groups of employees may be equally 'in the loop'. As a result, certain employee groups may have a larger response simply because word of mouth spreads more quickly within those groups. The degree of bias introduced by such issues depends on factors such as the size of the employer and the scope and breadth of the internal job listing.

The Phases of a Hiring Process

In addition to studying how the employer gets applications, the researcher needs a solid grasp on the multiple stages that make up the defendant-employer's hiring process. In practice, the hurdles in an employer's job-

A Diagram of the Hiring Process

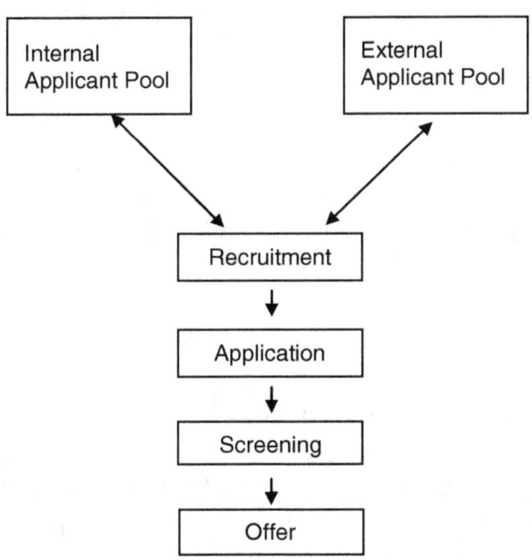

screening process can potentially have a significant effect on the resulting racial- gender- or age-based hiring patterns. Common sense and basic physiology suggest that an employer that administers a pre-employment test for a manufacturing position requires the job applicant to repeatedly lift 100-pound boxes employs fewer women than an employer that does not use the pre-employment test. In other instances, the effect of a pre-employment test that is related to a bona fide job requirement may be as important but not as clear.

Employment attorneys, compliance officers and others who deal with hiring data must recognize that there are many legitimate and nondiscriminatory factors that could account for deviations from the expected number of hires. These factors must be accounted for before a reliable statistical analysis of the employer's hiring pattern can be performed. We cover some of these factors in this section's discussion of a typical firm's hiring process.

Regardless of size, most companies use multiple stages, often referred to as multiple hurdles, in their hiring process to review the suitability of job applicants for employment. It is relatively rare for employers to hire the first person who walks through the door, even if they wanted to. To create a reliable and accurate analysis of the hiring process, the researcher must understand the discrete phases or hurdles that an applicant has to navigate before being offered a job. The number and type of hurdles that a job candidate faces can vary substantially from job to job.

For some jobs, the hurdles involve written document screening, pre-employment tests, physical testing, drug screening, and even scored interviews. Other positions have less formal, but still identifiable pre-employment hurdles that the successful job candidate must navigate before being offered a position.

Ironically, the type and formality of the pre-employment hurdles is not necessarily correlated with a job's salary or responsibilities. In some instances, high-level jobs with high responsibility and large compensation packages are filled internally with minimal pre-employment formality. In these instances, the job candidate's professional reputation or previous interactions with the employer may remove some of the layers of formality in the application process.

Job candidates applying for lower-level and lower-paying positions may actually face more pre-employment hurdles than job candidates for higher-level positions. The formality of the hiring process tends to be higher when most of the job candidates are not current employees. A more formal pre-employment process also tends to be used when the candidates are current employees with relatively short tenure with the employer.

In any event, it is important to clearly document the stages in the employer's hiring process and identify which job applicants made it to which hiring stages, as well as the reasons why job candidates left the hiring process. Generally speaking, the phases of a typical hiring process are the recruitment phase, application phase, screening phase, and employment-offer phase.

The following sections comprise a detailed discussion on the different phases of a typical hiring process. As we discuss the different phases of a hiring process, be aware that each phase may be composed of multiple sub-phases. For instance, the screening process may include a pre-employment test and multiple interviews while the screening process is simply a background check for other employers.

Recruitment Phase

The recruitment phase is the part of the hiring process that is dedicated to making individuals and potential job candidates aware of the employer's job openings. During the recruitment phase, the employer may use any number of different methods to get the word out about job openings. As discussed above, these methods include placing advertisements in the want ads of the local newspapers and relevant trade magazines or other industry publications, internal job postings, bulletin board posters, on-campus interviews, regional job fairs, and requests for current employees to spread the word about the job openings to potential job candidates. It is common for firms to use many different recruitment methods, some of which vary over time, for each type of job positions that the employer is attempting to fill. The employment attorney or compliance officer must be aware of how the various recruitment methods could indirectly impact the presence of minorities, women or other protected group of interest among the applicants.

Application Phase

The application phase is the part of the hiring process that is dedicated to collecting and reviewing the applications that were received during the recruitment phase.

Some employers have a pre-application screening process, or a system that limits or pre-determines which individuals will be allowed to apply for a position. Larger employers looking to fill a significant number of high-paying jobs that require relatively few job skills tend to receive an overwhelming number of applications. In these instances, some employers conduct a pre-application lottery, where the 'lottery winners' are allowed to submit an actual application for the job openings.

These types of pre-application lotteries should be more or less neutral (i.e., not favor any particular group of potential job candidates over another) if the recruitment techniques used to select the pre-application candidates were neutral. If not, the employment attorney or compliance officer will have to take care to ensure that any intentional or unintentional sample selection biases are accounted for in the hiring analysis.

Screening Phase

In the screening phase, employers remove applicants who do not fit pre-determined criteria. During the application phase, depending on the number of applications received, the employer may use any number of different screening methods to analyze the applications received during this phase of the hiring process. A typical employer will at a minimum begin with a basic document screening that removes clearly unqualified applicants from the pool of serious applicants. The process of application screening may be carried out in multiple sub-stages.

For instance, many employers first eliminate applications from individuals who do not meet the minimum requirements for a given job. Some employers then check the stated experience and education of the remaining applicants to determine whether they are relevant and appropriate for the job.

In the screening phase there is the potential for a set of bona fide job related criteria to create a disparity that appears to be discriminatory on the surface, when in fact the employer is not engaging in discriminatory behavior.

Employment Offer Phase

The employment offer phase is when the employee decides to accept the company's offer of employment. Although employers clearly select individuals for positions, it is ultimately the individual who chooses to work for the employer. This facet of the hiring process cannot be stressed enough. Some employers' screening process screens out not only individuals who are unqualified, but also those who for some reason do not have a strong interest in the job. In these instances, there is a high acceptance rate among the individuals selected by the employer. Conversely, the screening process will not be as effective if many of the individuals who are offered employment either directly or indirectly reject the offer. The discrimination findings can differ significantly when accounting for these factors.

Labor Market Perspective

So far, our discussion has focused on the different factors that affect the hiring process at the employee and employer level. However, employers do not make their hiring decisions in a vacuum. An employer's ultimate hiring decision is influenced by labor market factors. These factors, which cannot be controlled by the employer, will shape the final age, race, and gender distribution of the individuals who are ultimately employed. As discussed previously, without a thorough investigation by the employment attorney or compliance officer, these factors alone could yield hiring outcomes that appear discriminatory when in fact no discrimination has taken place.

In this section, we want to focus on the different labor market factors that need to be addressed in an analysis of allegations of discrimination concerning the hiring process. These include both supply- and demand-side labor market factors. Demand-side labor market factors affect the employer's hiring decisions in the labor market. Supply-side labor market factors affect an individual's decision to apply or accept employment offers.

A Brief (and Painless) Econ 101 Refresher

In order to have a common understanding, let's quickly revisit how a market works. This refresher will help, because a labor market works as any other market does. As you may recall from your high school or undergraduate economics courses, a market is composed of a demand-side curve and a supply-side curve. The demand side of the market, or the demand curve, shows all the products that would be demanded by consumers at each price. The supply side, or supply curve, shows all the products that would supplied to the market at different prices. The supply and demand curves intersect at the price that will prevail in the market for the product.

The labor market works in the same way. As shown in the figure below, the wage for a particular job is determined by the intersection of the demand and supply curves for labor. At this point, the key concept to understand about the labor market is not so much how the prevailing wage is determined, but rather what causes the labor market demand and labor market supply to increase or decrease.

We are interested in increases and decreases in the labor market demand and supply because it shows that, all else equal, a change in the demand or supply will result in a change to the number of employees demanded, no matter the price. These shifts and natural workings of the labor demand and labor supply curves can cause differences in the number of people that are hired for any particular set of jobs. Natural workings that are nondiscriminatory in nature may produce the appearance of discrimination against the protected group in question.

An increase in consumer demand, for the underlying products that an employer produces can affect the demand for different job positions differently. For example, during the high-tech boom experienced in the 1990s, the increase in demand for computer-related professionals greatly outstripped the demand for employees in manufacturing positions. Similarly, if certain demographic groups are more likely than others to be the suppliers of labor to fill these high-tech positions, then the resulting employee demographic breakdown can incorrect suggest that the employer discriminates against a particular protected group. Analyses that do not take labor market realities into account can produce unreliable results. In short, to be able to identify any potential discrimination, we must first account for the natural workings of the labor market.

Demand-Side Labor Market Factors

The workings of the labor market drive an employer's hiring decisions. Collectively, we refer to the hires made by a group of employers as their labor demand. Factors such as the number of other employers in the market that are competing for the same employees and the level of economic activity dictate much of the employer's hiring decision. In order to isolate any potential discrimination in the hiring process from the legitimate labor market factors, we must study, identify, and account for the relevant demand-side factors in the discrimination analysis.

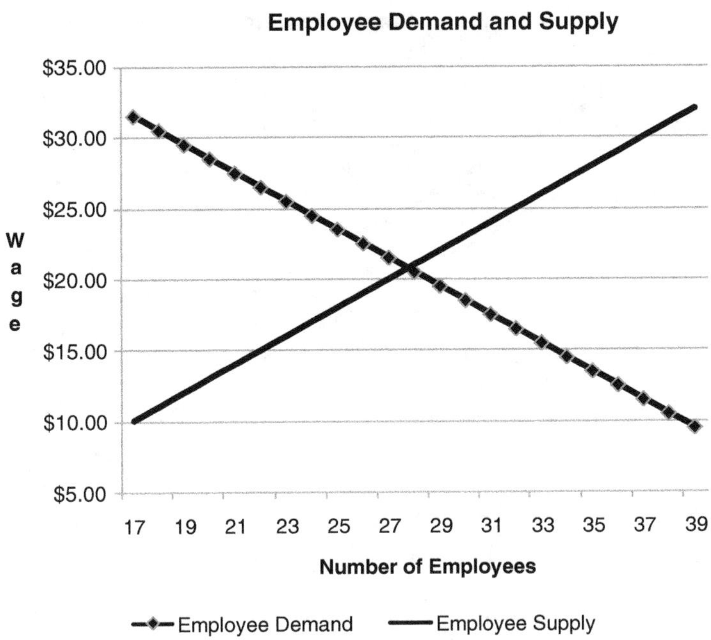

How Wages are Determined

An individual's wage is determined by the interplay between an employer's need for workers (employee demand) and the worker's desire to work for that employer (employee supply). In the graph above, the individual's wage is determined by the intersection of the employee demand and employee supply curves. The approximate wage rate for this employer is approximately $20 per hour. The employer will hire approximately 28 employees.

In general, if employee supply is held constant, factors that increase a firm's need for workers increase wages. Conversely, factors which cause an employer's need for workers to decrease have the effect of decreasing wages.

Holding employee demand constant, factors that increase an individual's desire to work for an employer will decrease wages. Conversely, factors that decrease an individual's desire to work for an employer will increase wages.

Many important demand-side labor market factors can impact the employer-defendant's hiring decision. These factors include the employer's product or service market, the condition of the economy as a whole, the regional economic condition that the employer faced, and prevailing industry-wide trends in the employer's product market.

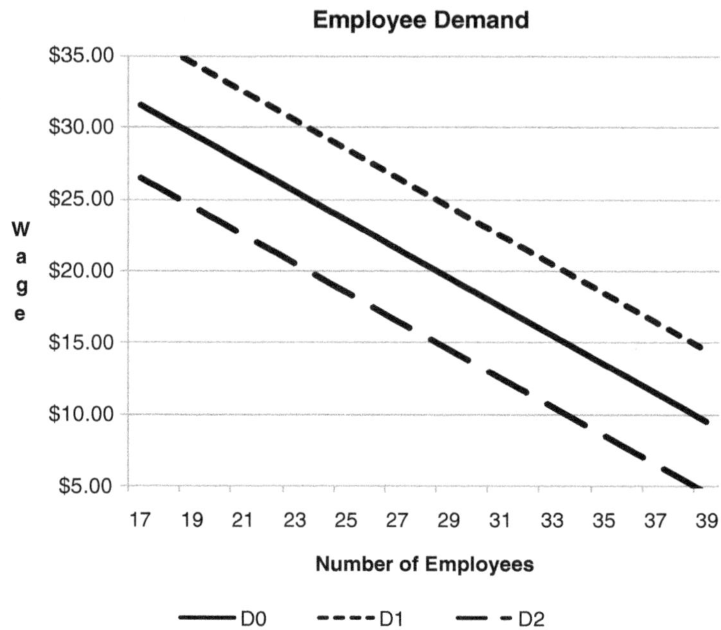

Changes in Employee Demand

Any change in the demand for employees means that the number of employees demanded by the employer has changed for every wage level. The figure above shows three different employee demand curves. The demand curve shifts vertically along the y-axis. An increase in the demand curve is shown as D1 and is shifted upward along the y-axis. Similarly, a decrease in the demand curve is shown in D2.

An increase in the demand for employees means that the number of employees demanded by the employer has increased for every wage level. For instance, an increase in demand could be represented by a shift of the demand curve from D0 to D1.

Conversely, a decrease in the demand for employees means that the number of employees demanded by the employer has decreased for every wage level. A decrease in demand could be represented by a shift of the demand curve from D0 to D2.

The factors that affect employee demand include (1) changes in the demand for the employer's product or service, (2) the state of the economy, (3) regional economic conditions, and (4) technological change.

Product and Service Market Effects

The demand for an employer's products and services is a major driver in its decisions to hire and fire workers. Holding other factors approximately constant across employers, the employer who is facing a 'hot market' for the products and services it sells is going to demand more workers. Similarly, employers in declining markets will generally have a lower demand for workers. The condition of a market could be determined by the relative selling price of the product or service and/or the number of units demanded by consumers in that market.

Economy wide effects

The economic condition of the overall economy is one factor that can have a significant effect on an employer's hiring activity and demand for employees. In most instances, there is a positive or negative statistical relationship between the employer's demand for workers and the economy. If the relationship between demand and the economy is positive, then as economic activity increases the employer's demand for workers increases.

Employers who produce luxury goods and services, such as high-tech electronics, that are in greater demand when the economy is strong tend to experience a positive increase in labor demand. The converse is true for employers whose demand runs counter to the overall economy. Law firms focused on bankruptcy law tend to do better when the economy sours, since if all else is equal, the number of bankruptcies tends to increase in economic downturns. Pawnshops are another example of a company with countercyclical product demand and labor demand.

The effect may not be as strong for some employers that hold on to their valuable employees even though the work may not warrant the staffing level. These organizations may find that it is more costly to train new employees, so they simply attempt to ride out the economic storm.

In any event, the major implication for the employment attorney or EEO compliance officer who is trying to make sense of the hiring discrimination allegations is that an employer's demand for workers may differ dramatically from year to year or even from month to month. The underlying statistical analysis of hiring rates must incorporate and account for this fact. Incorporating this type of information into the analysis may involve running separate statistical analyses for each year or using more complex methods to adjust the statistical model for the differing economic conditions that are reflected in the data.

If the statistical analysis of the employer's hiring data does not account for changes in the economy, then it may incorrectly suggest that a particular disparity is due to discrimination. More specific examples of this are found in later parts of this chapter.

Regional Economic Effects

An employer's hiring behavior may be directly affected by the regional economic conditions in which it operates. Regional economic conditions may differ from those of the overall economy. In some regions of the country, the local and/or state government may establish incentives and initiatives to encourage certain industries or business sectors to establish or expand operations in a particular geographical area. Depending on the scope of the incentives and the underlying pool of labor, the effect on hiring demand by employers that operate in the region could be quite far-reaching and significant.

The major implication is that, when performing a hiring analysis, it is often important to consider differences between the economic regions where an employer operates and conducts business. The economic region that should be considered could range from a portion of a city to parts of several cities or even several states.

Technological Effects

In addition to overall and regional economic conditions, the employer-defendant's labor market demand could be affected by a change in industry technological trends. These trends could either increase or decrease an employer's demand for employees.

For instance, in the late 1980s and 1990s, the speed and capabilities of personal computers increased rapidly. At the same time, the price of personal computers steadily declined and businesses moved from mainframe computers to individual personal computers. Accordingly, the demand for employees with skills and experience in administrating connected networks of personal computers soared in the 1990s. During the same period, demand for individuals with mainframe programming abilities died off almost completely.

In this instance, an analysis of an employer-defendant that employed both types of workers would experience two contradicting and conflicting labor force trends that would need to be explicitly accounted for in the analysis of its hiring data. In this situation, the analyst needs to review, study, and ultimately account for any significant trends within the employer's industry or industries.

Supply-Side Labor Market Factors

Individuals ultimately make the final decisions about when and where they will apply for employment, as well as where, when, and how they will supply their labor and to which firms.

Individuals' decisions are impacted by a number of factors, including the relevant human capital possessed by the individual worker, the state of the economy, and labor market trends within the applicable industry.

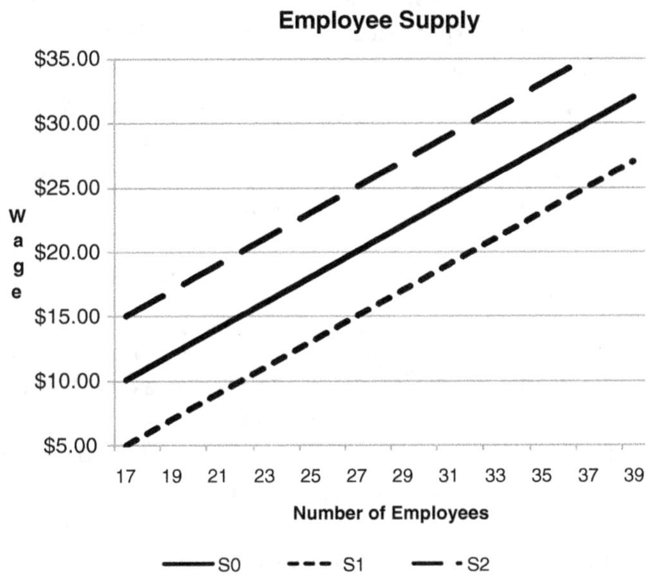

Changes in Employee Supply

A change in employee supply means that the number of employees willing to work for the employer has changed for every wage level. The figure above shows three different employee supply curves. The supply curve shifts horizontally along the x-axis. An increase in the supply curve is shown as S1 and is shifted to the right along the x-axis. Similarly, a decrease in the supply curve is shown in S2.

An increase in employee supply means that the number of employees willing to supply labor to the employer has increased for every wage level. An increase in supply would be represented by a shift of the supply curve from S0 to S1.

Conversely, a decrease employee supply means that the number of employees willing to work for the employer has decreased for every wage level. For instance, a decrease in supply could be represented by a shift of the supply curve from S0 to S2.

The factors that affect employee supply include (1) changes in human capital, (2) economy wide conditions, and (3) cultural capital.

Human Capital

Differences in the quantity and quality of human capital that an individual possesses can produce differing levels of success within a given employment selection process. Economists define human capital as the knowledge, skills, abilities and capacities possessed by a job applicant. A person's stock of human capital includes his or her education, on-the-job training, on-the-job experiences, investments in health, life and labor market experiences, employment opportunities, etc. In some applicant pools, the average level and quality of education varies across applicants. In these instances, education differences may be borne out in areas such as average school quality measures, performance on standard tests, average classroom performance and average educational attainment.

Economic Conditions

An individual's decision to apply for or accept a job offer is affected by the economic conditions in the overall economy, as well as that of the local economy. At the macroeconomic level, the number of applications and the quality of applicants can be correlated with the state of the economy. For instance, in the late 1990s, the overall expansion of the economy increased the number of job applications as people job-hopped in search of new and better positions. However, many employers reported interviewing and hiring 'lower-quality' individuals, because high demand forced employers to reach further into the labor pool.

Cultural Capital

The cultural background of an individual job applicant is an important, but frequently overlooked, factor that can be important in an analysis of alleged hiring discrimination. Empirical research has shown that the job applicant's cultural background, which includes shared experiences and the beliefs, traditions, habits, and values of the majority of that group, has a dramatic effect on the jobs that any given individual chooses to train for, apply for, and ultimately be employed in. This research suggests that there may be a tendency for individuals to gravitate toward employment in certain types of jobs. These tendencies for worker sorting may be evident in different racial groups, gender groups, nationalities, and age groups. As a result of culturally based job sorting, an employer may have application or hiring rates that differs from general workforce availability measures.

Conclusions and Chapter Summary

In this chapter, we provided a conceptual framework and understanding of a given employer's decision-making process in order to analyze allegations of hiring discrimination.

In the first part of the chapter, we described and discussed the hiring process from the employer's perspective. In particular, we explore why an employer hires individuals, internal versus external hiring pools, and the stages of a typical hiring process. In the second section of this chapter, we talked about the hiring behavior of an employer from a labor-market perspective. In this section we discussed the factors that employers consider when making hiring decisions.

Finally, we closed the chapter by putting all the pieces together and talking about their implications on the hiring analysis at the level of the employer and the labor market.

Hiring Discrimination Analysis

In this chapter, our goal is to provide a general framework to use when analyzing allegations of hiring discrimination. We focus on discrimination allegations involving the recruitment, application, and employment offer phases.

In the first section of the chapter, we discuss the statistical framework that is used to analyze discrimination allegations concerning the recruitment and application phases.

Applicant Flow Discrimination

Cases that use statistical evidence to analyze allegations of employer bias during the application phase tend to allege that the employer's recruitment methods directly or indirectly had a disparate impact on the rate at which protected group members applied to work for the employer. In some instances, the plaintiffs in these types of cases contend that the disparate impact is a consequence of the employer having selectively used recruitment methods that excluded the protected group from the application pool. Plaintiffs in these types of lawsuits often contend that the employer intentionally chose certain recruitment methods, such as on-campus interviews and word of mouth, so that minorities or other protected group members were not given the opportunity to apply.

In other instances, the plaintiffs allege a more subtle form of discrimination against the protected group. For instance, they may allege that the employer handles applications from the protected group differently. In a recent case involving a medical products manufacturer, the Office of Federal Contract Compliance Programs (OFCCP) claimed that female job candidates were having their employment applications disproportionately 'screened out' at the employer's call center. The end result of alleged disparate treatment of the applicants in this case is that fewer applications are considered from members of the protected group than would have been expected based on statistics regarding representation of the protected group in the workforce.

As these examples point out, hiring cases can involve claims of either disparate treatment or disparate impact. Either type of allegation lends itself to statistical analysis. While there are a number of different and reliable statistical methodologies, which can be used to analyze hiring discrimination allegations involving the recruitment and application phases, the statistical analysis used generally boils down to a single question:

The Research Question
Is there a statistically significant difference between the application rates of protected and non-protected group members in the relevant recruitment pool?

Recruitment-to-Application Rate

Generally, analysis of the research question involves calculating the application rate of the protected and non-protected group members in question.

$$Application\ Rate = \frac{Number\ of\ Individuals\ who\ Applied}{Number\ of\ Individuals\ in\ Recruitment\ Pool}$$

A basic analysis frequently involves comparing the application rates of protected and non-protected group members to those of a benchmark selection pool. There are a number of scientifically valid ways to make this comparison. While some are relatively straightforward calculations, others involve more complicated methods that account for multiple relevant employment factors.

Applicant Discrimination Model Factor	Description
Protected group application rate	Proportion of protected group members in the recruitment population who applied
Non-protected group member application rate	Proportion of non-protected group members in the recruitment population
How statistical significance is determined	Is the difference between the application rates of the protected and non-protected groups larger than three standard deviations?
Selection likelihood	Protected group application rate/non-protected group member application rate

It may be difficult to measure the number of individuals in a potential recruitment pool. In these instances, the analysis typically involves comparing the applicant pool to a proxy measure for the recruitment pool. For instance, in a racial discrimination case involving the hiring of product engineers at a software company, an analysis of application discrimination may compare the percentage of applications received from the protected group in question to the percentage of comparable software engineers found in the labor market as a whole. If the percentage of applicants from the protected group is less than the percentage of members in the potential recruitment pool, then this suggests that the employer received applications from the protected group at a lower-than-expected rate. Of course, the analysis also needs to consider the statistical significance of the application rate difference between the two groups of employees.

As stated above, analyses that use more advanced techniques, such as regression analysis, examine the same question as the basic model, but the statistical methodologies allow the researcher to analyze situations where the employers being analyzed are not all similarly situated. Essentially the only difference between the basic and advanced models is that the more advanced model adjusts the likelihood of applying for a given job position by the relevant employment related factors, such as location of application etc.

The use of advanced statistical techniques such as regression analysis is limited, because the required data generally is not available for the entire recruitment pool. The data needed to perform an advanced analysis of the application rate must cover a substantial portion of the recruitment pool and the factors that are believed to affect an applicant's decision to apply at the company. The determination and identification of these factors varies by company.

Screening Discrimination

An employer does not consider each and every application it receives. Most employers use some type of multiple hurdle process to identify the individuals who are most likely to succeed in the position. Testing and interviewing are two common phases in a typical multiple-hurdle employment process.

The **testing phase** involves pre-employment testing of the job applicants. Some employers conduct initial testing of job applicants, but the testing phase normally follows the application phase. The testing phase may include written tests of basic skills or job-related knowledge. Drug tests are usually administered after the application phase but before any written or other tests are taken by the applicant. Some employers use results obtained in the testing phase to determine who will be selected for an interview.

The **interview phase** involves meeting the applicant and discussing the job and the applicant's qualifications. During this phase, the employer interviews job candidates to further assess the fit of the potential employee with the company and the requirements of the job. The interview may be graded and scored by using any number of popular and generally accepted interview-scoring algorithms. Depending on the job and the employer, the interview stage may encompass multiple sub-stages, such as a phone interview, an on-campus interview, a job-fair interview, and/or an on-site interview. Each sub-stage may also be further divided, so the researcher and the ultimately the employment attorney must collect all the relevant information about each of the sub-stages of the interview phase.

Employment discrimination cases involving allegations of employer bias during the testing phase tend to contend that the employer's recruitment methods directly or indirectly had a disparate impact on the rate at which protected group members from the qualified application pool successfully made it to the testing and interview phases. From the plaintiff's perspective, the disparate impact on the protected group's interview rate may be the result of overt or subtle discrimination by the employer.

Plaintiffs may make allegations that the employer intentionally selected a testing or interview procedure or criterion that disqualified protected group members from the hiring process at a disproportional rate. In other cases, plaintiffs may charge that the supervisor or other individuals who are responsible for hiring more stringently evaluate the stated qualifications and experience of applicants from the protected group than from the non-protected group. For instance, the plaintiffs may contend that the employer who has a 'prior supervisory' job requirement for a position may accept any prior supervisory experience for non-minorities but (secretly) accept only job-specific supervisory experience for minorities.

In other instances, plaintiffs contend that the employer's discrimination is more overt and apparent. In hiring discrimination cases like this, plaintiffs have observed employer actions during the scoring of a written exam or during the interview phase that they believe is consistent with a bias against the protected group. These actions can include differential scoring on interviews and the subjective areas of a written test for members of the protected group. Sometimes it is alleged that the test itself is biased and the wording or administration of the test favors one group of job applicants over another.

As with application-related discrimination, many reliable statistical methodologies can be used to examine allegations of discrimination in the testing and interview phases. The actual research question boils down to a handful of common issues. One important part of a statistical analysis involving screening discrimination issues involves examining and comparing the screening rate of the protected group members with that of similarly situated non-protected group members.

In the basic model, the application rate is defined as:

$$\textit{Screening Rate} = \frac{\textit{Number of Individuals Who Were Screened}}{\textit{Number of Individuals Who Applied}}$$

Several caveats must be considered. First, the above formula assumes that the decisions to interview and test a job candidate are independent. The employer is not, for example, interviewing only employees who achieved a certain score on a written job-qualification test. If the decisions are not independent, such as when the employer requires a certain score on a test for an interview, then the number of qualified members in the relevant application comparison pool will be smaller than the total number of people who applied for the job position.

Second, to make reliable inferences concerning the allegation that protected group members are intentionally or unintentionally being interviewed or tested at a lower-than-expected rate, we must assume that the underlying pool of applications is not inherently biased. If the analyst or employment attorney suspects that application pool was tainted in some way, or if there are allegations to that effect, then these issues must be incorporated either directly or indirectly in the analysis.

Third, the comparison of interview or testing rates must involve members and employees who are truly similarly situated. If job applicants clearly differ on the surface in a number of important and relevant ways, then the selected statistical methodology must account for the relevant differences in an appropriate manner.

If the job applicants are clearly not similarly situated and there is sufficient data to perform the analysis, then the researcher may use a more sophisticated statistical methodology that allows him or her to account for multiple factors. The advanced techniques allow the analyst

Screening Discrimination Model Factor	Description
Protected group interview (or testing) rate	Proportion of protected group members in the relevant application population who were selected for an interview (or testing)
Non-protected group interview (or testing) rate	Proportion of non-protected group members in the relevant application population who were selected for interview (or testing)
How statistical significance is determined	Is the difference between the protected and non-protected group's interview (or testing) rate larger than three standard deviations?
Relative interview rate (or testing rate) likelihood	Protected group interview (or testing) rate / non-protected group member interview (or testing) rate

to create similarly situated comparison groups from the available groups of employees who are not inherently the same.

The research question concerning interview or testing rates is the same regardless of whether advanced or basic statistical models are used. The principal difference is that the advanced statistical model uses statistical methods to adjust the interview or testing rates by the appropriate factors that were used to make the decision, while the basic model does not make this adjustment.

The ability to perform a more advanced analysis that accounts for factors involved in the employer's decision to interview or test the applicants may be limited by the available personnel data. It is usually clear which applicants were qualified to be interviewed or tested, but in these types of analyses the data may not always be sufficiently complete to perform a multi-variable analysis of the decision process.

In particular, the researcher may find that the personnel information for the job applicants, who were not hired by the company, even if they made it to the interview stage, is less complete and may lack some of the information needed to perform a more advanced statistical analysis. The problems of data limitation are somewhat mitigated in situations where the employer performs rigorous application screening.

Employment Offer Discrimination

The employment offer phase of the hiring process involves determining and selecting which job candidates should receive an offer of employment. Like the other phases of the hiring process, the selection phase may be composed of multiple sub-stages. Individuals who make the ultimate decision may need to perform additional vetting of the remaining job candidates' qualifications, abilities, and interest in the job.

In these instances, the hiring process is more accurately characterized by the sub-stages of the selection phase. They may be clearly defined, such as when all candidates must take in-depth personality tests before undergoing a second interview, or they may be more loosely defined.

It is not always relevant to perform a separate analysis of all the sub-stages, but the analysis should nevertheless consider each sub-stage. In addition, individuals may have voluntarily opted out of the selection phase. In instances where the job candidates do not always accept the employer's offer, accounting for these individuals is also important. If opting out of the selection phase is an issue, then appropriate adjustments will have to be made to the starting pool of relevant job applicants.

In employer offer discrimination cases, the most common allegations are that an employer hires protected group members at a lower statistical rate than non-protected group members. Plaintiffs and employees who believe that they are victims of discrimination often contend that the employer makes hiring decisions either partially or entirely on preconceived statistical stereotypes about their particular race, gender, ethnicity, age, or other protected characteristic.

For instance, in gender discrimination cases, female job applicants for certain professional jobs may believe that the employer believes that they will not be as committed to the job as their male counterparts. In other instances, plaintiffs allege that the employer's hiring decisions are based on stereotypes about the motivation, inherent intellect, or suitability of different racial groups. The actual manifestation of the discrimination may be the result of the employer's intentional or subconscious decisions.

In addition, some plaintiffs feel that they are victims of discrimination that occurred when the employer chose not to hire members of their protected group because that is what the employer's customers or employees demanded. For instance, in a recent department store case, the plaintiffs alleged that the company disproportionally failed to hire minority applicants because it had a policy of favoring applicants with 'traditional' American appearances, which were almost always white or Caucasian. In other instances, racial discrimination cases have alleged that the employer disproportionally hired non-protected group members, because the employer's employees would supposedly not work well with the protected group members.

As in other phases of the hiring process, many reliable statistical methodologies can be used to examine allegations of discrimination. However, the actual research question in the selection phase generally boils down to a handful of common issues. One important part of a statistical analysis involving application discrimination issues is examining and comparing the selection rate of the protected group members and that of similarly situated non-protected group members. In the basic model, the selection rate is defined as:

$$\textit{Employment Rate} = \frac{\textit{Number of Individuals Offered Employment}}{\textit{Number of Individuals who Passed Screening}}$$

Several caveats must be considered when performing an analysis involving the selection phase of the hiring process. First, it may be difficult to construct bins of similarly situated job candidates for employers that do not have multiple phases in their hiring process. The employer may be considering the education, experience, and other qualification of each applicant at the time of the supervisor makes the hiring decision. In these situations, special care should be exercised to ensure that the individuals being analyzed are truly similarly situated, since the process lacks multiple stages to weed out clearly under-qualified or unqualified applicants. This may involve analyzing a smaller subset of the data or using more advanced statistical techniques.

Second, to make reliable inferences, the analysis should consider any potential bias that may have existed in the underlying pool of applicants from which the employer was making a selection.

Employment Discrimination Model Factor	**Description**
Protected group employment offer rate	Proportion of protected group members in the relevant application population who were offered employment with the company
Non-protected group employment offer rate	Proportion of non-protected group members in the relevant application population who were offered employment with the company
How statistical significance is determined	Is the difference between the protected and non-protected group's employment offer rate larger than three standard deviations?
Relative employment offer rate likelihood	Protected group employment offer rate / non-protected group member employment offer rate

Even in the later phases of the hiring process, the job candidates whom the employer is considering may not be similarly situated or possess equivalent or nearly equivalent qualifications. In these instances, it may be more appropriate to conduct a more advanced statistical analysis that accounts for the different decision factors in the model. This may involve the estimation of a multivariate regression model that includes multiple variables or measures the relevant factors that went into the employer's decision to make an employment offer.

Fortunately, data tends to be more complete in later phases of the hiring process. This is because the employer has already engaged in considerable due diligence to obtain the necessary information about each applicant. The more common problem that arises in these types of issues is that, although information is available about the job applicant, there are too few applicants to perform a reliable statistical analysis. However, if the data exists and is sufficiently complete, an advanced multivariate analysis of the hiring process can be quite insightful.

Case Study 1: Disparate Hiring

In this chapter, we provide the reader with several stylized case studies that illustrate the statistical techniques used to perform a statistical analysis of allegations of hiring discrimination.

The case study in this chapter focuses on an employer facing a gender discrimination lawsuit with allegations that it does not interview female candidates for employment as security guards.

Background

In this lawsuit, a large national security company is accused of discriminating against women who applied for security guard positions with the company. The company has offices in almost all major cities across the nation and hires more than 4,000 security guards nationwide each year. The company is divided into four regions (A through D) in the U.S. Each region comprises up to 12 regional sub-areas (I through XII) where new security guards are hired.

The hiring process for new security guards involves several stages. In the first stage (screening phase), applicants' documents are screened to see whether they meet basic requirements, and there is a background check and a drug test. In the second stage (testing phase), job candidates who successfully completed the first stage are given a standardized written test and basic physical exam.

In the third stage (interview phase), the job candidates who passed the physical test and achieved a satisfactory score (70 or higher) on the standardized test are eligible to be interviewed at the hiring supervisor's discretion. In the fourth and final stage (selection phase), job candidates who successfully interviewed with the employer are offered employment with the company as an entry level I security guard.

One allegation in the case is that the company discriminates against female applicants by selecting women for interviews at a disproportionally lower rate than that of men. According to the plaintiffs' pleadings, similarly situated female applicants were selected for interviews at less than one-third the rate of male applicants. Their data shows that out of the approximately 30,000 new security guard applicants nationwide who passed the first hiring stage, 9,300 (about 31%) were women. Overall, the employer interviews about 13% of the applicants who pass the hurdle in the first stage. However, only about 3% of the qualified female applicants and 12% of the qualified male applicants are interviewed for positions with the company.

The defendant in the case has provided the plaintiffs with a database that contains information on each applicant. The data shows each applicant's gender, years of formal education, years of relevant experience, whether the applicant has any previous supervisory experience, whether the applicant has any military experience, and whether the applicant was interviewed. The database also shows whether the applicant passed the physical exam and received a satisfactory score on the standardized test. Finally, the data contains information on the region and sub-region area where the applicant was interviewed and includes a unique identifier for each applicant.

An excerpt of the employer-provided data is shown below.

Database Excerpt – National Security Company

ID	Interview	Gender	Education	Experience	Supervisor	Military	Region	Area
1244	YES	M	12	0	NO	NO	A	VI
312	YES	F	13	1.5	NO	NO	A	VI
1274	NO	M	12	0.25	NO	NO	A	VI

Database Field Descriptions

The researcher's objective is to analyze the interview rates of male and female job applicants who passed the physical test and achieved a satisfactory score on the standardized test administered by the employer. In this portion of the case, the analysis must resolve several crucial issues. First, it must determine whether **similarly situated** female applicants are interviewed at a lower rate than **similarly situated** male job applicants. Second, if the interview rate is indeed lower for similarly situated female applicants, the analysis must determine whether that difference can be attributed to random chance.

Data Field	Description
ID	Employer-generated employee identification number
INTERVIEW	Variable equals YES if the applicant was interviewed
GENDER	M = Male and F = Female
EDUCATION	Number of years of formal education
EXPERIENCE	Number of years of previous experience as a security guard
SUPERVISOR	Variable equals YES if the applicant has previous supervisory experience as a security guard
MILITARY	Variable equals YES if the applicant has military experience
REGION	Employer-designated geographical division; variable equals A, B, C, or D
AREA	Employer-designated geographical division; variable equals a value between I and XII, inclusive

Formulation of the Statistical Hypothesis and Data Exploration

Formulating the statistical model involves using the facts of the case and information about the employer to create a statistical statement that can be tested by using the employer's hiring data. The actual test can be performed using any number of statistically valid methodologies.

In this case, we begin in the abstract and formulate the null hypothesis (i.e., what is assumed to be true prior to analyzing the data) and the alternative hypothesis. In this case, the null hypothesis is that the protective services company is not discriminating against female employees. Accordingly, the null hypothesis implies that any difference between the interview rates of the male and female job applicant groups is the result of random chance and not due to discrimination by the employer.

The alternative hypothesis is that the difference is unlikely to have been generated by random chance. The alternative hypothesis may be consistent with discrimination by the employer.

H_O: The employer is not discriminating against women by interviewing female applicants at a lower rate than male applicants.

Or

$H_o: IR_{female} = IR_{male}$

where IR_{female} *and* IR_{male} *are the interview rates for female and male applicants, respectively. The interview rate is defined as the number of applicants who were interviewed divided by the number of applicants who passed the physical test and scored 70 or more on the written test.*

One step that is often useful in any analysis is summarizing and looking at trends in the hiring data. This is often done over the course of the study and is not part of the formal report. It is also helpful to look at the raw tabulations or plots of the data.

Questions to Consider

- Are the individuals in the hiring analysis truly similarly situated? If not, what factors should be incorporated into the analysis to account for the differences?
- Do the female and male applicants generally have the same pre-application backgrounds?
- Does one group of applicants tend to have more relevant job experience than the other group?
- Are women and men generally applying to the same regions and sub-regions? Are there different opportunities in each of the company's regions and sub-regions?

The table below shows the summary statistics for the employer's interview data for male and female job applicants.

Hiring Data Summary Statistics – All Locations and Regions

	Female	**Male**
Interview rate	3.1%	12.4%
Average years of formal schooling	13.25	12
Average years of previous experience as security guard	1.5	2.75
Percentage with previous supervisory experience in protective services	12.3%	13.4%
Percentage with military experience	4.6%	9.8%

Questions to Consider

- When calculating summary statistics such as average experience, are there any significant differences across geographical regions?

- How could differences across regions affect the interpretation of the summary statistics?
- Do the summary statistics vary by gender or geographical region?
- What does the standard deviation of the summary statistics tell us in this case?

Motivating the Statistical Test

In this case, a number of different statistical tests were performed. One statistical test compared the number of interviews that actually occurred to the outcomes that would be expected if the employer were treating all similarly situated job applicants equally and fairly in the hiring process. If the employer is not discriminating, then the likelihood of selecting a similarly situated male or female applicant for an interview should be equal to the relative proportions of men and women in the qualified applicant pool. In other words, the expected interview outcomes of the company's hiring process should look more or less like the interview outcomes that would have been generated if the hiring supervisor were drawing applicant names from a hat.

The statistical test used is called the chi-squared statistic. It determines whether there is a statistically significant difference between the actual and expected number of female interviews, given the percentage of women who passed the standardized and physical test. The data for one of the security company's operational areas is shown below. This table shows the number of qualified security guards who were interviewed by the company by gender. This data is used to construct the chi-squared statistic.

Actual Interview Outcomes by Gender for the Protective Services Company – Area A, Region XI

	Interviewed		**Not Interviewed**		**Total Applicants**
	Number	Rate (%)	Number	Rate	
Female	3	4.34	66	95.65	69
Male	13	12.87	188	87.13	101
Total	16	9.41	154	90.59	170

Notes

1. The female interview rate is calculated by dividing the number of female applicants who were interviewed (3) by the total number of female applicants (69).

2. The male interview rate is calculated by dividing the number of male applicants who were interviewed (13) by the total number of male applicants (101).

As the table shows, the overall interview rate for female applicants is substantially less than that for applicants. The first row shows that the interview rate for female applicants was 4.34%, while the male interview rate nearly three times as high. The table also provides the information needed to calculate the expected hiring outcomes of a neutral and unbiased hiring process.

Assuming that the individuals are all similarly situated, fewer women should be selected, because there are fewer women in the application pool (69 women and 101 men). However, the **proportion** of female applicants who were interviewed should be approximately equal to the proportion of male applicants who were interviewed. That is, there should not be a statistically significant difference between the interview rates of male and female job applicants.

Determining the expected number of applicants who would have been interviewed by an unbiased hiring supervisor in this case is straightforward. We calculate the expected interview and non-interview rates for the security guards at the protective services company for all job applicants, assuming that gender is not an issue. That is:

Expected interview rate =

= Percentage of total qualified job applicants who were interviewed

= Number of interviews divided by the total number of qualified applicants

Expected non-interview rate =

= Percentage of total qualified job applicants who were not interviewed

= Number of applicants not interviewed divided by the total number of qualified applicants

Accordingly, the expected interview rate should be statistically the same for female and male job applicants. The expected non-interview rate should also be equivalent for female and male applicants. Once the expected rates are calculated for the interviewees and non-interviewees, the next step is to calculate the expected number of job applicants who would be interviewed (or not interviewed) for each applicant group. The number of female job applicants expected to be interviewed is equal to the total number of women multiplied by the expected interview rate. The numbers for the male applicants and the non-interviews are calculated in a similar manner.

That is:

Expected number of interviews =

= Expected percentage of the qualified job applicants who were interviewed

= Total number of qualified job applicants of the particular gender multiplied by the expected interview rate

Expected number of non-interviews =

= Expected percentage of the qualified applicants who were not interviewed

= Total number of qualified job applicants of the particular gender multiplied by the expected non-interview rate

The table below shows the expected number of interviews and non-interviews for female and male job applicants at the protective services company.

Expected Number of Job Interviews by Gender

	Number of Applicants	**Overall Interview Rate**	**Expected Number of Interviews**
	(1)	(2)	(1)×(2)
Female	69	9.41%	6.5
Male	101	9.41%	9.5

Actual Vs. Expected Job Interviews

	Actual Number of Interviews	**Expected Number of Interviews**	**Shortfall from Expected Number of Interviews**
	(1)	(2)	(1)–(2)
Female	3	6.5	−3.5
Male	13	9.5	+4.5

As the table shows, the expected number of interviews differs from the actual number of interviews. Since the hiring supervisor does not actually draw names from a hat when determining whom to interview for a security guard position, it is not surprising that the actual number of female interviews differs from the expected number of interviews. The important question is whether the difference between the expected and actual number of female interviews is statistically meaningful. Conceptually, answering this question is simple.

Our underlying motivation is to know the likelihood of obtaining the same number of female interviews as the protective services company if we randomly repeated the gender-neutral interview process many times. If it is very unlikely that a random and unbiased interview process would have generated the actual deviation between the expected and actual number of female interviews, then we conclude that the interview outcome for the protective company is not consistent with randomness or a gender-neutral process.

To perform the calculation, we need to know only the distribution of possible outcomes and the associated probabilities of occurrence for each of the interview outcomes that are possible in the hypothetical neutral process. Fortunately, these calculations have been done by others, so the analyst can use published tables or a computer program to obtain the answer.

One way we can address this issue is to use the chi-square test to analyze the deviation between the actual and expected interview outcomes using the chi-square test. To determine whether the deviation is statistically meaningful, we use our knowledge of the chi-square distribution.

Performing the Statistical Test

The chi-square test consists of several steps. First, we calculate the chi-square test statistic for our analysis using the actual and expected interview data.

$$\chi_T^2 = \sum_K \frac{(Actual_K - Expected_K)^2}{Expected_K}$$

$Actual_K$ is the actual number of job interviews, $Expected_K$ is the expected number of job interviews, and K is the number of interview classifications.

In our case study, the chi-square statistic is calculated as follows.

$$\chi_T^2 = \sum_2 \frac{(Actual_K - Expected_K)^2}{Expected_K} = \frac{(3-6.5)^2}{6.5} + \frac{(13-9.5)^2}{9.5} + \ldots = 3.49$$

The chi-square value (χ_T^2) that is calculated from the interview data is used to compare and test the statistical hypothesis. The chi-square value tells us the likelihood that the actual interview outcome was generated by a neutral and unbiased interview process. A larger chi-square test statistic indicates a lower likelihood of observing the actual outcome through random chance. In other words, the larger the chi-square test statistic, the

Interview Chi-Square Statistic Analysis

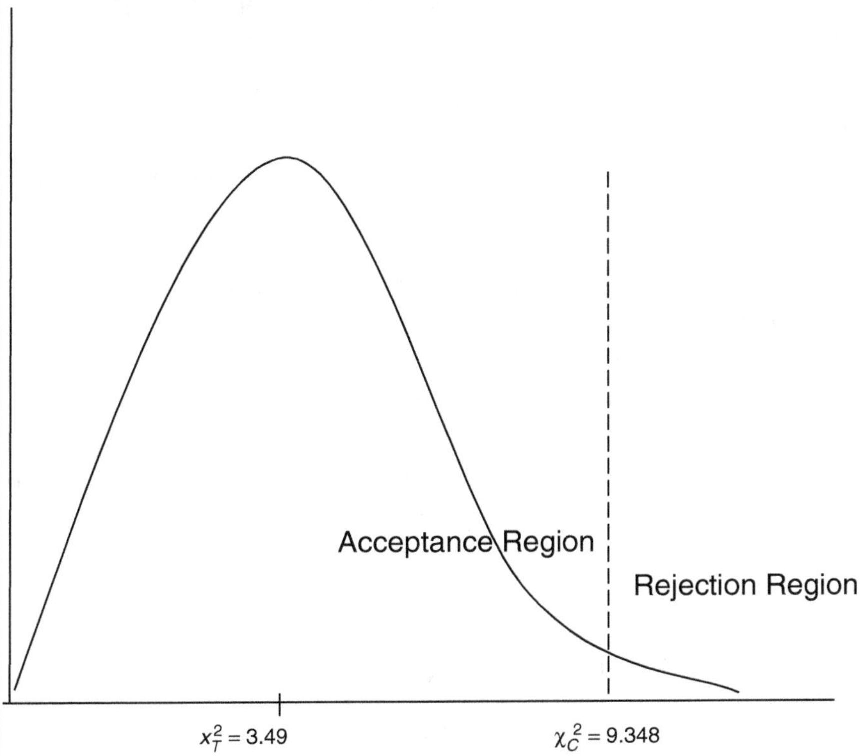

In our example, we have a test statistic value of 3.49. Since the test value is less than the critical value of 9.348, we accept the null hypothesis that the outcome could have been generated by a random, gender-neutral process.

less likely it is that our outcome would have been generated by a neutral and unbiased interview process.

Using the chi-square distribution and the pre-determined level of statistical significance, we determine the lowest possible value of the test statistic in step 1 that will cause a rejection of the null hypothesis (critical value, χ_c^2).

That is, if $\chi_A^2 > \chi_c^2$ then we reject the null hypothesis. The critical value used in these examples represents the 0.025 significance level. In other words, if we reject the null hypothesis, there is less than a two-and-a-half percent likelihood that random chance could have generated the interview outcome.

If the test statistic is larger than the critical value, then we reject the null hypothesis that the employer's interview process is neutral and unbiased.

In our example, we have a test statistic value of 3.49. Since the test value is less than the critical value, we accept the null hypothesis that the outcome could have been generated by a random, gender-neutral process.

Questions to Consider

- Are there any significant differences between regions when performing the statistical analysis at the regional level? What could account for these differences?
- Do you see any significant differences between the interviews conducted in each region? If so, what effect would they have on the analysis, if any?
- Why might you want to use a high threshold for statistical significance in these types of analyses?
- Why might you want to consider using a more advanced model? What would it look like if you did?

Case Study 2: Testing Discrimination

In this class-action lawsuit, a federal government agency is accused of administering a test that has a disparate impact on the selection rate of African-Americans into the Deputy Supervisor Program (DSP).

The DSP is a special program that trains agency employees to become supervisors. The employees take a test with written, math, and verbal portions.

The agency requires a total score of 75 on the test to be considered for admission into the program. The plaintiffs in the case allege that the written and verbal test cause a disparate negative impact on the selection rate of African-Americans into the coveted DSP. They contend that the test is not a business necessity for the Deputy Supervisor job.

In this early phase of litigation, the statistical analysis has two objectives. First, it must determine whether the test is correlated with on-the-job performance as a Deputy Supervisor. Second, it must determine whether there is a statistically significant difference between the performance of African-American and White test-takers.

Background

The federal agency that is being accused of discrimination employs more than 750,000 people nationwide. Each year, approximately 6,300 employees apply for admission into the competitive DSP, which is offered four times per year. All potential DSP candidates must be current employees in a line supervisor position in one of the country's four operational regions, have sufficiently high job-performance ratings, and have several recommendations before they are eligible to apply for the program.

Because many of the applicants are pre-screened locally before they are allowed to apply for a position, the DSP admission process is fairly

Database Excerpt – Federal Agency

Demographic Information Table

ID	Race	Gender	Highest Education	Date of Birth
1244	Act-DSP	M	Assoc	01/12/1962
312	Line Sup	M	Bachelors	11/12/1958
1274	Act-DSP	M	High School	06/01/1962
1098	Line Sup	F	High School	09/23/1955

Test Results Data Table

ID	Written Score	Math Score	Interview Score	Written Test Date	Math Test Date	DSP Select
1244	85	75	85	06/12/2006	06/12/2006	NO
312	76	72	87	06/12/2006	06/12/2006	NO
1274	92	95	96	06/12/2006	06/12/2006	YES

Job Position Data Table

ID	Job Title	Job Title Effective Date	Region	Supervisor
1274	Act-DSP-Temp	06/17/2005	I	NA
1274	Line Sup	04/19/2001	III	Jones
1274	Asst. Line Sup	01/03/1997	IV	Smith
1274	Operator	01/27/1995	V	Carnes

Job Performance Data Table

ID	Job title	Job Ranking	Job Performance Effective Date	Job Ranking	Rater
1274	Line Sup	1	4/15/05	98	Garcia
1274	Line Sup	1	4/15/04	91	Garcia
1274	Line Sup	1	4/15/03	95	Garcia
1274	Line Sup	1	4/15/02	93	Garcia

The employer's personnel database is organized into several different data tables that include several different types of employee data. The employer's database has separate data tables for DSP test results, past job positions, and job-performance data. The tables are linked through the unique employer identifier.

straightforward and includes only two stages. In the first stage, all applicants take written, math, and verbal tests, and participate in an interview. All DSP candidates are interviewed and scored using a well-recognized interview-scoring system.

An admission committee of five individuals selects which candidates will be admitted into the DSP based on their test and interview scores.

Data Field	Description
Demographic Data Fields	
Date of Birth	Employee's date of birth
Gender	Employee's gender: M = Male and F = Female
Highest Education	Highest completed education level
ID	Employer-generated employee identification number
Race	Employee's self-identified race
Job Testing Data Fields	
DSP Select	A Yes/No variable that shows whether the individual was selected for the DSP
Interview Score	Score (0-100) from the interview portion of the DSP selection process
Math Score	Score (0-100) received by employee on the math portion of the DSP entry test
Written Score	Score (0-100) received by employee on the written portion of the DSP entry test
Written/Math Test Dates	Date when the written or math test was taken
Job Position Data Fields	
Job Title Effective Date	Effective date when employee began working in the job position
Job Title	Title of employee's job
Region	Employer-designated geographical division, variable equals I, II, III,IV, V
Job Performance Data Fields	
Job Title	Date of job performance rating and ranking
Job Ranking	Relative ranking of employee within rating unit
Job Rating	Employee's job performance rating (1 to 5; 1 is the highest score)
Rater	Name of individual performing rating of employee

Although the admission committee follows relatively strict rules that govern the operation of the DSP, there is no set formula to determine who is admitted into the program. Each year, the admission committee varies from class to class (i.e., there are four different admission committees each year) and approximately 710 people nationwide are selected for the four annual classes of the DSP.

The plaintiffs in the case allege that the written and verbal tests, which they believe are not a business necessity for the job, cause a disparate negative impact on the selection of African Americans into the DSP. According to the plaintiffs' pleadings, simple data tabulations of the overall DSP data show that the selection rate of African-American line supervisors into the DSP was nearly half that of white line supervisors. The federal agency denies that the test has a disparate impact and strongly believes that the written and verbal tests are critically important determinants for the job of deputy supervisor.

In compliance with court orders, the employer-defendant has provided the plaintiffs with an electronic database of the DSP outcomes for the most recent year's four classes. The data contains an employee identifier, a classification number identifying the DSP class that the individual applied for, the individual's race, the outcome of the application process, and the operational unit from which the individual applied.

An excerpt of the agency-provided data is shown in the table below. The employer's personnel database is organized into several different data tables that include several different types of employee data. The employer's database has separate data tables for DSP test results, past job positions, and job-performance data. The tables are linked through the unique employer identifier.

Database Field Descriptions

As mentioned above, there are two primary statistical questions in this early phase of the litigation.

1. Is the score on the written portion of the DSP test correlated with on-the-job performance as a Deputy Supervisor?
2. Is there is a statistically significant difference between the performance of African-American and white test-takers on the written portion of the DSP test?

Is the score on the written portion of the DSP test correlated with on-the-job performance as a Deputy Supervisor?

One way to address this question is to examine the statistical correlation between the score on the written test and the numerical measure of job performance of new Deputy Supervisors. For this employer, the early performance of Deputy Supervisors in arguably most relevant because the employee is new and has relatively little experience in the position. As individuals progress in the job, their performance is generally more correlated with on-the-job experiences and knowledge that was obtained over the years while performing the job.

As the data tables above show, the employer requires each employee to be rated and ranked by his or her supervisor. The job rating is a numerical measure where 1 is the highest performance rating and 5 is the lowest performance rating. The employee's job ranking is based on the supervisor's relative ranking of the employee within the rating unit. An employee's ranking is a number between 0 and 100 and is usually expressed as a percentile (i.e. 25%, 50%, 75%, or 95%).

The correlation between test performance and first-year job performance can be studied by examining the statistical correlation between the employee's score and rating. To begin, a standard correlation coefficient can be used to measure the strength of correlation between the two numerical measures. The correlation coefficient represents the strength of the relationship between two variables and takes a value between +1 and −1. A correlation coefficient of +1 means that the two variables are completely positively related and move together (i.e., when one value goes up (or down), the other goes up (or down)). A correlation coefficient of −1 means that the two values move in opposite directions. The closer the value is to +1 or −1, the stronger the relationship. A standard test

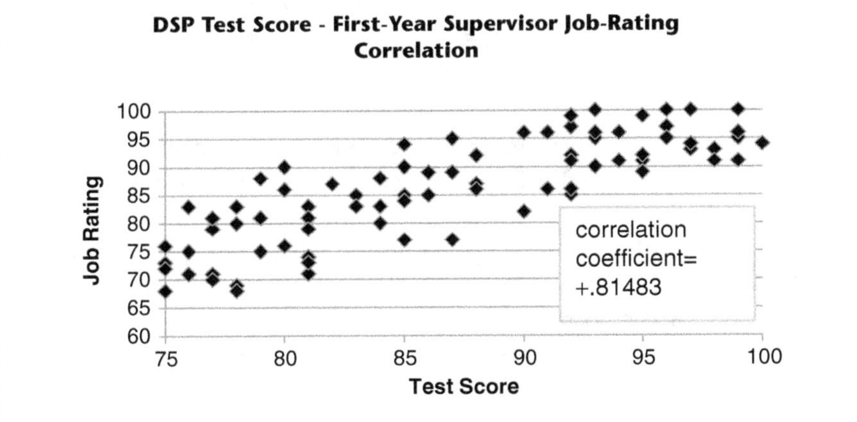

The correlation coefficient represents the strength of the relationship between two variables and takes a value between +1 and −1. A correlation coefficient of +1 means that the two variables are completely positively related and move together (i.e., when one value goes up (or down), the other goes up (or down)). A correlation coefficient of −1 means that the two values move in opposite directions. The closer the value is to +1 or −1, the stronger the relationship is. A standard test of statistical significance can be used to determine whether the measured correlation is consistent with random chance.

of statistical significance can be used to determine whether the measured correlation is consistent with random chance.

In this case, we used the data to extract the first job-performance ratings for Deputy Supervisors and the score they received on the written portion of the DSP exam. There were 99 usable data observations in the employer's database.

In our analysis, the correlation between the score on the DSP test and performance during the first year as a Deputy Supervisor is positively correlated. The figure below shows a graph of the data for the 99 Deputy Supervisors whom we studied, as well as the correlation coefficient.

As shown in the figure, the correlation coefficient is 0.81483. This means that individuals who perform better on the written portion of the DSP test also tend to receive higher first-year job-performance ratings as a Deputy Supervisor. Since the correlation coefficient is close to +1, there is a very strong positive correlation between the two variables. Although the calculation is not shown, the correlation is statistically significant and therefore is unlikely to been caused by random chance alone.

The calculation of the correlation coefficient for two variables (x and y) is as follows.

$$\textit{correlation coefficient} = \frac{\frac{1}{n}\sum_{i=1}^{n}(x_i - \bar{x})(y_i - \bar{y})}{\sqrt{\frac{1}{n-1}\sum_{i=1}^{n}(x_i - \bar{x})^2} \cdot \sqrt{\frac{1}{n-1}\sum_{i=1}^{n}(y_i - \bar{y})^2}}$$

In this formula, n is the number of data points (or observations), x is the test score, and y is the first-year job-performance rating of deputy supervisors. The symbols $\bar{x}$ and $\bar{y}$ are the average written test score and average first-year job-performance rating of the deputy supervisors whom were studied.

Our analysis of the correlation suggests that the written portion of the DSP test is indeed a good measure of how well a person will perform in the Deputy Supervisor position.

Is there a statistically significant difference between the performance of African-American and white test-takers on the written portion of the DSP test?

Having determined that the written portion of the test is related to job performance, the second question can now be tackled. First, we must determine whether **similarly situated** African-Americans have an average test score that differs from that of **similarly situated** white DSP test-takers. Second, if the average test score is lower for similarly situated African-American test-takers, we must determine whether the difference in test scores can be attributed to random chance.

In this case, we formulate the statistical model by using the facts of the case and information about the employer to create a statistical statement that can be tested against the data. The test of statistical significance can be performed using any number of statistically valid and generally accepted methodologies. We will discuss a few of these methodologies in the following section.

We begin by formulating the null hypothesis (i.e., what is assumed to be true prior to analyzing the data) and the alternative hypothesis. In this case, the null hypothesis is that the DSP does not have a disparate impact on African-American employees. Accordingly, the null hypothesis implies that any difference between the test scores of African-American and white test-takers is the result of random chance and is not due to discrimination by the employer.

The alternative hypothesis is that the difference is unlikely to have been generated by random chance. The alternative hypothesis may be viewed as being consistent with discrimination by the employer. In other words, acceptance of the alternative hypothesis suggests that the test does in fact have a disparate impact on African-American test-takers.

The null and alternative hypotheses can be written as follows.

Null Hypothesis (H_O): The written portion of the DSP test does not have a negative disparate impact on African-American test-takers.

Or

H_0: *Average Written Test Score* $_{African-American}$= *Average Written Test Score*$_{White}$

Versus the...

Alternative Hypothesis (H_O): The written portion of the DSP test does have a disparate impact on African-American test-takers.

Or

H_A: *Average Written Test Score* $_{African-American}$ $\neq$ *Average Written Test Score*$_{White}$

Conceptually, we can use our knowledge of the expected outcomes under the null hypothesis of no disparate impact to formulate a statistical test for analyzing the testing scores. First, we need to think about what the distribution of test scores should look like in a 'normal' situation. Assuming we have a relatively large number of test outcomes, we would expect the test scores for both African-American and white test-takers to follow a normal distribution, or what is referred to as a bell curve.

With a bell curve, the majority of the test score outcomes for both groups should coalesce around the mean test score for each group. Extremely low test scores and extremely high test scores should occur infrequently. The mean test score and the actual shape of the bell curve for each racial group of test-takers may differ. However, the test scores for each group can be expected to follow a normal distribution.

The figure below shows the separate bell curves for all 149 African-American and 507 white DSP test-takers. As shown, African-American test-takers had an average score of 67.5 on the written portion of the DSP entry test. White test-takers had an average test score of 76.2 on the written portion of the DSP entry test. The relatively wider shape of the bell curve for African-Americans shows that they had a wider range of test outcomes than white test takers did. As discussed in previous chapters, the variation in the outcomes can also be seen by looking at the standard deviation of the test scores.

DSP Test Score Distributions

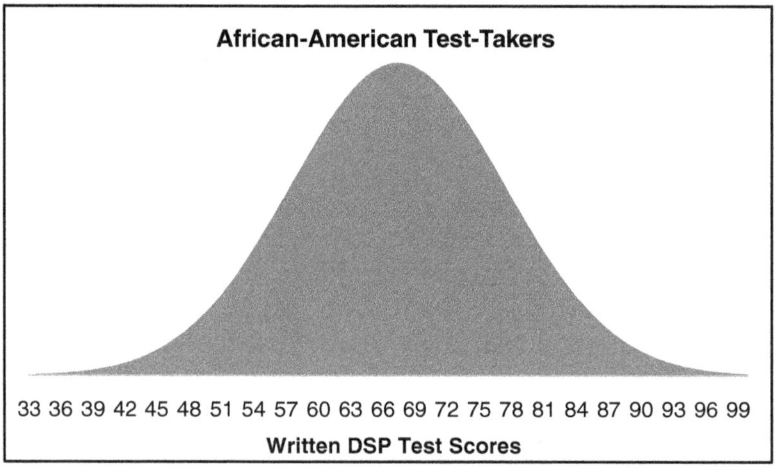

The average DSP score for African-American test-takers is 67.5 with a standard deviation of 10 points.

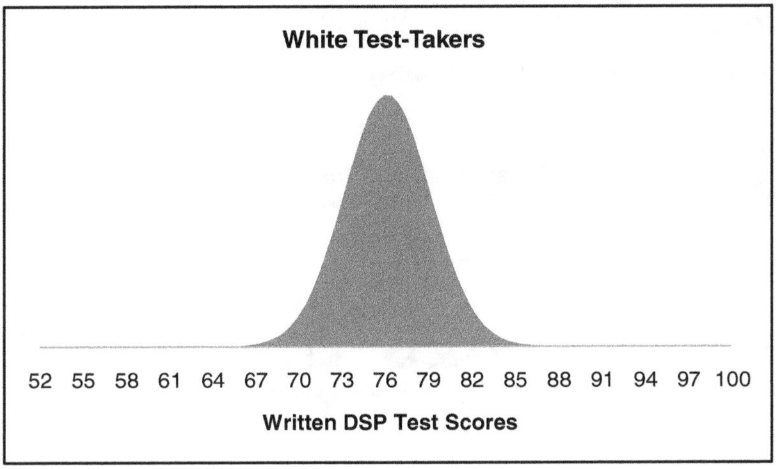

The average DSP score for white test-takers is 76.2 with a standard deviation of three points.

Now that we can statistically describe the distribution of test scores for each group of test-takers, we can develop the statistical test to examine the hypothesis that there is no statistically significant difference between the average test scores of African-American and white test-takers.

Recall our null hypothesis:

H_o : *Average Written Test Score*$_{African-American}$ = *Average Written Test Score*$_{White}$

We can rewrite this as:

$$H_O : \overline{X}_1 - \overline{X}_2 = 0$$

where $\overline{X}_1$ is the average score for African-American test-takers and $\overline{X}_2$ is the average score for white test-takers. Writing the null hypothesis this way allows us to derive the expected outcomes from a random (hypothetical) experiment that compares the expected outcomes of the two testing distributions.

Since we know the shapes of the statistical distributions that generated the test scores, statistical principles tell us that the expected outcomes of a hypothetical experiment in which we draw from the two distributions will follow a bell-shaped curve. The expected outcomes from our new statistical distribution can then be used to test the hypothesis that the test scores from the two racial groups are not statistically different from one another. Our new statistical distribution is shown in the figure below.

Sampling Distribution for the Difference Between Two Means

Drawing from this distribution,

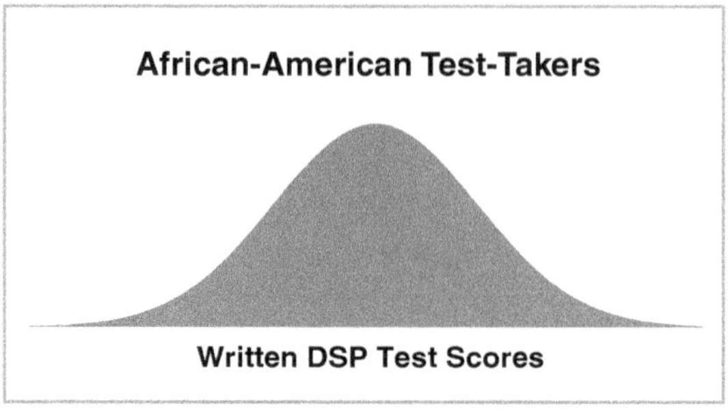

and then this distribution,

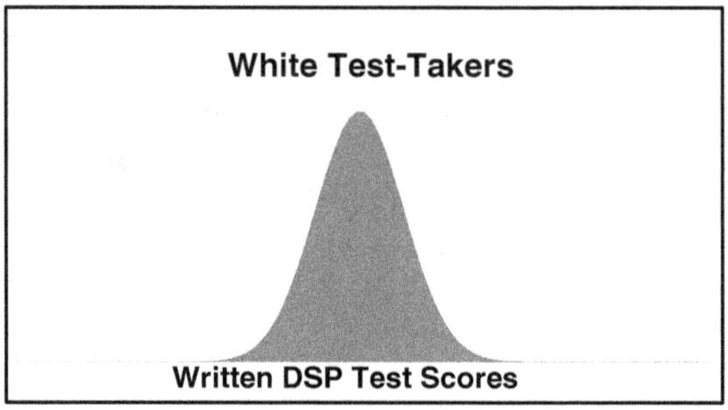

results in:

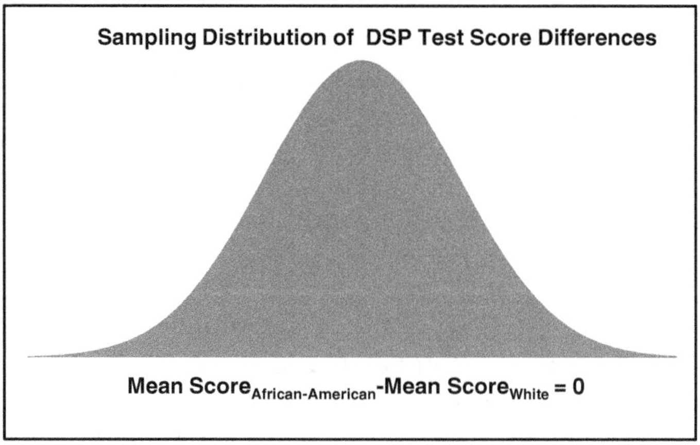

Using our sampling distribution for the DSP test score differences, we can now test the hypothesis. We begin by calculating the test statistic for our data. If the test statistic that we calculate from the data exceeds our threshold, then we will reject the null hypothesis that the difference between the two average test scores of African-Americans and whites is statistically the same (i.e., that the difference is equal to zero).

$$z = \frac{(\bar{x} - \bar{y})}{\sqrt{\sigma_{\bar{x}}^2/n + \sigma_{\bar{y}}^2/n}}$$

Note: The values for $\sigma_{\bar{x}}^2$ and $\sigma_{\bar{y}}^2$ were calculated from the provided dataset. The calculation of the values is not shown.

The standard normal value (Z_T) that is calculated from the testing data is used to compare and test the statistical hypothesis. The standard normal value tells us the likelihood that the actual testing outcome would have been generated if African-American and white test-takers had the same average test scores. The larger the standard normal test statistic value is, the lower the likelihood is that our test difference outcome was generated by random chance.

Using the standard normal distribution and the pre-determined level of statistical significance (z_c), we can evaluate the hypothesis.

If $z_T > z_{0.025}$, we reject the null hypothesis. The critical value that we use in this example represents the 0.025 significance level. Using the 0.025 significance level means that if we reject the null hypothesis, there is less than a two-and-a-half percent likelihood that random chance could have generated the observed interview outcome.

The test value for our analysis, based on the testing outcome data, is as follows.

$$z_T = \frac{(76.2 - 67.5)}{\sqrt{9/149 + 100/507}} = 17.14$$

The test statistic and critical values for our hypothesis test are shown in the figure below.

The calculated z-statistic for our data is 17.14, which is larger than the critical value of 2.25 that is associated with the 0.025 significance level. This means that we should reject the hypothesis that the mean test scores are statistically equivalent for African-American test-takers and white test-takers. In other words, the difference in test-score performance is statistically significant. A z-statistic of 17.14 means that there is less than a one-in-a-billion chance that the difference in test scores would

Two Population Test Example Graph

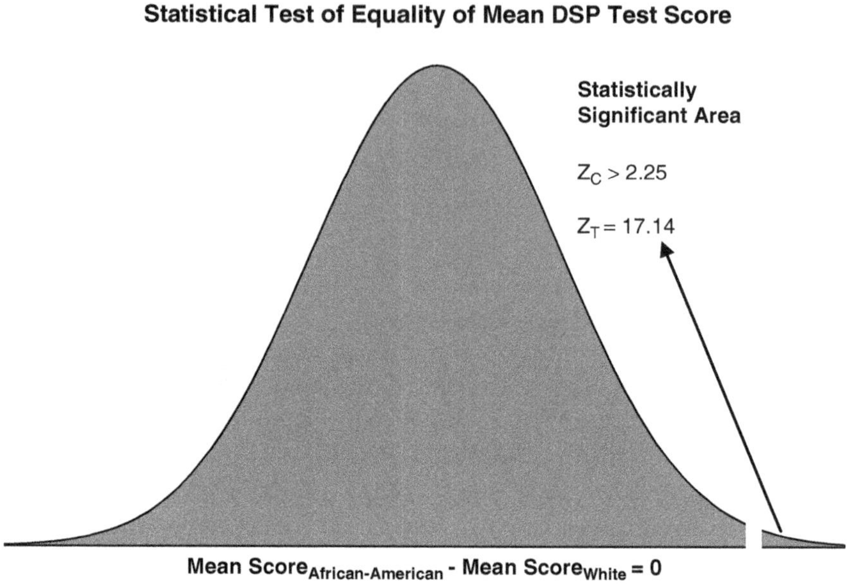

The z-statistic for our data is 17.14, which is larger than the critical value of 2.25 that is associated with the 0.025 significance level. A z-statistic of 17.14 means that there is less than a one-in-a-billion chance that the difference in test scores would have been generated by random chance if the mean test performance of the two groups were in fact equal. This means that we should reject the hypothesis that the mean test scores are statistically equivalent for African-American and white test-takers. In other words, the difference in test-score performance is statistically significant.

The statistically significant region can vary by study and type of research. Some employment cases, such as *Casteneda v. Partida*, have suggested that differences that are greater than two or three standard deviations are significant. See the earlier chapters for more discussion on the concept of statistical significance.

have been generated by random chance if the mean test performance of the two groups were in fact equal.

Questions to Consider

- Are the individuals in the testing analysis truly similarly situated? If not, what factors should be incorporated into the analysis to account for the differences?
- Do the African-American and white DSP test-takers generally have the same pre-testing backgrounds?

- Does the experience level in related job positions vary?
- Are there any other variables, such as prior experience, that can explain the difference in test scores?

Data Exploration and Things to Think About

One step that often proves useful in a disparate-impact analysis is summarizing and examining trends in the testing data. For instance, it may be useful to examine trends and relationships between a test-taker's score, education level, and prior job experience. Much of this type of analysis is done over the course of the study and is not part of the formal report. Often it is simply helpful to look at raw tabulations or plots of the data.

Salary Discrimination Analyses

Even when performing exactly the same job, it is common for employees to be paid differently.

In this chapter, we examine allegations of salary discrimination. As before, the ultimate goal of our employment analysis is to determine the likelihood that our employment data was generated by an unbiased salary process. As we now know, if we determine that there is a low or small likelihood that an unbiased process generated our data, then it may suggest some type of bias against the protected group.

The main difference between the methodologies discussed in this chapter and those of previous chapters is that now we are considering the effects of many different employment-related factors on discrimination analysis. In many real-world situations, even employees who work in exactly the same job most likely differ in some important employment-related aspect. For instance, in many jobs, it would not be surprising to learn that even if all other employment factors were held equal, employees with longer job tenure have a significantly higher salary than do less senior employees. The statistical methods introduced in the preceding chapters do not provide an efficient way to perform an analysis in these types of situations.

This chapter begins with an introduction to the linear regression model. This is a common statistical technique that allows the discrimination researcher to account for individual effects of relevant employment factors such as the employee's job tenure, education, or salary on the employment outcomes.

After we study the basic linear regression model, we will provide an introduction to salary data and the use of linear regression in a salary analysis. We close the chapter with a discussion of the role that human capital plays in determining an individuals' salary.

Motivation for the Linear Regression Model in Employment Discrimination Cases

At the heart of employment discrimination allegations is the idea that employees that are otherwise similarly situated are treated or impacted differently by the employer's actions. However, it is difficult, especially in salary discrimination cases, to determine who is similarly situated. Many legitimate employment factors simultaneously influence the salary determination process for any given individual.

As an example, let's consider 250 salespeople working for a department store. The store's compensation staff is examining their salary. The department's management considers all the employees to be similarly situated. The only difference that is noted is that the employees were hired at different times and consequently have differing job tenure. It is alleged that African-American salespersons earn less than similarly situated white salespersons.

The job tenure and average salary for African-American and white salespeople is shown in the table below. African-American salespeople had an average salary of $52,750, while white salespeople had an average salary of $59,462.

Within the department store, employees with longer job tenure tend to earn more than employees with shorter job tenure. The average salary for individuals with 3 to 5 years of experience is $53,333, while the average salary of individuals with 6 to 10 years is $57,209. The premium placed on job tenure at the department store reflects the value of the employee's experience, store-specific knowledge, and on-the-job training.

Salary Summary by Job Tenure for a Department Store

In a situation where job tenure is related to an employee's compensation, it is appropriate to use a statistical approach that accounts for this factor. As a heuristic example, let's begin with a simple stratified salary approach. That is, we begin by looking at the average salary by race for each of the different job-tenure groups. Slicing the data to account for variation in job tenure allows us to examine the relationship between job tenure and salary while simultaneously considering the potential correlation between the employee's race and salary.

After we account for differences in job tenure, the alleged disparities of the aggregate salary data disappear. In fact, African-American salespersons have higher salaries than white salespersons in each of the job-tenure

Job Tenure (in Years)	**Average Salary by Job Tenure for all Employees**	**White Salespeople**		**African-American Salespeople**	
		Number of Employees	Average Salary	Number of Employees	Average Salary
0 – 2	$46,154	10	$36,000	55	$48,000
3 – 5	$53,333	30	$48,000	60	$56,000
6 – 10	$57,209	40	$57,000	3	$60,000
> 10	$73,077	50	$73,000	2	$75,000
Average	**$57,443**		**$59,462**		**$52,750**

In the example, the compensation staff at the department store is looking at the salary of a cohort of 250 salespeople. All of the employees are considered similarly situated by the department management. The only difference that is noted is that the employees were hired at different times and consequently have different lengths of job tenure with the department store. It is alleged that African-American salespersons earn less than similarly situated White salespersons.

Within the department store, employees with longer job tenure tend to earn more than employees with shorter job tenure. The average salary for individuals with 3 to 5 years of experience is $53,333, while the average salary of individuals with 6 to 10 years is $57,209. The premium placed on job tenure at the department store reflects the value of the employee's experience, store-specific knowledge, and on-the-job training.

groups. The average salary for African-American salespersons with up to two years of experience is $48,000, while similarly situated white salespersons earn $36,000 on average. A similar pattern emerges for the other job-tenure salary groups shown in the table.

How can different analyses on the same data yield such radically different interpretations?

In this example, accounting for job tenure is the key difference. On average, African-American salespersons had shorter job tenure than white salespersons. Nearly 50% (55 out of 120) of the African-American employees had been with the department store for two or fewer years.

In contrast, less than 10% (10 out of 130) of the white salespersons had been with the department store for two or fewer years. Since the department store's compensation was tied to job tenure, a salary analysis that did not account for tenure would erroneously imply a salary disparity between similarly situated employees when it fact there was none.

In this example and similar settings, the statistical salary analysis must account for multiple relevant employment factors. In most instances, an employer's compensation system is based on many different factors, so a statistical analysis should potentially account for multiple employment factors simultaneously. The regression models discussed in this chapter provide us with a way to perform such a task. We will discuss the **salary regression model**, which is a mathematical equation that shows the independent effect that each employment factor has on the determination of an employee's salary. The next sections of this chapter begin by discussing the data that is used in salary regression models.

Salary Data

Before we talk about the regression model in detail, we need to spend a little time discussing the data that goes into a salary regression model. Employee data is used to measure the independent effects of each employment factor. In general, the data is created and entered into a database as employee transactions, such as salary changes and promotions, occur.

The salary and other types of employment data are typically maintained by the human resources department or a similar department in a personnel-record management computer program such as those provided by Oracle, PeopleSoft, SAP, and SAS. The programs used by human resource personnel typically have a user-friendly interface for making entries and updating personnel files.

The data must be exported from the program in a form that is useful for a statistical salary analysis. This means taking data from the form in the human-resource record management system and converting it into another, usually electronic, format. Depending on the program, the company may provide the data in hardcopy or in a raw electronic format.

Raw electronic data may come in many file formats, including ASCII (text) and spreadsheet formats such as Microsoft Excel. Popular formats for text files include comma-delimited (each entry in the data file is separated by a comma), tab-delimited (each entry in the data file is separated by a tab character), and space-delimited (each entry in the data file is separated by a space) files.

After company-level data has been received, a dataset is constructed from the raw electronic data, organizing it into one table of uniquely defined rows and columns. The most common datasets are employee-data snapshots and are referred to as **cross-sectional datasets**. Each row of a

Electronic Salary Data

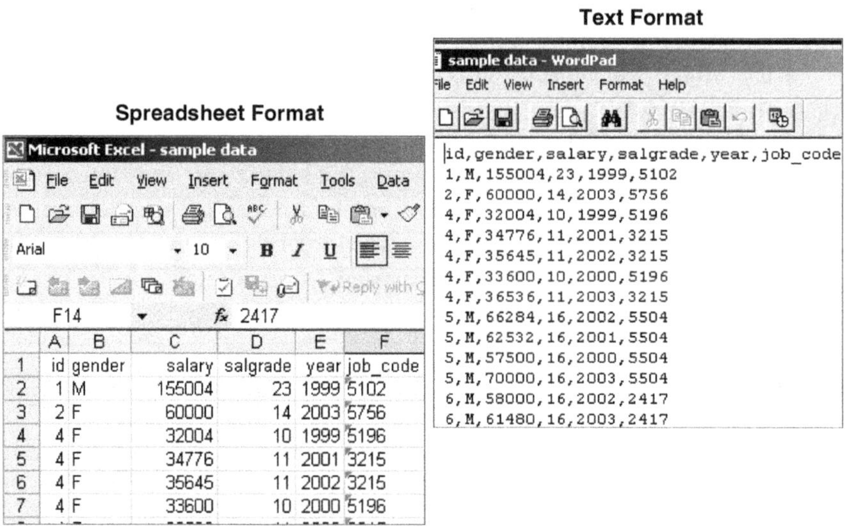

Raw electronic salary data may come in many file formats, including ASCII (text) and spreadsheet formats such as Microsoft Excel. Popular formats for text files include comma-delimited (each entry in the data file is separated by a comma), tab-delimited (each entry in the data file is separated by a tab character), and space-delimited (each entry in the data file is separated by a space) files.

cross-sectional dataset contains employment factors for one employee at a given point in time. Each column contains information about one, and only one, employment factor, such as gender, salary, etc.

Often, annual data snapshots are combined to create an employee dataset that spans multiple years. A dataset that has a year-end snapshot for employee records that span multiple years is referred to as a panel dataset. The figure below presents a sample analysis dataset screenshot from a commonly used statistical program.

Introduction to the Use of Linear Regression in a Salary Analysis

Having discussed salary data, we can now talk about how to use linear regression techniques to construct measures that will allow us to make comparisons among individuals who are similarly situated. To motivate

Looking at Analysis Datasets

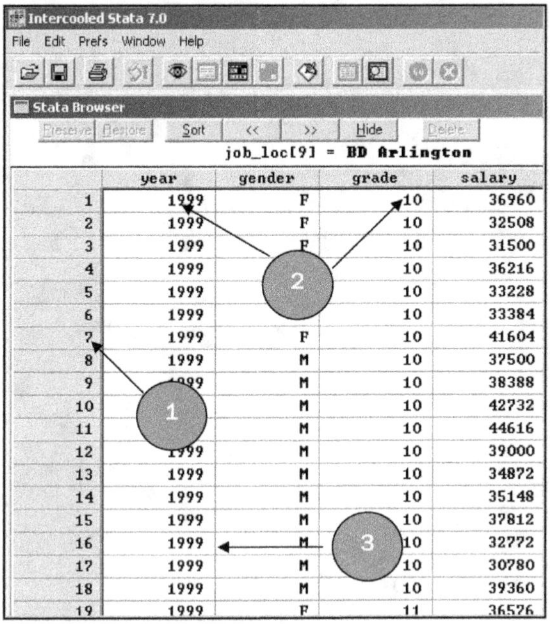

	year	gender	grade	salary
1	1999	F	10	36960
2	1999	F	10	32508
3	1999	F	10	31500
4	1999		10	36216
5	1999		10	33228
6	1999		10	33384
7	1999	F	10	41604
8	1999	M	10	37500
9	[illegible]	M	10	38388
10		M	10	42732
11		M	10	44616
12	[illegible]	M	10	39000
13	1999	M	10	34872
14	1999	M	10	35148
15	1999	M	10	37812
16	1999	M	10	32772
17	1999	M	10	30780
18	1999	M	10	39360
19	1999	F	11	36576

A Typical Analysis Dataset

1. Each row of the dataset contains employment factors for one employee at a given point in time.
2. Each column contains information about one and only employment factor, such as the salary grade at a given point in time.
3. This is a panel dataset, because it contains employee records for multiple years.

the discussion, consider the scatter diagram shown in the figure below. The figure shows and plots the salary of African-American and white employees from the department store example. In the diagram, job ratings are plotted against the employee's salary. It is assumed that the individuals are similarly situated in every way other than job ratings.

This figure demonstrates several important things about the company's salary determination process. First, the salary of all employees tends to increase with their job ratings. You can see this by drawing an imaginary line that fits through the main part of the data. The imaginary line that you draw has an upward slope, which means that the employees' salaries tend to increase with job rating.

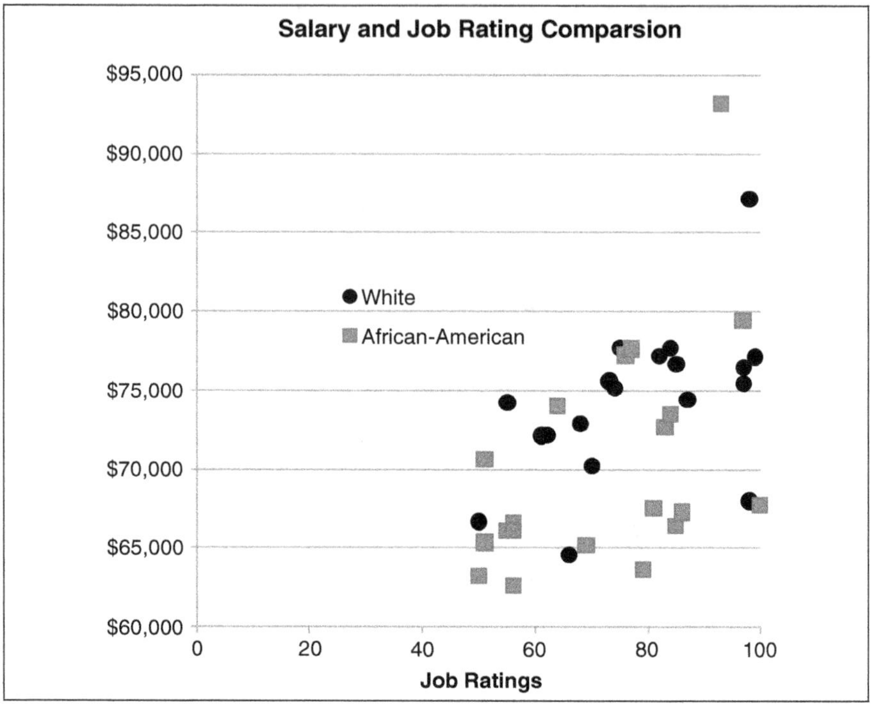

Second, African-American employees tend to have lower salaries and lower job ratings than white employees. You can see this by looking at where most of the squares that represent African-American employees' salaries are located in relation to the circles that represent white employees' salaries in the graph. Most of the squares are below the circles in the graph.

Third, eyeballing the data suggests that even after accounting for job ratings, African-American employees tend to earn less than white employees. Consider the employees who had a rating between 60 and 80. In this range, African-American employees tend to earn less than white employees who are in the same approximate job rating deciles. This can be seen simply by observing that most circles are above similarly situated squares in the graph, indicating a higher salary.

The ultimate goal of our salary analysis is to incorporate information about the employees' job ratings into the salary model. We want to see whether the eyeballed effect that we perceive in the data holds up to a more thorough statistical analysis. In brief, our approach is as follows.

1. Estimate the mathematical salary equation.

2. Check the fit.
3. Determine the statistical significance and make inferences.

The approach we use to estimate our salary regression model is described in detail below.

Estimating the Mathematical Salary Equation

First we will use the analysis dataset created in the first step of the salary analysis to construct a mathematical representation of the employment factors that are correlated with an employee's salary. As mentioned above, the mathematical representation of these factors is referred to as a salary regression model. The mathematical process of constructing a salary regression model is called estimating the model.

Many generally accepted methods are used to estimate the salary regression model. The most common model is the linear regression model, which assumes, among other things, that salary can be represented as a linear function (i.e., a straight-line function) of the employment factors. The linear regression model is frequently estimated using the ordinary least squares (OLS) method.

The relationship between salary and the employment or demographic factor of interest is captured by the slope of the line that we fit through our data. A little more formally, since our data is assumed to be linear, we can describe the relationship using the following formula:

$$y_i = \beta_0 + \beta_1 x_1 + \epsilon_i$$

where, the β terms are called coefficients and ϵ is the error term.

Recall from algebra that the slope of the line is represented by β_1 in the equation. The slope tells us how the demographic factor is correlated with the salary variable. The variable x_1 is the parameter used in the regression model. In practice, there will usually be multiple parameters that account for the multiple employment variable(s) of interest and other explanatory variables. The coefficient tells us what effect a change in the parameters has on the dependent variable. In our examples, the dependent variable is salary.

For example, if the objective is to explain what determines salary at a firm, then a mathematical model can be formulated with salary as the dependent variable (variable of interest) on the left side of the equality sign (=). On the right side of the equality sign lie the independent variables (also called explanatory variables), which determine salary, such as the employee's age, years of schooling, and years of work experience.

Using mathematical notation, a salary model can be written as follows:

$$Salary = b_0 + b_1 x + b_2 x_2 + b_3 x_3 + \varepsilon$$

$$Salary = b_0 + b_1\ Age + b_2\ Years\ of\ Schooling + b_3\ Years\ of\ Work\ Experience + \varepsilon$$

The model coefficients, b_0, b_1, b_2, and b_3, show the magnitude of the explanatory variables' effect on the variable of interest (salary). The last term, ε, is an error term. The error term is used to account for random deviations in the dependent variables.

The OLS method is commonly used to estimate the model coefficients, b_0, b_1, b_2, and b_3. OLS aims to find the parameter values that allow us to fit the best line through the salary data. We want the line to be as close as possible to all of the data points, which means that some of the data points will lie above the line and others will lie below it.

The most common way to fit the line is to find the line that produces the lowest sum of squares. The line that is closest to all the data points is determined by selecting the line that minimizes the sum of the squared distances from the line to each salary observation. The distances are squared because this allows us to ignore negative numbers and better accounts for large and small distances from the line. Many nuances must be considered in the actual estimation and implementation of the employment salary regression model, but the above discussion captures the essential elements of the process.

Let's revisit the department store example to see how the linear regression model works in practice. To simplify issues for the moment, let's estimate a separate regression line for only the African-American employees. The figure below plots the job-rating data versus salary for African-American employees. The best-fit line for the salary data is shown by the dotted line that goes through the center of the salary data.

The linear regression line for the African-American employees shows us the relationship between the dependent variable (salary) on the vertical y-axis and the independent variable (job rating) on the horizontal x-axis. In our example, the line for African-American employees is:

$$\mathrm{y} = 297.85\mathrm{x} + 51,062 = 297.85 * \mathrm{Job\ \ Rating} + 51,062$$

Since the job rating model coefficient (279.85) is positive, the equation shows a positive effect between an African-American employee's salary and his or her job rating. The slope tells us how much of an increase in salary is related to an increase in job ratings.

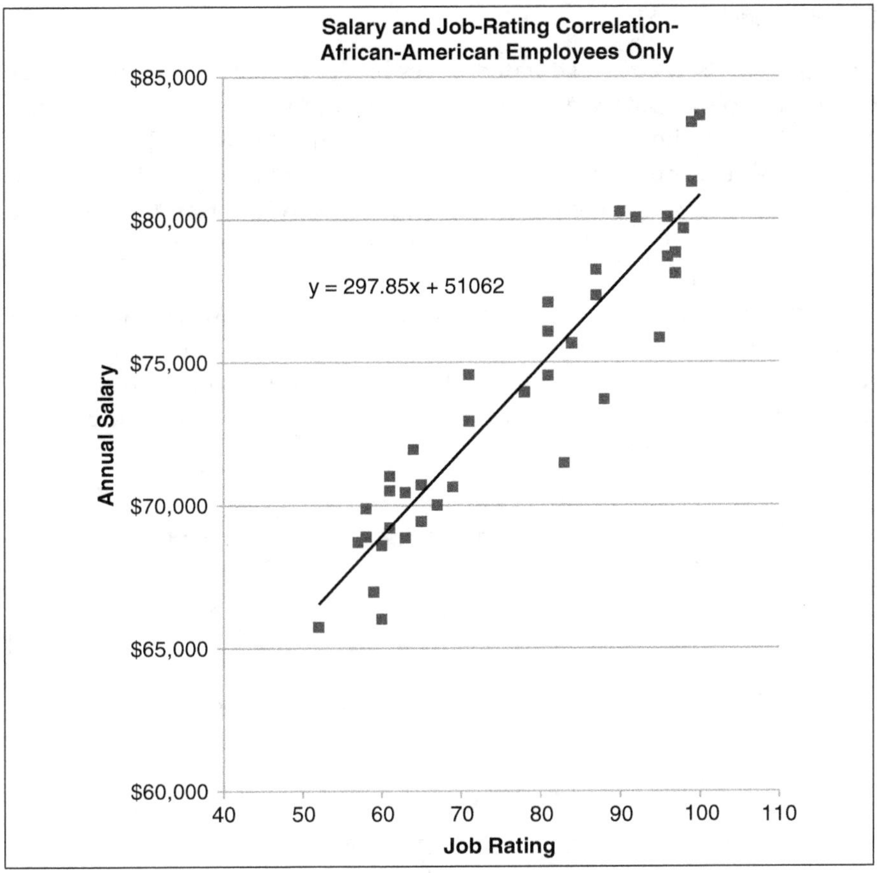

In this example, the job-rating coefficient of 297.85 means that a one-point increase in the job rating is correlated with a $297.85 increase in the annual salary of African-American employees. Because the salary relationship is linear, a ten-point increase in the job rating is correlated with a $2,978.50 increase in the annual salary.

In addition, we can use the estimated salary regression line to determine or predict the salary of different employees. For instance, our regression equation predicts that an African-American employee with a job rating of 80 should earn $74,890. That is,

$$y = 297.85x + 51,062 = (297.85 * 80) + 51,062 = \$74,890$$

As with any statistical procedure, there is statistical error and it can be calculated using standard mathematical formulas.

Check the Model Fit

Now that we know the estimated effect of a particular model parameter on an employee's salary, we want to determine how well our estimated model line fits the employee data. To assess the fit of our linear salary model, we determine whether the salary data points are sufficiently close to our estimated salary regression line. Additionally, we want to determine whether the effect on salary that we have estimated for our employment factor is 'real' or due simply to random chance.

To do this, we must introduce the concept of a **standard error** (S_b). In this case, standard error refers to the deviation of the y values (salary) from the estimated best-fit salary line. The figure below shows two different salary regression models with two different standard error measures.

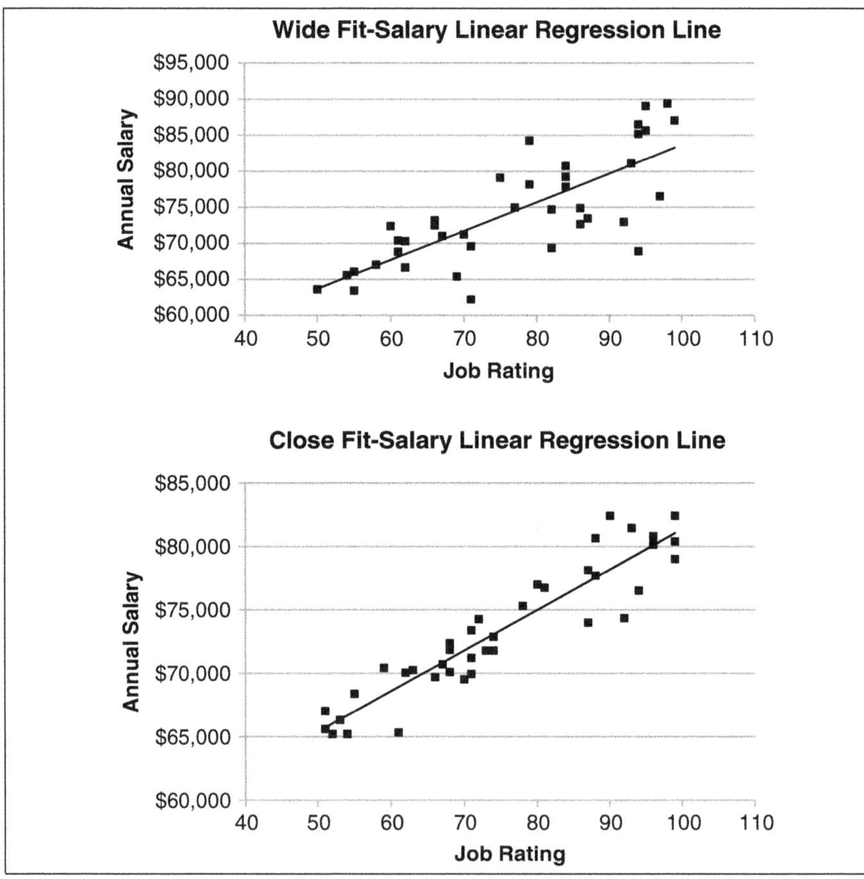

The salary regression model in the top panel shows a linear regression model where the data is relatively disperse in relation to the best-fit line. That is, relative to the linear regression model in the lower panel, the actual salary observations are, on average, farther away from the linear salary regression line. The salary regression model in the top panel has a higher measure of standard error than the salary regression model in the lower panel.

All else being equal, we want the coefficient estimated from the data to be large relative to the estimated standard error.

When estimating a regression, we calculate the standard error (S_b) for each of the employment factors, such as job ratings and location, that we include in our salary determination model. The standard error is calculated in most statistical programs when an OLS procedure is run. The formula for calculating the standard error for our model parameters can be found in any statistics book.

Determine Statistical Significance and Make Inferences

The previous chapters have taught us that sheer randomness could be responsible for observed employment outcomes. In other words, the estimated salary effect may be the result of random chance. In order to make inferences regarding the effect of different employment factors on the salary determination process, we must be able to rule out the possibility that random chance is driving our linear regression results. We must also be able to rule out the possibility that any relationship between the salary determination process and the individual's protected class status is not driven by random chance.

How do we determine whether random chance is driving our results? We first determine what the expected results would be if randomness had produced them. Then we compare our actual salaries to the randomly generated outcome and determine how close the two outcomes are. If the comparison exercise suggests that the statistical results are unlikely to have been generated by sheer randomness, then we conclude that the employment factor has an effect on the salary determination process. (Note: The concepts below are similar to the sampling distribution discussion presented in previous chapters.)

Consider the following randomness experiment. Let's say that a given employer has 1,000 employees. For our experiment, we will estimate a linear regression for a sample of 100 employees. Our linear regression model will include a factor for job ratings. As discussed above, we will have both a regression coefficient (b_1) that shows the effect of the job rating on salary and the standard error (S_{b_1}) associated with the job-rating parameter. For our experiment, we will look at the ratio of the regression coefficient to the standard error by calculating the following test statistic (t).

$$t = \frac{b_1}{S_{b_1}}$$

Each time we select 100 individuals, we make this calculation using the coefficient (b) and standard error (s) obtained from our best-fit linear regression line. Then we select a new sample of 100 employees and re-estimate our linear regression model. We will continue this process many times, say 1,000 times, recording the outcome of each of the 1,000 experiments.

Standard statistics show that if we continue doing this, the final distribution of coefficient-to-standard-error ratios will resemble the normal distribution that we discussed earlier. In other words, we expect the outcomes of our randomness experiment, on average, to follow a curve that is very similar to the hump- or bell-shaped curve distribution that we described previously.

The distribution of our test statistic is shown in the figure below where the light-grey area represents the statistical rejection region. If our test statistic falls in this region, then we will reject the null hypothesis that our results are due to random chance. Accordingly, we conclude that the employment factor being studied has an effect on the salary determination process.

More specifically, we use this information to determine whether our outcome is statistically significant. To determine whether the test statistic and the employment factor's purported effect are statistically significant, we will compare the calculated test statistic to the expected outcomes of randomness (as shown in figure above). If the outcome falls within the main part of the distribution, we accept the proposition that the salary effect is most likely due to random chance. In other words, we expect a similar outcome. In this case, we say that the effect is statistically insignificant.

In contrast, if the calculated test statistic falls outside of the main part of the distribution, we reject the proposition that random chance was driving the salary outcomes. We reject the proposition because our model tells us there is a very small chance that the calculated test statistic (t)

Student's T-Distribution with Shaded Rejection Regions

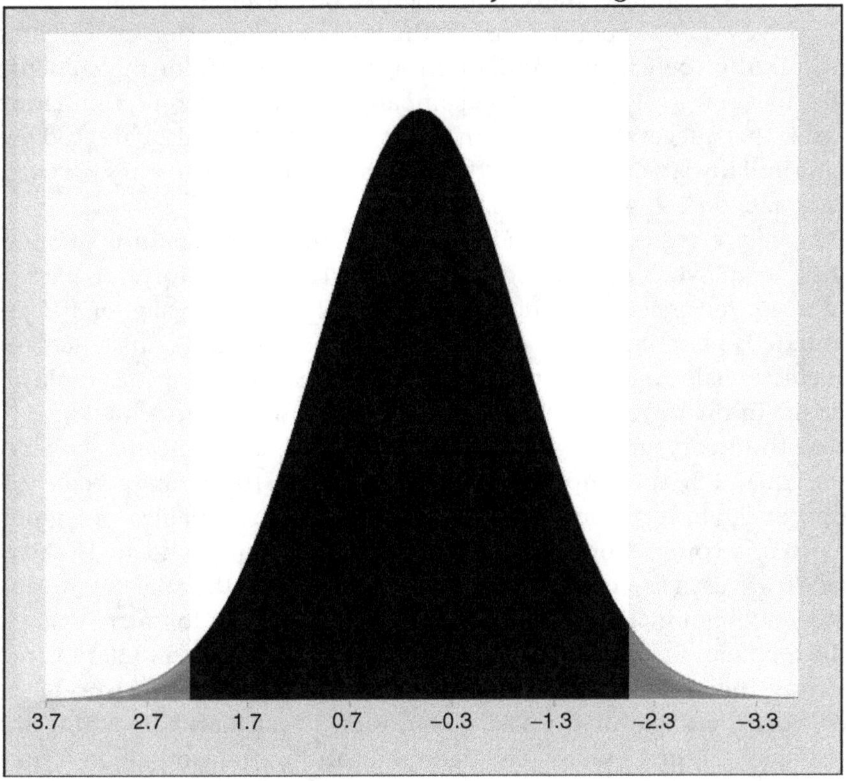

We can use the information from the student's T-distribution to tell us about the statistical importance of our coefficient of interest. We use this information to determine whether the results calculated for any particular outcome are consistent with the randomness exhibited by our experiment. In other words, the effect of race, gender or age that we have observed is real and is not the result of sheer randomness. As before, if there is a small probability that random chance has generated the coefficient, then we will conclude that the effect is real (i.e., consistent with disparate treatment or impact of the employer's action).

If we determine that our outcome has a small chance of being generated through this type of random experiment, then we say that we reject the hypothesis that our employment factor of interest is being driven solely by random chance.

In the graph above, we would reject the null hypothesis if the test statistic calculated from our data fell within the shaded rejection region.

would have been generated by sheer random chance. In this case, we say that the effect of the employment factor is statistically significant.

To drive home the point, consider the following regression table, which presents the coefficient, standard error, and t-value (from the student's t-distribution) for XYZ, Inc. The company faces a gender-discrimination lawsuit that alleges that women in salary grades 9, 10, and 11 are paid less than similarly situated males at the company. The company has provided salary data on 1,494 employees.

The salary regression includes independent or explanatory variables for the employee's gender and salary grade. The explanatory variables in the salary regression are indicator variables that have a value of 1 if the attribute is present and 0 if the attribute is not present. For instance, the variable female equals 1 if the employee is female and 0 if the employee is male. In the regression, males are the comparison group.

For the salary grade, grade 10 and grade 11 are indicator variables that equal 1 if the employee is in salary grade 10 or salary grade 11, respectively. In regression models that use indicator variables, one group is used as a comparison group. In this case, individuals who are in salary grade 9 are used as a comparison group. Accordingly, the salary regression model does not include a salary grade indicator variable for salary grade 9.

In the analysis, the actual dollar value of the employee's salary is not used as the dependent variable in the salary regression. Instead, the dependent variable in the salary regression is calculated by taking the natural logarithm of salary. The natural logarithm transformation is used because it allows us to translate the coefficients more easily and has other desirable statistical properties that are outside the scope of this book.

By examining the regression table, we can gain insights on the nature, size, and statistical significance of the employment factor impact. The nature of the employment factor's impact can be determined by examining the sign of the coefficient on the independent explanatory variable. In the table, the negative sign on the female variable shows that females earn less than males on average. Similarly, the table shows that all employees in grade 10, regardless of gender, earn more than employees in grade 9. The same is true for individuals in salary grade 11.

The size of the employment factor's impact can be determined by examining the size of the model coefficient on the statistical variable of interest. In the table, since the natural logarithm of salary is the dependent variable, the coefficients can be interpreted as percentage changes. The table shows a value of –0.065 for the female indicator variable. This means that female employees earn 6.5% less than men. Similarly, the

Salary Regression Table for XYZ, Inc.			
VARIABLE	**COEF**	**STD ERR**	**T-Value (Number of Standard Deviations)**
(1)	**(2)**	**(3)**	**(4)**
constant	10.710	2.658	4.029
female	–0.065	0.057	–1.140
grade10	0.150	0.045	3.333
grade11	0.195	0.036	5.401

Variable	**Description**
constant	y-intercept value
female	Indicator variable that equals 1 if the employee is female
grade10	Indicator variable that equals 1 if the employee is in salary grade 10
grade11	Indicator variable that equals 1 if the employee is in salary grade 11

value 0.150 means that employees in grade 10 earn 15.0% more than employees in grade 9.

The statistical significance of the salary impact can be determined by examining the t-value associated with the coefficient of the employment factors at issue. When working with regression output like that shown in the table below, the statistical significance of a given salary disparity is determined by examining the numerical values for the standard deviations (from the t-distribution) shown in column (4). As discussed previously, numerical values that are more than two or three standard deviations from the mean are typically considered to be statistically significant in employment cases.

The t-value for the coefficient on the female variable is –1.140. Accordingly, the results in the table suggest that the salary difference between male and female employees is not statistically significant. That is although the average salary of male employees is higher than that of female employees (the number in column (2) is negative), the difference is not statistically significant (the number of standard deviation in column (4) is less than 3.0). In contrast, and as expected, the salary bump related to being in a higher salary grade is statistically significant. The table shows t-values of 3.333 and 5.401 for the grade 10 and grade 11 employment factors.

The final step in the analysis involves model diagnostics, or determining how well the estimated salary or other employment model fits the data. Many generally accepted routines and methodologies can be used. A discussion of these methodologies can be found in the reference section and keyword dictionary found at the end of this textbook.

In the next section, we dive a little deeper into the discussion of human capital and its role in determining an individual's salary.

Spotlight: Role of Human Capital in Salary Determination

The accuracy of the salary discrimination models discussed above often hinges on how the attorney and his or her experts account for the unique attributes that each employee brings to the job and the complex relationship between those attributes and the employee's ultimate salary.

Inaccurately accounting for employees' unique job-related abilities, which labor economists collectively refer to as **human capital**, can create unreliable statistical models of an employer's compensation system. Faulty compensation models often lead to the mistaken belief that there is discrimination when in fact there is none, or mask discrimination when it does exist.

In this section, we discuss the human capital factors that employment attorneys need to think about when investigating allegations of salary discrimination.

We begin the section by discussing the effect that human capital has on an employee's salary. In the second section, we discuss how courts have weighed human capital factors in their decisions in salary discrimination cases.

In the third and final section, we discuss the specific information that employment attorneys need to obtain from the employer's human-resource personnel while investigating the allegations.

The Concept of an Employee's Human Capital Investment

Think of a mid-level manager at a company with 100 similarly situated managers. Would it surprise you to learn that each of the 100 individuals, even if they all started at exactly the same time, had a different salary? Probably not.

Why? Because even a cursory examination of most employers' compensation structures quickly reveals myriad employment factors that have nothing to do with race, gender, or nationality and determine an individual's salary. All these factors must be accounted for in some way before a valid statistical inference can be made regarding any observed pay disparities.

One of the most important determinants of a person's salary is called human capital, which is defined as the knowledge, skills, and unique abilities that an employee brings to a job. Human capital investments include things such as the employee's formal education, job training, and labor market experience.

Investments in human capital are often compared to the physical capital investments made by a company. A company acquires physical capital such as new factories or production machinery if it believes it will ultimately increase the company's overall profitability. In other words, the company makes an investment in new physical capital if it believes that it can earn an adequate return on its investment and improve the bottom line.

Employees make similar decisions when deciding to acquire additional human capital such as education and job training. An employee acquires additional job training if he or she believes that the training will make him or her more valuable in the labor market or to a particular employer. The additional value that the training or other human capital factor adds to the 'employee's bottom line' is called the return on human capital.

Unfortunately, it is much more difficult to quantify human capital investments and their return than physical capital investments made by companies. The information that is collected from an employer forms the basis for the human capital measures that will be used in the statistical analysis of allegations of salary discrimination. Needless to say, the accuracy and thoroughness of the human capital measures collected by the attorney is critically important.

The labor economist's or statistician's measurement or mismeasurement of these human capital factors can turn an employment discrimination case on its ear.

Why Accurate Measurement of Human Capital Investments is Crucial

Conventional labor-market thinking and economic research strongly suggest that human capital factors play a significant role in determining how much a person is paid. This is true not only in determining why people in different jobs are paid differently, but also in studying why people in the same job are paid differently.

Think of all the factors that determine a person's salary as a 'salary pie'. The salary determination factors used to make the salary pie include the human capital factors that we have already discussed, as well as institutional factors such as the employee's geographical location or other employer-specific issues. These other employer-specific issues include more subtle factors such as differences in responsibility levels that are not necessarily reflected in the job title alone.

Intangible salary determination factors and job-related attributes such as the employee's innate desire to succeed ('fire in the belly') are difficult, but not always impossible, to measure.

For many positions, human capital factors comprise the lion's share of the salary pie. In some instances, human capital factors may explain up to 75% of the salary variation among employees. Even within the same job, an employment attorney may observe a substantial variation in earnings between different groups of employees. Often the earning variation is due to the differences in the quantity and quality of employees' education, previous job assignments, or factors related to the employees' attachment to the employer. Accordingly, 20% or more of the person's salary can be explained by institution factors such as the job location.

The remaining 5% or so of an employee's salary variation can be quite nettlesome in some statistical analyses of allegations of salary discrimination. This is particularly true when job-related factors are important but difficult to measure. For example, in the service industry, some employees may be better than others at customer service and interaction, and therefore earn a higher salary and bonuses. In theory, it may be possible to account for the employee's customer service abilities, but in practice, it is often difficult to measure the employee's ability with complete certainty. Incorrectly accounting for the intangibles can lead to faulty inferences regarding salary discrimination by the employer.

In sum, while the percentages vary across employers, in most cases human capital is a very important salary determinant factor. Inaccurately modeling an employee's human capital can cause employment attorneys to wrongly attribute (or fail to attribute) legitimate differences in salary to an individual's race, gender or nationality.

The Courts' View on Human Capital

For quite a while, courts have placed significant importance on human capital factors when weighing statistical evidence in motions to exclude evidence, for summary judgment, and for class certification in salary discrimination cases.

One recent case that is particularly insightful is the *Cooper Michaels et al. v. Southern Company, Georgia Power Company*. In this case, African-American workers alleged that Georgia Southern discriminated against them in terms of pay and promotions. The court, which denied the plaintiffs' motion for class certification, clearly states the problem with the plaintiffs' statistical expert's model, especially on its failure to account for human capital. The district court decision in the case was affirmed on appeal by the 11th Circuit Appeals court.

In its denial of the plaintiffs' motion for class certification, the district court observed that although the plaintiffs' expert statistician did have some measures for the individuals' education, her measures were inadequate and unconvincing. In particular, the court noted that the quality of the educational institutions was not accounted for by the plaintiffs' statistician.

As the district court observed, "[the plaintiffs' expert]'s reports did not take into account the type or level of acquired skills of job applicants. [The plaintiffs' expert]'s "education" component failed to take into account the field of study, the relevance of that field to any position in question, or the quality of the educational institutions involved, factors which may be important in some managers' employment decisions."

In addition to the problems with the plaintiffs' statistician's education measures, the court also took issue with other human capital factors such as job-specific experience. In the end, the court ruled that it was "impossible to determine what the [salary and promotions] gaps [we]re, whether they [we]re statistically significant, or whether factors other than race [we]re involved."

The Georgia Southern case is not an isolated case and there are many similar examples, including *Coleman v. Exxon* in the United States Federal Court in Texas. Other cases that have addressed the human capital issue are listed in the reference section.

The Bottom Line

Courts recognize the unique attributes that an employee brings to a job and the complex relationship between those attributes and the employee's ultimate salary.

What can be done to ensure that statistical analysis includes the right measures of human capital?

1. Learn about employees' individual jobs.
2. Participate in tours of the plant and/or employer.
3. Listen to the stories of human-resource staff members about trends at the company.
4. Look for outliers in the company. Some of the statistical analysis may be driven by the results of a few individuals.

Conclusions and Chapter Summary

In this chapter, we examined allegations of salary discrimination. As before, the ultimate goal of our employment analysis was to determine the likelihood that our employment data was generated by an unbiased salary process. The main difference between the methodologies discussed in this chapter and those of the previous two chapters is that we looked at methods allowing us to consider the effects of many different employment-related factors on the discrimination analysis.

This chapter began with an introduction to the linear regression model. After we studied the basic linear regression model, we then provided an introduction to salary data and the use of linear regression in a salary analysis. The chapter closed with a discussion of the role that human capital plays in determining an individual's salary.

Promotion Discrimination Analyses

Generally, a job promotion involves an increase in title, rank, authority, responsibility, and/or pay for an individual employee. For any given employee, the likelihood of being promoted can be affected by many factors.

In this chapter, we examine analyses of promotion discrimination. We begin by looking at the definition of a job promotion and the factors in an employer's job-promotion decision. Following this discussion, we describe several different methodologies that are used to analyze promotion discrimination. We provide several examples to illustrate the underlying principles of each of these methodologies.

Defining a Promotion

Before we can think about how promotion analyses are performed, we need to what constitutes a promotion. Generally, a job promotion involves an increase in title, rank, authority, responsibility, and/or pay for an individual employee. The definition of a promotion may vary among employers. In some instances, an individual's promotion may include an increase in responsibility and authority, but may not result in a significant change in compensation.

For instance, managers in retail and heavily commission-based occupations sometimes receive lower total compensation when they move into the ranks of middle management, because their compensation is no longer as dependent on variable commissions and overtime. In other instances, a job promotion may involve a significant increase in salary, but little change in the employee's day-to-day responsibilities.

Job Promotion Factors

Regardless of how a job promotion is defined, an employee's likelihood of being promoted can be affected by many factors. Clearly **job performance** is one factor that enters into an employer's decision to promote an employee. Job performance may be measured by an employer in a number of ways, but these generally fall into either a job-rating or job-ranking evaluation system. Some companies use both a rating and a ranking evaluation system.

In a **job-rating system**, the job performance of the employees is rated by a supervisor or team of supervisors. These systems usually have a pre-established set of ratings and job criteria that the supervisors consider when evaluating each employee. For example, an employer may rate each employee on a 1-to-5 scale in areas such as job knowledge, dependability, and communication skills.

In a **job-ranking system,** the job performance of each employee is compared to and ranked against that of all other employees in the ranking unit. As with the rating system, a job-ranking system generally has a set of pre-established criteria for the rankers to consider in their evaluations. In pure ranking systems, the actual job performance of similarly ranked individuals may vary across different ranking units within a single employer.

In addition to job performance, **job seniority** and career progression ladders can also affect an employee's chance of being promoted. In some job positions, the length of time that the employee has been with the company, in a particular job, or in a particular salary group figures into the promotion decision. Conceptually, job seniority reflects the accumulation of employer-specific expertise, knowledge and skills that are valuable to that specific employer. For certain jobs, as an employee's seniority increases, the likelihood of earning a promotion should also increase if other job promotion factors are held constant.

An employee's education is another factor that could impact the likelihood of receiving a promotion. A person's formal, informal, and on-the-job training indicates the employee's potential to succeed in a position with greater responsibilities.

Finally, factors that are not easily measured by the employer can affect the chance of receiving a promotion. Some of these factors are intangible and can include things such as one's innate desire to succeed, superior social skills, and above-average professional and social maturity. Although these factors are not easy to measure, the statistical analysis should attempt to consider and incorporate them when they are arguably part of the decision-making process for promotions.

Promotion Research Methodology

The allegations in a promotion case are similar to those in other types of discrimination cases in that the plaintiffs believe they were denied a promotion because of their race, gender, age or other attribute of a protected group. However, in a promotion analysis it is important to study the exact mechanism through which the discrimination has allegedly affected the employee's likelihood of receiving a promotion. Specifically, the employee may allege that the employer's discrimination caused him or her to not be promoted, to take a longer time to be promoted, or to receive a smaller promotion than that which would have been expected in the absence of discrimination. Let's start with the first research question.

In the first instance, the research question would be:

> Is there a **statistically significant** difference between the promotion rates of the protected and non-protected group members in the units being studied?
>
> Or,
>
> What is the probability that an unbiased and protected-group-neutral promotion process would have generated the observed employment outcome being studied?

Data Collection

The first stage of the analysis is collection of the relevant data. In a promotion case, this data can be provided at a unit level or an employee level. At a unit level, the data may include aggregate employee counts by protected group status and other types of unit-level calculated statistics. Data at the employee level may include the outcome of the promotion process, any interview scores, past and current job-performance measures, formal education, and other employee-specific information. The level at which the data is provided affects the type of statistical test that can be performed.

During the data-collection process, one concern is to ensure that the information reflects the employer units that were being considered during the promotion process. This requires obtaining information on the supervisor and/or teams that are responsible for employee evaluations, rankings and ultimately job promotions. In some instances, it may require conducting sub-analyses based on different units and supervisors.

Hypothesis Testing

As discussed in detail in previous chapters, the null hypothesis is that the employer's promotion process was unbiased and protected-group-status neutral. The null hypothesis can be written as follows.

> **H_O:** The employer's promotion process is unbiased and protected-group neutral and the difference between the groups' promotion rates is consistent with random chance.

Depending on the level of detail of the data and information available about the promotion process, statistical testing of the null hypothesis can be performed by using a number of different statistical tests, including the binomial test, Fisher Exact test, chi-square test, and limited dependent-variable models such as the logistic regression model. As discussed in previous chapters, the statistics generated by these methods are used to accept or reject the null hypothesis. A more detailed example is presented in the following section of this chapter.

Time to Promotion

In an analysis of the time to promotion, we are studying the time it takes for different groups of employees to be promoted to the next level. For instance if a promotion is defined as an increase to the next salary grade, then we would study the time it takes for an employee to be promoted from one grade to the next, perhaps from salary grade 10 to salary grade 11.

The job promotion factors and the general method of setting up the research hypotheses that we considered above are similar to those involved in answering the promotion-rate question. Depending on the type of data available, the appropriate statistical test may be a **Z-test** or **t-test of the difference between two means** or a time-duration model such the **Cox proportional hazards** model.

Size of Promotion

Some promotion cases involve allegations that the protected group member received a smaller promotion than similarly situated non-protected group members. The size of a promotion can be measured in terms of a salary increase or a change in employment conditions. In these cases, statistical tests that examine the difference between means (or medians) and linear regression models that consider the different employment factors are common.

A Fixed Promotion Probability Example

We will start with a simple example. Assume that we have a department composed of 100 similarly situated employees. Of the 100 employees, 50 are men and 50 are women. Furthermore, it has been determined from past promotion experiences that each employee has a ten-percent chance of being promoted in any given year. This year, the company has authorized the department to promote 20 employees. The employer ended up promoting 13 men and seven women.

From the perspective of a labor economist or statistician, a gender-neutral promotion process in this example looks a lot like the classic example of a person selecting 20 balls from a bowl filled with yellow and green balls. The person randomly selects one ball from the bowl, notes the color of the ball on a piece of paper, and then puts the ball back into the bowl. This process of drawing a ball, noting the color, and replacing the ball in the bowl continues until all 20 balls have been selected.

A Question to Consider
Q: Why do you put the balls back in the bowl in this example? **A:** The balls are put back into the bowl so that the probability of selecting a yellow or green ball is the same in each of the ball selections. In our example, it is assumed that each employee has a fixed ten-percent chance of being promoted, so putting the balls back into the bowl is necessary. This process is called sampling with replacement.

Since, theoretically, we know how the underlying employment process works, we can calculate the expected employment outcome that would be obtained if discrimination were not a factor. More importantly, we can calculate the probability that an unbiased employment process would have generated the employment outcomes in question.

Going back to our promotion example, if the promotion process were neutral, we would expect that half of the 20 promotions would be earned by female employees, because 50 of the 100 employees in the promotion pool are female. If we assume that an employment-selection process works in the manner described above (as in the ball drawing exercise), then the expected number of employees selected from the protected group can be shown to be equal to the total number of employment selections times the proportion of protected-group employees in the selection pool. That is,

$$Expected\ Promotions = E(X) = np$$

where n is the number of promotions and p is the proportion of protected-class employees in the department.

As illustrated in the coin-flipping example, although we expect that half of the promotions will go to women, it is not uncommon to observe a situation where the actual outcome deviates from this expected promotion outcome. By using what we know (or have assumed) about the employment process, we can calculate exactly how likely it is that our actual promotion outcome would have been generated by an unbiased promotion process. If we find that it is extremely unlikely that an unbiased promotion process could have generated our data, then we may conclude that the employment outcome is consistent with some type of bias.

To calculate the probability that only seven women would have been promoted in our example, we use a special and well-known formula that mathematically describes our employment process. The formula is called the **binomial distribution** and is presented in the equation below.

$$\Pr(X = x) = \binom{n}{x} p^x q^{n-x}$$

In this formula, n is the number of promotions, x is the number of women who are promoted, p is the proportion of female employees, and q is the proportion of male employees.

Although the mathematical formula looks complicated, it requires nothing more than a series of simple multiplication operations. The probability that only seven women received one of the 20 promotions is calculated as follows.

$$\Pr(X = 7) = \binom{20}{7} 0.5^7 0.5^{20-7} = \binom{20}{7} 0.5^7 0.5^{13}$$

Note:

$$\binom{n}{k} = \frac{n!}{k!(n-k)!}$$

and

$$n! = n(n-1)(n-2)\cdots 1$$

$$\text{So: } \binom{20}{7} = \frac{20!}{7!(20-7)!} = \frac{20!}{7!(13!)} = 77,520$$

Plugging the numbers into the formula yields:

$$\Pr(X = 7) = (77,250) \times 0.5^7 \times 0.5^{13} = 7.37\%$$

Thus, the probability of seven females and 13 males being promoted is 7.37%. These probabilities can also be found in tables in many statistical textbooks.

Note that the probability of seven or fewer women being promoted is greater than the probability of having exactly seven women be promoted. The probability of having seven or fewer females promoted is greater because the former considers the probability of an outcome where 6, 5, 4, 3, 2, 1, and 0 women are promoted. The total probability of having seven or fewer women be promoted is determined by summing the probabilities of each lesser number of promotions. The specific calculation is as follows.

$$\Pr(X \leq 7) = \sum_{k=0}^{7} \Pr(X = k) = 13.16\%$$

Hence, the probability of observing the given promotion outcome, or worse, from an unbiased promotion process is 13.16%. Generally, a finding that is less than 1-5% is viewed as statistically significant and hence not consistent with randomness. The above promotion process with a probability of 13.16% is not statistically significant and therefore is consistent with a non-biased employment process.

A Non-Fixed Promotion Probability Example

To examine another important statistic used in employment discrimination analyses, let's introduce another example and study a company that has recently made a number of promotions in its engineering department.

The engineering department was composed of 24 employees, 16 of whom were in the protected class of employees who are 40 years of age or older. All of the employees in the department are assumed to be similarly situated by management. The engineering department promoted ten employees. All of the employees who were promoted were less than 40 years of age.

Is it likely that an age-neutral promotion process could have generated these results?

As with the previous promotion example, we must first determine what the distribution of expected employment outcomes would look like in the absence of discrimination. Then we can use the range of expected employment outcomes to calculate the probability that an age-neutral process would have resulted in only employees under age 40 being promoted.

From the perspective of a labor economist or statistician, an age-neutral promotion process would look a lot like the classic example of a person selecting balls from a bowl as discussed above. However, unlike the previous promotion example, the balls are not placed back into the bowl after noting the color. The person randomly selects one ball from the bowl, notes the color of the ball on a piece of paper, and then discards the ball.

This process of drawing a ball, noting its color, and discarding it continues until all ten balls have been selected from the bowl. In this analogy, the bowl originally contained 24 yellow and green balls, and when the process ended, 14 balls remained.

Why do we not put the balls back in the bowl in this promotion example?

In the promotion analogy, the balls are not put back into the bowl, because a person can be promoted only once in this example. Consequently, the probability of selecting an employee who is in the protected age group changes after the first employment promotion has been made. When the first theoretical promotion was made in the department, there was a 16/24 (number of employees in protected age group/total number of employees) or 2/3 (67%) chance of selecting a person who was 40 years of age or older. For the second promotion, the probability of selecting a person 40 years of age or older falls because an employee in the protected age group has already been selected. At that point, the probability of selecting a person in the protected age groups is 15/23 (65%).

A Question to Consider
Q: What effect does discarding the balls have on the exercise?
A: Discarding the balls after selecting them causes the probability of selecting a ball of a particular color to change for each selection. Think about a person who draws two balls from a bowl that originally had five balls: three yellow and two green.
Before any balls are drawn, the probability of drawing a yellow ball is 3/5 and the probability of drawing a green ball is 2/5. If a yellow ball is randomly drawn on the first draw, four balls are left in the bowl: two yellow and two green.
For the second draw, the probability of drawing a yellow ball is 2/4 and the probability of drawing a green ball is 2/4.
This process is called sampling without replacement.

Again, because we know how the underlying promotion process works theoretically, we can calculate the employment outcome that would be expected if discrimination were not a factor. More importantly, we can calculate the probability that an unbiased employment process would have generated the employment outcomes in question.

Going back to our promotion example, if the promotion process were neutral, we would expect that 16/24 or 2/3 of the ten promotions would involve engineers 40 years of age or older. If we assume that an employment selection process works as described above (as in the ball-drawing exercise), then, like the promotion example above, the expected number of protected-group employees selected for promotion is equal to the total number of employment selections times the proportion of protected-group employees in the selection pool. That is,

$$E(X) = np$$

where n is the number of employees who are promoted and p is the proportion of protected-class employees.

As before, although we have an expectation concerning the number of promotions that would involve employees who are 40 years of age or older, it is not uncommon to observe a situation where the actual outcome deviates from this expected promotion outcome.

By using what we know (or have assumed) about the employment process, we can calculate exactly how likely it is that our observed employment promotion outcome would have been generated by an unbiased promotion process. If we find it unlikely that an unbiased promotion process could have generated our data, then we may conclude that the employment outcome is consistent with some type of bias.

To calculate the probability that only employees under the age of 40 would have been promoted in our example, we use a well-known formula that mathematically describes this type of employment process. The formula is called the **hypergeometric distribution** and is presented in the equation below. Although the mathematical formula looks complicated, it requires nothing more than a series of simple arithmetic operations.

$$f(x|A, B, n) = \frac{\binom{A}{x}\binom{B}{n-x}}{\binom{A+B}{n}}$$

The probability that only employees over the age of 40 would have been promoted is calculated as follows.

$$f(10|16, 8, 10) = \frac{\binom{16}{10}\binom{8}{10-10}}{\binom{16+8}{10}} = \frac{\binom{16}{10}\binom{8}{0}}{\binom{24}{10}}$$

Recall that

$$\binom{n}{k} = \frac{n!}{k!(n-k)!}$$

and

$$n! = n(n-1)(n-2)\cdots 1$$

so, we have

$$\binom{16}{10} = \frac{16!}{10!(16-10)!} = \frac{16!}{10! * 6!} = 8008$$

$$\binom{8}{0} = \frac{8!}{0!(8-0)!} = \frac{8!}{1 * 8!} = 1$$

$$\binom{24}{10} = \frac{24!}{10!(24-10)!} = \frac{24!}{10! * 14!} = 1,961,256$$

Plugging these values into our hypergeometric equation yields:

$$f(10|16, 8, 10) = \frac{8008 * 1}{1,961,256} = 0.00408$$

Thus, the probability that only employees who are 40 years of age or less are promoted is less than 0.5%. As mentioned previously, a finding that is less than 1-5% is generally considered to be statistically significant and hence inconsistent with randomness. This promotion process has a statistically significant probability of 0.5% and hence is inconsistent with a non-biased employment process.

Advanced Job Promotion Analysis

The two examples above are similar in that they both assume that the individuals who are being studied are similarly situated. It is assumed, or is a fact, that the employees in the promotion analysis have similar employment factors such as experience, education, job responsibilities, and more. In some situations, the analysis is conducted for individuals who have different employment factors.

With a sufficient number of individuals, it may be possible to stratify the employees and perform the analyses described in the previous example for each employee stratification. If this type of sub-analysis is not feasible, then a more advanced approach is required. The logistic regression approach is an example of such of an approach and is presented in the following section.

Consider an employer that uses a ranking evaluation system and uses those employee rankings in the promotion decision. Each employee is ranked on a scale from 0 to 100. We were provided data for 427 employees. Of the 427 employees, 35% are 40 years of age or older. Each of the employees are similar in terms of employment conditions, such as job title, responsibilities, and job tenure. For the purposes of our analysis, the only difference between the employees is their ranking and age. The table below shows the data for some of the employees in the company.

To determine whether an individual's age is correlated with his or her likelihood of receiving a job promotion, we use what is called **logistic regression**. The logistic regression methodology provides us with a mathematical factor called a coefficient. The coefficient in the promotion logistic regression model tells us what effect, if any, the employment factor has on the likelihood of being promoted. A positive coefficient means that an increase in the employment factor is correlated with an increase in the probability of being promoted.

Specifically, the probability of a promotion (p) can be written as:

$$p = \frac{e^{\beta_0} + \beta_1 x}{1 + e^{\beta_0} + \beta_1 x}$$

In this equation, e is the exponential function, β_0 is a constant number, and β_1 is the mathematical coefficient that describes the effect of the employment factor on the probability of promotion. The variable x is an employment factor, such as job ranking or age. Although only one variable is shown, the model can be expanded to include multiple employment factors.

The equation above can be simplified by taking the natural logarithm of p, yielding

$$\ln(p) = ln\left(\frac{e^{\beta_0} + \beta_1 x}{1 + e^{\beta_0} + \beta_1 x}\right)$$

$$= \beta_0 + \beta_1 x$$

The promotion logistic regression coefficients can be used to calculate the promotion-related odds ratio. We can calculate odds ratios for each of the employment factors that we are studying. The promotion odds ratio is a statistic that tells us, for a unit change in any given employment factor, how much more likely than not an employee is to earn a promotion.

For instance, one factor in the logistic regression model tells us whether the person in the data is 40 years of age or older. This variable is equal to 0 if the person is under 40 and 1 if the person is 40 or older. The promotion odds ratio for the age variable calculated from the logistic regression equation would tell us how much more likely a person who is 40 years of age or older is to receive a job promotion than a person who is under the age of 40.

A promotion odds ratio that is equal to 1 means that the older employee is as likely as the younger employee to earn a job promotion. A promotion odds ratio that is less than 1 means that the older worker is less likely to earn a job promotion. An odds ratio that is greater than 1 means that the older worker is more likely to earn a promotion than the younger worker.

$$OR = \frac{Probability\ of\ Earning\ a\ Promotion}{Probability\ of\ Not\ Earning\ a\ Promotion} = \frac{p}{(1-p)}$$

By re-arranging the above equations, the odds ratio (OR) can be written as:

$$OR = e^{\beta_1}$$

where e is the exponential function and β_1 is the mathematical coefficient that describes the effect of the employment factor on the probability of earning a promotion.

The promotion odds ratio can be calculated by exponentiating the logistic regression equation shown above. Most statistical analysis programs calculate the odds ratio from the logistic regression equation automatically.

As with the promotion statistical tests that we discussed previously, we must determine whether the odds ratio estimated through our logistic regression equation is statistically significant. That is we test to see whether we can reject the null hypothesis that the underlying employment factor is not correlated to the likelihood of an individual earning a promotion. We test to see whether we can reject the null hypothesis that the logistic regression coefficient (discussed above) on the promotion variable is equal to zero. Standard z-test statistics are used in the hypothesis-testing procedure. Additional statistics tests can determine the accuracy or fit of the promotion logistic regression model to the employment data. These statistical tests can be found in any of the logistic regression textbooks that are referenced in this book.

Example

Let's return to the promotion example we discussed earlier. Two employment factors, job ranking and age group, are accounted for in the promotion logistic regression function. The equation below shows the logistic function for promotions in that example. For the purposes of the example, assume that the measured effects concerning job rankings and age are statistically significant.

The natural log *ln()* of the promotion probability (p) equation is written as:

$$\ln(p) = ln\left(\frac{e^{-0.448+.11x_1\ 1.16x_2}}{1+e^{-0.448+.11x_1\ 1.16x_2}}\right)$$

As expected, the mathematical coefficient of 0.11 in the equation implies a positive relationship between the person's job ranking and the probability of a job promotion. In addition, the mathematical coefficient of 1.16 in the equation implies a positive correlation between earning a promotion and being in the protected age group of 40 years and older.

The coefficient can be transformed into an odds ratio to more easily interpret the effect of each of the employment factors. Specifically, the odds ratios are:

$$OR_{job\ rankings} = e^{\beta_1} = e^{.11} = 1.11$$

$$OR_{Age\ 40\ plus} = e^{B_2} = e^{1.16} = 3.19$$

The odds ratios of 1.11 for job ranking means that a one-unit increase in the job ranking increases the odds of a promotion by a factor of 1.11. Similarly, the odds ratio of 3.19 for the age group means that individuals who are age 40 and older are 3.19 times more likely than individuals who are under the age of 40 to earn a job promotion. In this example, the data does not suggest a bias against older workers.

The illustrative graph below shows the predicted probabilities associated with each job performance ranking for employees who are under 40 and for those who are 40 or older. An employee who is under the age of 40 and receives a job performance ranking of 32 has a 0.28 probability of receiving a promotion. In contrast, an employee who is 40 years of age or older and receives a job performance ranking of 32 has a 0.55 probability

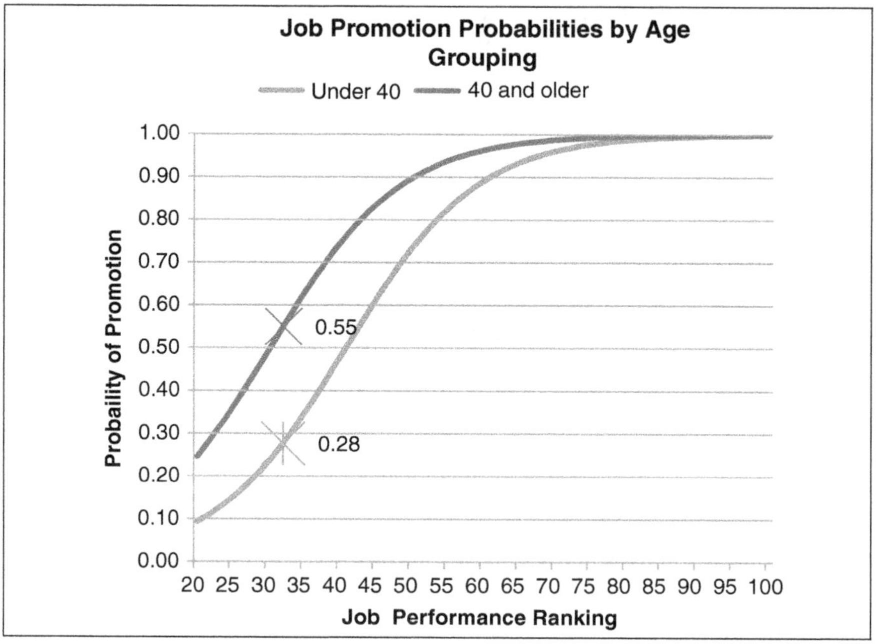

of receiving a promotion. In this instance, the data does not suggest a bias against older employees.

Conclusions and Chapter Summary

In this chapter, we examined promotion discrimination analyses. We began by looking at the definition of a promotion and the factors in an employer's promotion decision. Then we described several methodologies that are used to analyze promotion discrimination. We gave several examples to illustrate the underlying principles of each of these methodologies.

Section IV

Statistics and Economics in Action

Statistics and economics are not spectator sports. The best way to learn how statistics and economics are useful in employment discrimination analyses is to examine how they are used in practice.

In this section, we present a detailed dictionary of important statistical terms that arise in statistical analyses of employment discrimination. The dictionary of statistical terms contains a definition of the term and in many instances a worked out example that is employment related.

Following the statistical dictionary, there is a section that discusses the various types of publicly available labor market data. The data discussed in this section is commonly used to provide additional insights on an employer's company-level data. For instance, the data discussed in this section can be used to provide information on external labor availability pools in hiring discrimination cases and to provide compensation benchmarks in salary discrimination cases.

In addition to the section on labor market data, we also provide a list of legal cases that have relied on statistical analysis in some portion of the legal proceedings. The list of cases includes federal court, state court, and Supreme Court cases. The list also includes cases where the statistical evidence has been challenged under *Daubert* or related cases. In the final section, we provide a bibliography of employment related economic and statistics articles and textbooks.

Dictionary of Statistical Employment Terms

Terms

A

Absolute Value, *n.* magnitude of a number or the distance of a number from zero.

Discussion: Absolute value is often used in employment cases when reporting differences between an employee's salary and the average employee salary.

Example: In this case, assume the average employee earns a salary of $60,000 a year. The plaintiff only earns $50,000 a year. What is the difference between the plaintiff's salary and the average employee's salary? The difference or absolute value of the difference is:

$$|\$50,000 - \$60,000| = \$10,000$$

In this case, the plaintiff earns $10,000 less than the average employee.

See Also: Range

Addition Law, *n.* the Addition Law states that the probability of event A or event B occurring is equal to the probability of event A occurring plus the probability of event B occurring, less the probability of both event A and event B occurring. Formally:

$$\Pr(A \text{ or } B) = \Pr(A) + \Pr(B) - \Pr(A \text{ and } B)$$

Discussion: Visually, the addition law can be drawn using sets.

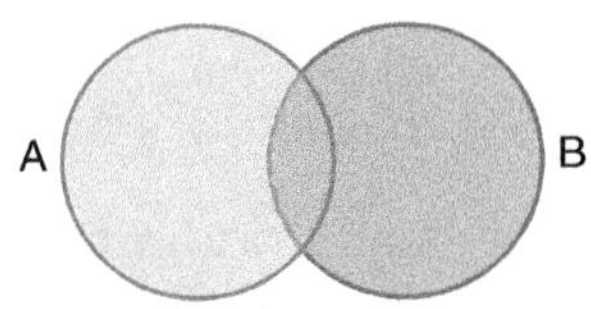

If the light circle is the probability of A and the dark circle is the probability of B, then the probability of A or B is the light circle plus the dark circle minus the overlap between the two circles. The overlap is subtracted to avoid double-counting.

Example: Consider an electronics company facing allegations of discrimination against hiring female and African-American applicants. If all applicants are equally well-qualified for a position, then the outcome of the hiring process should be the same as if the applicants' names were drawn from a hat. That is, each applicant has an equal chance of being hired. To test our hypothesis of nondiscrimination, we wish to calculate the probability that one female or one African-American is hired. The applicant pool consists of the following:

	Male Applicants	**Female Applicants**	**Total**
White Applicants	4	2	6
African-American Applicants	1	3	4
Total	5	5	10

Based on the table above, the probability of hiring a female, African-American, and African-American female applicant, respectively, are as follows:

$$\text{Pr(female hired)} = \frac{\text{5 females}}{\text{10 applicants}} = 50\%$$

$$\text{Pr(African-American hired)} = \frac{\text{4 African-Americans}}{\text{10 applicants}} = 40\%$$

$$\text{Pr(African-American female hired)} = \frac{\text{3 African-American females}}{\text{10 applicants}} = 30\%$$

Hence, the probability that a female or an African-American applicant will be hired is:

$$\Pr(A \text{ or } B) = \Pr(A) + \Pr(B) - \Pr(A \text{ and } B) = 50\% + 40\% - 30\% = 60\%$$

The last term (the probability of an African-American female being hired) is subtracted to avoid double-counting those applicants who are both female and African-American.

See also: Cross-tabulation, probability

Adverse Impact, *n.* an outcome of a selection process that results in fewer benefits or greater burdens being placed on the protected class.

Discussion: Adverse impact can be an intentional or unintentional effect of a particular event in the selection process.

Example: In *Griggs v. Duke Power Company*, the plaintiff filed a class action alleging racial discrimination in its policy for transfer to higher pay grades. The defendant required employees to pass two separate aptitude tests and to possess a high school education. The plaintiffs argued that these requirements were not necessary for the jobs and that they had a disproportionate negative impact on African-American employees. In this case, statistical evidence was used to demonstrate the adverse impact on African-American employees.

See also: Disparate application, disparate impact, disparate treatment, hypothesis testing, statistical significance.

Aggregate, *n.* single variable or value that results from combining multiple variables.

Discussion: In a hiring discrimination case, it is common to break down annual hiring data into smaller, discrete hiring periods. Intuitively, this separation makes sense. Individuals who applied for jobs in September cannot be hired for job openings in March.

Example: In *Hogan v. Pierce*, the plaintiffs alleged that African-Americans were wrongfully denied promotion opportunities. In fact, no African-Americans were promoted by the employer. However, each promotion period considered very few individuals, African-American or otherwise. When the promotions were analyzed by promotion period, the differences in promotion rates were not statistically significant for every promotion period that was analyzed. When the promotion data was aggregated using the Mantel-Haenszel Odds Ratio, a statistically significant difference in promotion rates was found.

See also: Hypothesis testing, Mantel-Haenszel Odds Ratio, statistical significance, Wald test.

Alternative Hypothesis, *n.* the statement believed to be true if the null hypothesis is rejected.

Discussion: In employment discrimination cases, the alternative hypothesis is that the data generated by the defendant-employer's employment policies and procedures are NOT consistent with unbiased and nondiscriminatory behavior by the employer. It is important to understand that even if we reject null hypothesis and accept the alternative hypothesis, we are not stating that the firm discriminated against the protected group of employees. We can never say that based on the results of our statistical hypothesis test.

Example: Assume we are testing the null hypothesis that the average salaries of women and men are equal, versus the alternative hypothesis that their average salaries are not equal. We will reject the null hypothesis if the average salary of women is so much less than that of men that it is unlikely that a random and unbiased salary determination process would have produced the outcome. We will also reject the null hypothesis that the average salary is the same for the protected and unprotected groups, and the implicit assumption that all groups are compensated equally for the same work, if we find that the average salary of male employees is so much more than that of females employees at the company.

See also: Hypothesis testing, null hypothesis, statistical significance.

Analysis of Variance (ANOVA), *n.* a way to determine the extent to which variance in the data can be attributed to a particular cause.

Discussion: ANOVA can be used to compare the equivalence of several groups' mean values. In the test, the null hypothesis is that the true mean is the same for each group. In an employment litigation setting, it might be used to compare the average wages of members of the protected class to that of members of the non-protected class.

Example: Suppose an economist is interested in comparing the hourly wages of male employees to the hourly wages of female employees. The salaries are as follows:

Male: \$5, \$6, \$5, \$7.50, \$10

Female: \$4, \$4.50, \$12, \$5, \$5

ANOVA is calculated as follows. First, calculate the sum of squares for each group. The formula for the sum of squares is:

$$\sum X^2 = \sum x^2 - \frac{(\sum x)^2}{n}$$

where x is the observed salary, n is the total number of individuals in the pool, and X is the deviation of the observation from the mean.

Male:

$$\sum X_m^2 = 5^2 + 6^2 + 5^2 + 7.5^2 + 10^2 - \frac{(5 + 6 + 5 + 7.5 + 10)^2}{5}$$

$$\sum X_m^2 = 242.25 - \frac{(33.5)^2}{5} = 17.8$$

Female:

$$\sum X_f^2 = 4^2 + 4.5^2 + 12^2 + 5^2 + 5^2 - \frac{(4 + 4.5 + 12 + 5 + 5)^2}{5}$$

$$\sum X_f^2 = 230.25 - \frac{(30.5)^2}{5} = 44.2$$

Next, use the sum of squares result:

$$\sum x_T^2 = \sum x_B^2 + \sum x_W^2$$

That is, the total sum of squares is equal to the sum of squares between the groups plus the sum of squares within the groups. In this example, the total sum of squares is:

$$\sum X_T^2 = 242.25 + 230.25 - \frac{(33.5 + 30.5)^2}{10} = 62.9$$

Between the groups, the sum of squares is:

$$\sum X_B^2 = \frac{33.5^2}{5} + \frac{30.5^2}{5} - \frac{(33.5 + 30.5)^2}{10} = 0.9$$

Within the groups, the sum of squares is:

$$\sum X_W^2 = \sum X_T^2 - \sum X_B^2 = 62.9 - 0.9 = 62$$

The between-group variance is:

$$\hat{\sigma}_B^2 = \frac{\sum X_B^2}{k - 1} = \frac{0.9}{2 - 1} = 0.9$$

where k is the number of groups. The within-group variance is:

$$\hat{\sigma}_W^2 = \frac{\sum X_W^2}{n - k} = \frac{62}{10 - 2} = 7.75$$

The F-test can then be used to determine whether there is a statistically significant difference between the hourly wages of males and females. In this case:

$$F = \frac{\sigma_B^2}{\sigma_W^2} = \frac{0.9}{7.75} = 0.12$$

At the 1% level, $F_1^8 = 5981$. If our F statistics equals 5981, then there is only a one-percent chance that randomness could have produced the observed outcome or one even more disparate.

In our case, the F-statistic is equal to 0.12. Since $0.12 < 5981$, our findings suggest that there is no statistically significant disparity between male and female hourly wages at the 1% level.

Similarly, at the 5% level, $F_1^8 = 238.9$. If our F statistics equals 238.9, then there is only a five-percent chance that randomness could have produced the observed outcome or one even more disparate. In our case, the F-statistic is still less than the critical value. That is, since $0.12 < 238.9$, there is no statistically significant disparity between male and female hourly wages at the 5% level using ANOVA.

See also: F-test, hypothesis testing, mean, null hypothesis, sum of squares, variance.

Applicant Flow Data, *n.* company data that contains the files and applications of individuals who responded to a position announcement.

Discussion: Depending on the manner in which an employer receives applications, the application data may contain individual hardcopy resumes and/or standardized electronic application data. As a result, the application contained in the data from one source may be somewhat standardized and include the same set of information for all applicants. Other application sources may result only in an individually prepared (and non-standard) resume submitted by the applicant.

Regardless of the employer, the applicant data will most likely be the most incomplete and varied type of employment data encountered by the employment attorney in a discrimination case. It is common for companies to maintain only minimal documentation on the individuals who applied for a given job position. This practice is common in part because the large majority of applications received by firms are submitted by individuals who are unqualified for the position or who show only a passing interest in the position.

It is important to keep in mind that not all individuals included in the applicant flow data are applicants. With the increasing popularity of internet-based recruiting and job searching, clarification was needed to determine which potential applicants are indeed applicants. In 2005, OFCCP released its final definition of an internet applicant, stating that an individual must meet the following criteria:

- The individual submits an expression of interest in employment through the internet or other electronic means.
- The company considers the individual for employment in a particular position.
- The individual's expression of interest indicates that he or she meets the basic qualifications for the position.
- The individual at no point prior to receiving an offer of employment indicates that he or she is no longer interested in the position.

Bottom line: Although an individual may be on the applicant flow log, if he or she does not meet all of the above criteria, the individual may not need to be included in statistical employment analyses.

See also: Pool.

Availability, *n.* the percentage of the protected group available for the hiring decision being made.

Discussion: Availability is an important criterion for determining the relevant baseline for analyses.

Example: Consider a medical research company located in Houston, Texas. The company is being investigated by OFCCP for failure to hire enough African-American biotechnology scientists. Unfortunately, the company did not maintain applicant flow records. In cases where adequate records are not maintained, OFCCP may use external data, such as the percentage of African-Americans with a degree in biology, as a measure of the applicant pool. These types of external data measures can be problematic because they do not always accurately measure the labor availability of the group in question.

See also: Applicant flow, benchmark, pool.

Average, *n.* a measure of central tendency; typical or normal.

Discussion: The term "average" is generally used to refer to the mean value of data. Informally, it can also be used to refer to something that is typical or normal, such as the average employee's clocking patterns or the average employee's shift.

See also: Mean.

B

Bar Chart, *n.* a way to display data using rectangles whose lengths are proportional to the frequency of the data they represent.

Discussion: Bar charts can be used to graphically illustrate many aspects of employment data.

Example: The bar chart below compares the percentage of women working as software engineers at Company XYZ to the percentage of women working as software engineers at other companies in the region. Bar charts are an easy way to display descriptive employment data visually.

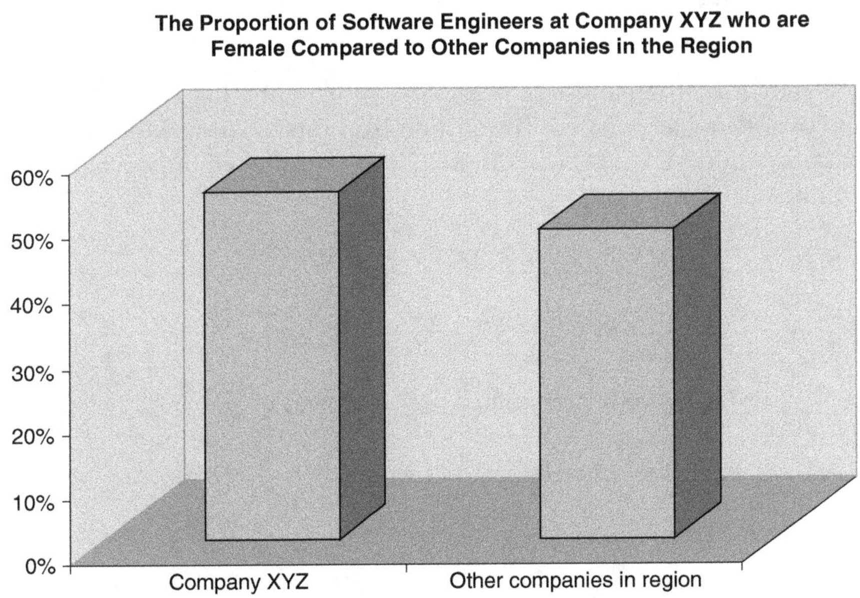

See also: Graph, percentage.

Bayes' Theorem, *n.* states

$$\Pr(A|B) = \frac{\Pr(B|A)\Pr(A)}{\Pr(B|A)\Pr(A) + \Pr(B|A')\Pr(A')}$$

where Pr(A|B) is the probability that event A will occur given that event B has already occurred.

Discussion: Event A′ is the event "not A". For example, if event A is the employee being male, Event A' would be the employee not being male, or being female.

Example: Consider an engineering company that lays off a portion of its workforce. The company is subsequently sued for discriminating against workers who are 40 years of age or more. The cross-tabulation table below shows terminations by age bracket.

	Employees Below the Age of 40	Employees Age 40 and Over	**Total**
Terminated	5	10	**15**
Not Terminated	15	10	**25**
Total	**20**	**20**	**40**

Let event A be the employee being age 40 or more. Let event B be the employee being terminated. The economist wants to know the probability that an employee is age 40 or more, given that the employee has been terminated. Then:

$$\Pr(A) = \Pr(\text{40 and over}) = \frac{20}{40} = 50\%$$

$$\Pr(A') = \Pr(\text{below 40}) = \frac{20}{40} = 50\%$$

$$\Pr(B|A) = \Pr(\text{terminated} \mid \text{40 and over}) = \frac{10}{20} = 50\%$$

$$\Pr(B|A') = \Pr(\text{terminated} \mid \text{below 40}) = \frac{5}{20} = 25\%$$

Using Bayes' Theorem:

$$\Pr(\text{40 and over} \mid \text{terminated}) = \frac{\frac{10}{20} \times \frac{20}{40}}{\frac{10}{20} \times \frac{20}{40} \times \frac{5}{20} \times \frac{20}{40}} = 66.67\%$$

There is a two-out-of-three chance that an employee is age 40 or older, given that the employee has been terminated. We can verify this statement from the data in the table above:

$$\Pr(40 \text{ and over} \mid \text{terminated}) = \frac{10}{15} = 66.67\%$$

See also: Cross tabulation, percentage, probability.

Benchmark, *n.* a measure of the composition of individuals who make up an application or external labor pool.

Discussion: Common benchmarks in hiring discrimination cases include U.S. Census data or EEO-1 data. Determining the correct benchmark to use in employment cases may require careful refinement of the data to ensure that the benchmark is an accurate comparison group.

Example: Consider a case where a police officer is accused of racially profiling African-American motorists in Houston, Texas. Data from the 2000 Census may be used to determine the comparison pool or benchmark for the officer's traffic citations. Determining the proper benchmark for traffic citations is difficult, because it is impossible to determine exactly who was driving and committing traffic violations at the time the citations were issued. Two issues must be accounted for in this example.

First, the Census data does not include information concerning whether individuals drive on a regular basis. To better capture the number and race of individuals driving where traffic citations were issued, two additional cuts of Census data can be considered. In the first cut, the analysis can be limited to determining the number of African-Americans in the area as a percentage of the population aged fifteen and older. This cut limits the analysis solely to individuals who are old enough to posses either a Texas driver's license or learner's permit. In the second cut, the analysis can be limited to individuals residing in a household with access to at least one vehicle. This cut limits the analysis to individuals most likely to be driving because it excludes households without a vehicle.

Second, even if there were a perfect measure of who drives regularly, Census data does not provide information on where individuals drive. According to data from the National Household Travel Survey, the average driver travels more than 33 miles a day in the city in which the police officer works. This degree of mobility means that individuals may be driving in a geographical area outside of where they live. To account for this mobility, multiple geographical regions should be used as benchmarks in the analysis.

See also: Applicant flow data, availability, hypothesis testing.

Bernoulli Distribution, *n.* a random variable, X, has a Bernoulli distribution if the random variable can take only the values 0 and 1 and the probabilities of these values are:

$$\Pr(X = 1) = p \text{ and } \Pr(X = 0) = 1 - p$$

Discussion: The Bernoulli distribution can be used in many employment situations because there are often only two outcomes. An individual is either hired or not, promoted or not, and terminated or not. In each of these cases, economists would denote hirings, promotions, or terminations as X equal to one. The "or not" would be denoted as X equal to zero.

See also: Bernoulli's Theorem, binary event, probability.

Bernoulli's Theorem, *n.* states that if the probability of success in any trial is p, then the probability of exactly r successes in n independent trials is:

$$C_r^n p^r (1 - p)^{n-r}$$

where:

$$C_r^n = \frac{n!}{(n-r)!r!}$$

and:

$$n! = 1 \times 2 \times \ldots \times n$$

Example: Consider a simple, completely unrealistic promotion example. Instead of a traditional promotion process, a marketing firm decides to base promotions on a roll of the dice. An individual is promoted if an even number is rolled on a standard, six-sided die. If an odd number is rolled, the individual is not promoted. Hence, the probability of promotion is:

$$p = \frac{3}{6} = \frac{1}{2}$$

Five individuals are eligible for promotion (n = 5). The company wants to determine the probability that exactly four individuals will be promoted (r = 4). This is calculated as follows:

$$C_4^5\left(\frac{1}{2}\right)^4\left(1-\frac{1}{2}\right)^{5-4} = \frac{5!}{(5-4)!4!}\cdot\frac{1}{16}\cdot\frac{1}{2} = 5\cdot\frac{1}{32} = 15.6\%$$

See also: Bernoulli distribution, hypothesis testing, probability.

Bias, *n.* a systematic error in a statistical result.

Discussion: This type of error, if relevant, must be taken into account when interpreting the results of any statistical test.

Example: Assume an economist wishes to determine the tenure for assembly employees hired during 2002 at a manufacturing plant. Termination data is available only for 2002 and 2003. The economist does not know whether or when an employee was terminated if he or she was not terminated on or before December 31, 2003. Most of the assembly employees do not remain at the company for longer than six months.

For calculation purposes, the economist decides to assume that all manufacturing employees not terminated on or before December 31, 2003 were terminated January 1, 2004. If the economist calculates the average tenure based on this assumption, the result will be right-biased. This means that the calculated average tenure is likely to be lower than the true average tenure (including termination data for 2004, 2005, 2006, etc.).

See also: Mean, median, skew, variance.

Binary Event, *n.* an event with only two possible outcomes or values.

Discussion: Many employment decisions are binary events. A person is either hired or not, promoted or not, or terminated or not.

See also: Bernoulli distribution.

Binomial Coefficients, *n.* coefficients used to calculate certain probability distributions.

Discussion: Two notations are generally used for binomial coefficients:

(a) C_r^n

(b) $\binom{n}{r}$

The formula for calculating binomial coefficients is:

$$C_r^n = \frac{n!}{(n-r)!r!}$$

where r is the number of successes, n is the number of independent trials, and:

$$n! = 1 \times 2 \times \ldots \times n$$

Binomial coefficients can also be used to determine the number of combinations that exist where n is the number of choices and r is the number of slots.

Example: Assume an employer is restructuring due to budget concerns. Twenty salespersons are affected by the restructuring and only five positions are available on the new sales force. How many different sales group compositions are there?

$$C_5^{20} = \frac{20!}{(20-5)!5!} = \frac{20!}{15! \cdot 5!} = 15,504$$

There are more than 15,000 different combinations.

See also: Bernoulli's Theorem, combination, permutation.

Binomial Distribution, *n.* a distribution where a random variable, X, takes discrete values 0, 1, . . . , n and the probabilities of these values are:

$$\Pr(X = x) = \binom{n}{x} p^x q^{n-x}$$

where $q = 1 - p$

Discussion: The Bernoulli distribution is a special case of the binomial distribution where X can equal only 0 or 1. Note that this equation is the same as Bernoulli's Theorem for most employment cases. The binomial distribution can be used in employment discrimination cases in which employees are similarly situated.

Example: Assume that a department is composed of 100 similarly situated employees. Of the 100 employees, 50 are male and 50 are female. Furthermore, it has been determined from previous promotion experience that each employee has a ten percent chance of being promoted in any given year. The company has authorized the department to promote 20 employees. Thirteen males and seven females were promoted.

From the perspective of a labor economist, a gender-neutral promotion process in this example looks a lot like the classic example of a person selecting 20 balls from a bowl containing yellow and green balls. In this example, which appears in most statistics textbooks in one form or another, a person randomly selects one ball from the bowl, notes the color of the ball on a piece of paper, and then puts the ball back into the bowl. This process of drawing a ball, noting its color, and replacing it in the bowl continues until all 20 balls have been selected.

In our example, the binomial distribution is used to compute the probability that only seven women would be promoted. In the equation above, n is the number of promotions, x is the number of women promoted, p is the proportion of female employees, and q is the proportion of male employees.

Although the mathematical formula looks complicated, it requires nothing more than a series of simple mathematical operations. The probability that women received only seven of the 20 promotions is calculated as follows:

$$\Pr(X = 7) = \binom{20}{7} 0.5^7 0.5^{20-7} = \binom{20}{7} 0.5^7 0.5^{13}$$

Using the binomial coefficient formula:

$$\binom{20}{7} = \frac{20!}{7!(20-7)!} = \frac{20!}{7!(13!)} = 77,520$$

Plugging values into the formula yields:

$$\Pr(X = 7) = 7.39\%$$

Thus the probability of seven females and 13 males being promoted is 7.39%. These probabilities can also be found in tables in many statistical textbooks. Note that the probability of seven or fewer females being promoted is greater, as follows:

$$\Pr(X \leq 7) = \sum_{k=0}^{7} \Pr(X = k) = 13.16\%$$

Hence, the probability of observing the given promotion outcome or one in which even fewer females were promoted from an unbiased promotion process is 13.16%.

Note that the number of selections (seven) in this case is small enough for computational simplicity. The binomial distribution is appropriate when the number of selections is large (30 or more). This may be common in hiring, termination, and promotion decisions for which the number of selections is small. In these cases, a Fisher Exact test is more appropriate.

Also note that this test is appropriate only when the probability of selection remains constant after each selection is made. That is, the probability of a selection being made from the protected class needs to remain roughly the same. The company should not decide to hire more or fewer of the protected class after each selection is made.

See also: Bernoulli distribution, Bernoulli's theorem, binomial coefficient, Fisher Exact test, percentage.

Bivariate Distribution, *n.* the distribution of two random variables.

Discussion: Employment cases center on the relationship between the variable that describes protective status (such as race, gender, or age) and the variable that describes the alleged discrimination (such as salary, promotion status, or hiring status).

Example: An economist may wish to use a cross-tabulation to compare the bivariate distribution of age and salary:

Salary	Employees Below the Age of 30	Employees Age 30–39	Employees Age 40 and over
$25,000–$39,999	11	5	2
$40,000–$59,999	1	10	7
$60,000–$74,999	0	3	15

In this case, a simple cross-tabulation reveals that older employees generally have higher salaries. To determine the level of this association, the economist may wish to draw a scatter diagram, such as the one below, to show the bivariate distribution visually.

The economist will also calculate the correlation coefficient to determine more precisely the level of association between the two variables.

See also: Correlation, cross tabulation, scattergram.

Box-and-Whisker Plot, *n.* a special diagram used to visually show the distribution of data.

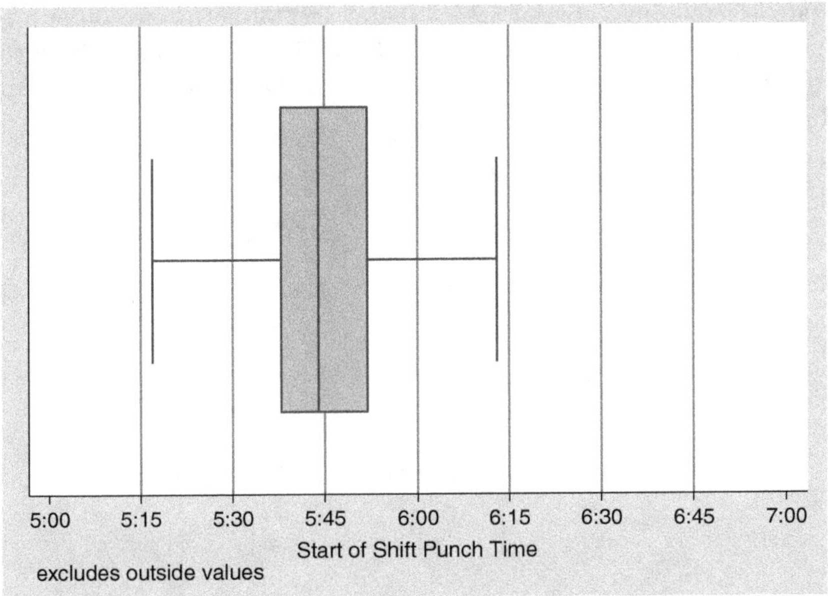

Discussion: In wage-and-hour cases, a box-and-whisker plot might be used to show the median punch-in time for a group of employees.

Example: Consider a wage-and-hour case for a manufacturing company. The plaintiffs allege that the company edited punch times and used time-clock rounding rules so that employees were not paid for the 15 to 30 minutes of work performed before the scheduled start of their shift. The company's employees' shifts began at 6:00 AM, but according to the allegations, employees were required to be at their station at least 15 minutes before their shift and often clocked in up to 30 minutes before the scheduled start of their shift.

A box-and-whisker plot of morning punch times is shown below.

The median punch time is the vertical line in the middle of the rectangle, slightly before 5:45 AM. The two ends of the rectangle represent the lower and upper quartiles. The left portion of the rectangle is the lower quartile. Roughly 25% of employees clock in between 5:38 AM and 5:45 AM. The right portion of the rectangle is the upper quartile.

Roughly 25% of employees clock in between 5:45 AM and 5:52 AM. This means that 50% of employees clock in between the times shown by the rectangle – roughly between 5:38 AM and 5:52 AM. The two outer lines are drawn at the 10th and 90th percentiles. This means that 90% of the punch times fall between those two lines – roughly between 5:15 AM and 6:15 AM.

See also: Graph, median, quartile.

C

Cardinal Number, *n.* a number that denotes quantity, not order.

Discussion: An individual's salary would be a cardinal number, because it tells how much income he or she earns. An individual's salary grade would not be a cardinal number, because it ranks his or her salary on a scale.

See Also: Ordinal number.

Categorical Scale, *n.* a scale that sorts variables into categories that are exhaustive, exclusive, and clearly defined.

Discussion: In the current context, the term "exhaustive" means that every observation (or individual in employment cases) must fit into at least one category. "Exclusive" means that every observation can fall into only one category. "Clearly defined" means there is no doubt regarding to which category each observation belongs. Categories in employment cases may include, but are not limited to, age, sex, race, job title, salary grade, and education level.

See Also: Exhaustive, exclusive.

Causation, *n.* the production of an effect by an event or cause.

Discussion: Although employment statistics may suggest evidence of discrimination in employment cases, they cannot prove that discrimination caused the observed employment disparities. Employment statistics can show only whether there is a statistically significant disparity between the expected and observed employment outcome.

See Also: Hypothesis testing, statistical significance.

Central Limit Theorem, *n.* states that if a random sample of size n is taken from any distribution with mean μ and variance σ^2, then the sample mean will have a distribution that is approximately normal with mean μ and variance = $\frac{\sigma^2}{n}$.

Discussion: As the sample size increases, the distribution more closely approaches the normal distribution. Many statistics in employment discrimination cases use the central limit theorem by assuming the data has a normal distribution. In cases with small sample sizes, it may be more appropriate to use non-parametric tests, such as the Fisher Exact test, which do not assume a normal distribution.

See Also: Hypothesis testing, normal distribution, t-test, statistical significance.

Certainty, *n.* a condition or event that occurs with a probability equal to one (or 100%) is said to occur with certainty.

Example: Assume a company is concerned about disparities in hiring by gender for a data entry position. The economist interviews human-resources personnel and determines that hiring decisions are based solely on performance on a standardized test. If an applicant scores higher than 75 on the standardized test, he or she will be hired. In this example, the economist may decide to first examine the difference in test scores for men and women instead of the difference in hiring rate, because hiring occurs with certainty if the applicant scores higher than 75 on the test.

See Also: Probability.

Chi-Squared Distribution, *n.* the distribution of $\chi^2 = X_1^2 + X_2^2 + \ldots + X_n^2$ where $X_1^2, X_2^2, \ldots, X_n^2$ are independent normal random variables with a mean of zero and a variance of 1.

Discussion: This distribution has n degrees of freedom. The chi-squared distribution is the underlying basis for many statistical tests, including the chi-squared test.

See Also: Chi-squared test, hypothesis testing.

Chi-Squared Test, *n.* a test used to determine whether there is an association between two random variables.

Discussion: The test statistic is calculated as:

$$\chi^2 = \sum \frac{(\text{Actual Outcome} - \text{Expected Outcome})^2}{\text{Expected Outcome}}$$

Example: Two-hundred similarly situated employees, 100 men and 100 women, work as servers for a cruise line. Due to poor sales, the cruise line must lay off 75 employees. The observed termination outcome is that 50 women and 25 men are terminated.

Gender	Not Terminated	Terminated	**Total**
Female	50	50	**100**
Male	75	25	**100**
Total	**125**	**75**	**200**

To calculate the chi-squared test statistic, we first compute the expected outcome. In a gender-neutral termination process, the expected number of female terminations would be:

$$\text{Number of female employees} \times \frac{\text{Number of terminations}}{\text{Total number of employees}}$$

Similarly, the expected number of male terminations would be:

$$\text{Number of male employees} \times \frac{\text{Number of terminations}}{\text{Total number of employees}}$$

Using the formulas above, we can construct a table with the expected layoff outcome.

Gender	Not Terminated	Terminated	**Total**
Female	62.5	37.5	**100**
Male	62.5	37.5	**100**
Total	**125**	**75**	**200**

The chi-squared test statistic is then:

$$\chi^2 = \frac{(50 - 62.5)^2}{62.5} + \frac{(50 - 37.5)^2}{37.5} + \frac{(75 - 62.5)^2}{62.5} + \frac{(25 - 37.5)^2}{37.5}$$

$$\chi^2 = 13.33$$

The number of degrees of freedom is (r – 1)*(c – 1) where r and c are the number of possible values that each of the variables (termination status and gender) can take. We look up the chi-squared statistic from a table to determine whether the outcome is statistically significant.

In this case, each of the variables can take one of only two values – female or male and terminated or not terminated. Hence, the degree of freedom is 1, (2 – 1)*(2 – 1). Using a table that gives chi-squared probability values, we can see that, at the 1% level, $\chi^2(1) = 6.63 < 13.33$. In this example, the deviation between the expected and actual termination outcome is statistically significant at the 1% level.

Sample STATA output:

```
tab female term, chi

         |  term
female   |  0     1    | Total
---------+-------------+------
0        |  75    25   | 100
1        |  50    50   | 100
---------+-------------+------
Total    |  125   75   | 200

Pearson chi 2(1) = 13.3333   Pr = 0.000
```

Note that the expected numbers in the table above are relatively large. The chi-squared test is appropriate when there are at least five predicted values in every cell. In cases where there are relatively few hires, terminations, or promotions, the chi-squared test is not appropriate. If the number of hires, terminations or promotions is small, the Fisher Exact test is a more appropriate choice.

The chi-squared test also requires that the probability of selection be constant for each decision. This assumption essentially requires the data to be from one hiring, promotion, or termination event so that everyone has an equal probability of being hired, promoted, or terminated. That is, it is important that everyone included in the table be in the pool of potential hires, promotions, or terminations.

See Also: Cross-tabulation, Fisher Exact test, hypothesis testing, statistical significance.

Class, *n.* a collection or group of people, things, or variable values that share a common characteristic.

Discussion: Before a class-action lawsuit can proceed, the plaintiffs must have the class certified. There are two basic requirements for class certification. First, a well-defined community of interest must exist among the class members. Second, the class must be ascertained easily. Statistical tests can often rebut these requirements. For example, statistical tests can be performed to determine whether common questions of fact predominate. We can examine the variations and commonalities among class members. Similarly, we can test whether the class representatives' claims and experience are typical of other potential class members. In employment discrimination cases, this often involves testing whether there is a statistically significant disparate or adverse impact on the protected class. In wage-and-hour cases, this may involve simply analyzing the punch activities of the class representative compared to those of other employees.

See Also: Adverse impact, statistically significant.

Cluster Sampling, *n.* a method of sampling in which individuals are grouped into small clusters and a simple random sample is drawn from each cluster.

Discussion: Cluster sampling often groups people together by location.

Example: Consider a wage-and-hour misclassification claim where employees worked for a chain of grocery stores. Plaintiffs claim the employees were forced to work during their lunch break and did not enjoy a duty-free meal period. The economist wishes to address this claim using a survey of the potential class members.

Because the store locations are so disperse, drawing a random sample of the employees is expensive. The store's policies are sufficiently homogenous that the economist decides to use cluster sampling and survey only those employees who work near major metropolitan areas. This method decreases the cost of the survey and allows a larger sample to be drawn.

See Also: Homogeneous, simple random sample, survey.

Coded Data, *n.* data that has been translated from its original form into a standardized form that makes it simpler to perform data analyses.

Discussion: Coded data is especially useful when dealing with surveys. Surveys often ask respondents to check a box to answer a question. When creating a database from survey responses, the checkmarks must be entered as letters or numbers. Respondents may have left boxes blank or may have checked multiple boxes, and these types of human errors must be coded systematically into the survey database.

Example: Consider the following survey question:

3. What is your marital status?

☐ Single	☐ Separated
☐ Married, living with spouse	☐ Divorced
☐ Married, not living with spouse	☐ Widowed

Two variables might be used to code this question. The first variable, q3, would contain the respondent's answer as follows:

- E – single
- F – married, living with spouse
- G – married, not living with spouse
- H – separated
- I – divorced
- J – widowed

A second variable, q3_c, would contain comments on any errors in the survey response as follows:

- –9999 – question's answer is error-free
- –999 – multiple answers to a single-answer question
- –99 – not checked

By coding the data in this way, it is easier for the economist to analyze data while excluding erroneous or suspect survey responses. After the survey data has been entered into a spreadsheet, the economist may choose to further code the data. For example, if the economist's analysis were concerned only with whether the respondent is married, the economist could choose to create a new variable, "married", that could be coded using a common convention: 0 if the respondent is unmarried and 1 if the respondent is married.

See Also: Binary event, data dictionary, survey.

Coefficient, *n.* a number or constant factor in front of variables in an algebraic equation.

Discussion: In the linear equation $y = 6x + 3$, 6 is the coefficient for x. In employment litigation, linear regression analysis is sometimes used to assess the impact that various factors have on the observed employment outcome. In these cases, the coefficient in front of the variable of interest (e.g., race, gender, or age) is examined to determine what impact, if any, the variable of interest has on the observed outcome.

For example, if the coefficient is negative for women in a salary regression, then being a woman has a negative impact on one's salary. Statistical tests can then be used to determine whether the coefficient is statistically significant. If the coefficient is equal to zero or if a statistical significance test shows that the coefficient is not statistically different from zero, then gender has no impact on salary.

Example: The STATA output below is from a salary regression for workers with a college degree. The first column of numbers labeled "Coef." gives the coefficients for the dependent variables in the salary regression. As you can see, the coefficient for the female variable is approximately -0.35. A negative coefficient in this example means that females have a lower average salary than male employees.

```
. educ = Bachelors

      Source |       SS       df       MS              Number of obs =   15330
-------------+------------------------------           F(  7, 15322) =  317.29
       Model |  1255.[illegible]66     7  179.423666           Prob > F      =  0.0000
    Residual |  8664.[illegible]93 15322  .56548022            R-squared     =  0.1266
-------------+------------------------------           Adj R-squared =  0.1262
       Total |  992[illegible]9 15329  .647155952           Root MSE      =  .75198

------------------------------------------------------------------------------
         inc |      Coef.   Std. Err.      t    P>|t|     [95% Conf. Interval]
-------------+----------------------------------------------------------------
      female |  -.3518044   .0123054   -28.59   0.000    -.3759245   -.3276843
       black |  -.1205785   .0221088    -5.45   0.000    -.1639144   -.0772427
      indian |  -.0892178   .0850171    -1.05   0.294    -.2558615    .0774259
       asian |  -.0566266   .0247676    -2.29   0.022    -.1051741   -.0080791
    hispanic |  -.2051414   .0247628    -8.28   0.000    -.2536794   -.1566033
       exper |   .0550911   .0018359    30.01   0.000     .0514925    .0586896
      exper2 |  -.0010939   .0000448   -24.44   0.000    -.0011816   -.0010061
       _cons |   10.33805   .0183995   561.86   0.000     10.30198    10.37411
------------------------------------------------------------------------------
```

See Also: Linear regression, variable.

Coefficient of Determination, *n.* a measure of how well data fits a regression line. Mathematically, the coefficient of determination is defined as:

$$r^2 = \frac{\text{Explained variance}}{\text{Total variance}}$$

Discussion: The coefficient of determination, or r-squared, takes values between 0 and 1. A value near zero means that none of the variables in the regression explain or fit the data very well. For example, if salary were regressed only on shoe size, the coefficient of determination would be expected to be very small because shoe size is not likely to determine salary.

Conversely, a coefficient of determination value that is near one means that the variables in the regression explain the data very well. For example, if a company based salary solely on age, such that they paid an employee his or her age as an hourly wage (i.e., \$40/hour for 40-year-old employees and \$37/hour for 37-year-old employees), then a regression of salary on age would have a coefficient of determination of one. In other words, all of the variance in salary would be explained by the age variable in this completely unrealistic example.

Example: In the STATA output below for a salary regression, the coefficient of determination is found on the upper right-hand side below the number of observations and the results of the F-test.

The coefficient of determination or r-squared is approximately 0.13. This means that 13% of the variation in salary is explained by the variables in the regression.

```
educ = Bachelors

  Source |       SS       df       MS              Number of obs =   15330
---------+------------------------------           F(  7, 15322) =  317.29
   Model |  1255.96566     7  179.423666           Prob > F      =  0.0000
Residual |  8664.28793 15322   .56548022   ------> R-squared     =  0.1266
---------+------------------------------           Adj R-squared =  0.1262
   Total |  9920.25359 15329  .647155952           Root MSE      =  .75198

------------------------------------------------------------------------------
     inc |      Coef.   Std. Err.       t     P>|t|       [95% Conf. Interval]
---------+--------------------------------------------------------------------
  female |  -.3518044   .0123054    -28.59   0.000      -.3759245   -.3276843
   black |  -.1205785   .0221088     -5.45   0.000      -.1639144   -.0772427
  indian |  -.0892178   .0850171     -1.05   0.294      -.2558615    .0774259
   asian |  -.0566266   .0247676     -2.29   0.022      -.1051741   -.0080791
hispanic |  -.2051414   .0247628     -8.28   0.000      -.2536794   -.1566033
   exper |   .0550911   .0018359     30.01   0.000       .0514925    .0586896
  exper2 |  -.0010939   .0000448    -24.44   0.000      -.0011816   -.0010061
   _cons |   10.33805   .0183995    561.86   0.000       10.30198    10.37411
------------------------------------------------------------------------------
```

See Also: Error, linear regression, variance.

Cohort, *n.* a group of individuals within a population who have experienced the same event within the same time period.

Discussion: Cohorts are used to examine groups of similarly situated individuals in employment discrimination cases.

See Also: Adverse impact, hypothesis testing.

Combination, *n.* all possible ways of selecting items from a set when the order of selection is of no importance.

Discussion: The number of ways of selecting r objects from a total of n, all different is denoted by:

$$C_r^n = \frac{n!}{(n-r)!r!}$$

This formula is the same as the binomial expansion.

Example: If three letters are selected from the set A, B, C, and D, there are four possible combinations: ABC, ABD, ACD, and BCD. Using the formula yields:

$$C_3^4 = \frac{4!}{(4-3)!3!} = 4$$

See Also: Permutation, probability.

Complementary Events, *n.* events that are both exclusive and exhaustive.

Discussion: Many employment outcomes are complementary events.

Example: The employment outcomes "an applicant is hired" and "an applicant is not hired" are complementary events. A single applicant cannot be both hired and not hired (exclusive) and he or she must be either hired or not hired (exhaustive).

See Also: Binary event, exclusive, exhaustive.

Conditional Probability, *n.* the probability of an event occurring, given that some other event has already occurred.

Discussion: The probability of event A occurring, given that event B has already occurred, is denoted as Pr(A|B). Algebraically, conditional probability is defined as:

$$\Pr(A|B) = \frac{\Pr(A \cap B)}{\Pr(B)}$$

Where $\Pr(A \cap B)$ is the probability that event A and event B will occur.

Example: Conditional probabilities are especially important in multistage employment processes. Consider a hiring case that has two stages. In the first stage, the employer reviews resumes. About 20% of the applicants who submit resumes are selected for an interview.

In the second stage, the employer interviews applicants who passed the first stage based on their resumes. The employer hires about five percent of all applicants. The economist wants to know the probability that an applicant will be hired, given that he or she is selected for an interview. In this example, event A is being hired and event B is being selected for an interview. Hence:

$$\Pr(\text{hired}|\text{interviewed}) = \frac{\Pr(\text{hired and interviewed})}{\Pr(\text{interviewed})} = \frac{5\%}{20\%} = \frac{1}{4} = 25\%$$

So, if an applicant is interviewed, he or she has a 25% chance of being hired.

See Also: Conditional event, probability.

Conditioning Event, *n.* an event that is known to have occurred.

Discussion: In the conditional probability below, event B is the conditional event.

$$\Pr(A|B) = \frac{\Pr(A \cap B)}{\Pr(B)}$$

Example: Consider a hiring case that has two stages. In the first stage, the employer reviews resumes. About 20% of the applicants who submit resumes are selected for an interview. In the second stage, the employer interviews applicants who passed the first stage based on their resumes. The employer hires about five percent of all applicants. The economist wants to know the probability that an applicant will be hired, given that he or she is selected for an interview. In this example, being selected for an interview is the conditioning event.

See Also: Conditional probability, probability.

Confidence Interval, *n.* an interval such that the value of an estimate of a parameter has a stated probability of falling within a determined range.

Discussion: If the 95% confidence interval of a salary mean is from $40,000 to $47,500, there is a 95% probability that the average salary falls between $40,000 and $47,500. Confidence intervals are especially important in regression analyses and statistical tests because they help determine statistical significance.

Example: Consider the STATA output below for a regression of salary on demographic factors for individuals with a college degree. The 95% confidence intervals are listed in the two right-hand columns:

· educ = Bachelors

Source	SS	df	MS
Model	1255.96566	7	179.423666
Residual	8664.28793	15322	.56548022
Total	9920.25359	15329	.647155952

Number	15330
F(7,	17.29
Prob >	.0000
R-squar	.1266
Adj R-s	.1262
Root	[illegible]

inc	Coef.	Std. Err.	t	P>|t|	[95% Conf.	Interval]
female	-.3518044	.0123054	-28.59	0.000	-.3759245	-.3276843
black	-.1205785	.0221088	-5.45	0.000	-.1639144	-.0772427
indian	-.0892178	.0850171	-1.05	0.294	-.2558615	.0774259
asian	-.0566266	.0247676	-2.29	0.022	-.1051741	-.0080791
hispanic	-.2051414	.0247628	-8.28	0.000	-.2536794	-.1566033
exper	.0550911	.0018359	30.01	0.000	.0514925	.0586896
exper2	-.0010939	.0000448	-24.44	0.000	-.0011816	-.0010061
_cons	10.33805	.0183995	561.86	0.000	10.30198	10.37411

The 95% confidence interval for the female coefficient is approximately −0.38 to −0.33. That is, we are 95% sure that the female coefficient is between −0.38 and −0.33.

The range of a confidence interval depends on the variance of the data. If the variance of the data is large, then the confidence interval will be very wide. Because there is more noise in the data, it is more difficult to obtain a precise estimate. In datasets with large variance, it is more difficult to obtain a statistically significant result. If the variance of the data is small, then the confidence interval is more likely to be small. Because there is less noise in the data, it is easier to obtain a more precise estimate.

The formula for a 95% confidence interval for a one-population mean is defined as:

$$\left(\bar{x} - 1.96\frac{\sigma}{\sqrt{n}}, \bar{x} + 1.96\frac{\sigma}{\sqrt{n}}\right)$$

where $\bar{x}$ is the sample mean, n is the sample size, and σ is the variance.

See Also: Linear regression, mean, sample size, variance.

Consistent, *adj.* the larger the sample size becomes, the closer the estimate approaches its true value.

Discussion: Formally:

$$\lim_{n \to \infty} \hat{\theta}_n = \theta$$

More simply put, an estimate is consistent if the estimate increases in accuracy as the sample size increases.

See Also: Mean, sample size.

Constant, *n.* a value or algebraic expression that remains invariant or unchanged.

Example: In the equation y = $6x + 3$, 3 is a constant.

See Also: Coefficient, variable.

Continuity Correction, *n.* a mathematical adjustment to a confidence interval formula.

See Also: Bernoulli trial, binomial distribution, normal distribution, standard deviation.

Continuous Variable, *n.* a variable that may take any value.

Example: Generally, an individual's salary is a continuous variable. It can be any non-negative real number.

See Also: Discrete, dummy variable, variable.

Correlation, *n.* the interdependency of two or more random variables.

Discussion: Two variables are said to be correlated if changes in the value of one variable are related to changes in the values of another variable. The two variables are positively correlated if increases in one variable are related to increases in the values of another variable, or if decreases in one variable are related to decreases in another variable. In other words, the direction of change is the same for two variables that are positively correlated. Two variables are negatively correlated if increases in one variable are related to decreases in another variable. The direction of change is opposite for two variables that are negatively correlated.

Example: In most retirement plans, an employee's pension depends on the number of years of his or her service to the employer. In this example, years of service and the value of the pension are positively correlated.

See Also: Correlation coefficient, covariance.

Correlation Coefficients, *n.* a measurement of the extent to which two variables are related.

Discussion: A correlation coefficient of zero means there is no correlation between two variables. A negative correlation coefficient means that as one variable grows larger, the other variable grows smaller. A positive correlation coefficient implies that as one variable grows larger, the other variable also increases.

Among other things, correlation coefficients can be used to determine whether there is a relationship between race or gender and salary. A correlation coefficient close to zero implies there is little relationship between the two variables.

The correlation coefficient, defined as $\rho(X, Y)$, is equal to:

$$\rho(X, Y) = \frac{Cov(X, Y)}{\sigma_X \sigma_Y}$$

where Cov(X,Y) is the covariance between variable X and Y and $\sigma_X . \sigma_Y$ are the standard deviations (the square root of variance) for X and Y, respectively. Algebraically, this equation is equivalent to:

$$\rho(X, Y) = \frac{\frac{1}{n}\sum_{i=1}^{n}(x_i - \bar{x})(y_i - \bar{y})}{\sqrt{\frac{1}{n-1}\sum_{i=1}^{n}(x_i - \bar{x})^2} \cdot \sqrt{\frac{1}{n-1}\sum_{i=1}^{n}(y_i - \bar{y})^2}}$$

Example: In a hiring gender-discrimination case, the plaintiffs want to know whether there is a correlation between the employee's gender and whether or not he or she is hired.

The plaintiffs test this initial claim by determining the correlation coefficient between the employee's gender and hiring status.

	Not Hired	**Hired**	**Total**
Male Applicant	8	8	16
Female Applicant	4	2	6
Total	12	10	22

The covariance is calculated as:

$$\begin{aligned} Cov(X, Y) &= \frac{1}{n}\sum_{i=1}^{n}(x_i - \bar{x})(y_i - \bar{y}) \\ &= \frac{1}{22}\left(8 \cdot \left(0 - \frac{6}{22}\right) \cdot \left(0 - \frac{10}{22}\right) + 8 \cdot \left(0 - \frac{6}{22}\right) \cdot \left(1 - \frac{10}{22}\right)\right. \\ &\quad \left. + 4 \cdot \left(1 - \frac{6}{22}\right) \cdot \left(0 - \frac{10}{22}\right) + 2 \cdot \left(1 - \frac{6}{22}\right) \cdot \left(1 - \frac{10}{22}\right)\right) \\ &= \frac{1}{22}\left(\frac{120}{121} - \frac{144}{121} - \frac{160}{121} + \frac{96}{121}\right) = -\frac{4}{121} = -0.033 \end{aligned}$$

The standard deviation of gender status is:

$$\sigma_X = \sqrt{\frac{1}{22 - 1}\left(16 \cdot \left(0 - \frac{6}{22}\right)^2 + 6 \cdot \left(1 - \frac{6}{22}\right)^2\right)} = 0.46$$

The standard deviation of hiring status is:

$$\sigma_Y = \sqrt{\frac{1}{22 - 1}\left(12 \cdot \left(0 - \frac{10}{22}\right)^2 + 10 \cdot \left(1 - \frac{12}{22}\right)^2\right)} = 0.51$$

The correlation coefficient is:

$$\rho(X, Y) = \frac{-0.033}{0.45 \cdot 0.51} = -0.15$$

The negative sign indicates that females are less likely to be hired than males. However, the correlation coefficient is relatively close to zero, implying that the correlation is weak. Statistical tests would need to be performed to determine whether the correlation coefficient is statistically different from zero.

See Also: Correlation, covariance, mean, standard deviation, variance.

Covariance, *n.* the variation between two variables, X and Y.

Discussion: Formally, covariance is given as the following equation:

$$Cov(X, Y) = \frac{1}{n} \sum_{i=1}^{n} (x_i - \bar{x})(y_i - \bar{y})$$

where n is the sample size, $\bar{x}$ is the sample mean of x, and $\bar{y}$ is the sample mean of y. Covariance is used to calculate the correlation coefficient.

Example: Consider the termination data below:

	Not Terminated	**Terminated**	**Total**
Employees Under Age 40	20	5	25
Employees Age 40 and Older	10	15	25
Total	30	20	50

Let the age variable, x, equal zero if the employee is younger than 40, and one if the employee is age 40 and over. Let the termination variable, y, equal zero if the employee is not terminated and one if the employee is terminated. The means are as follows:

$$\bar{x} = \frac{\text{25 employees age 40 and over}}{\text{50 total employees}} = 0.5$$

$$\bar{y} = \frac{\text{20 employees terminated}}{\text{50 total employees}} = 0.4$$

For each cell in the table above, we need to calculate $(x_i - \bar{x})(y_i - \bar{y})$.

Employee Type and Termination Status	**Number of Employees of this Type**	$(x_i - \bar{x})(y_i - \bar{y})$
Employees Under Age 40, Not Terminated	20	$(0 - 0.5)(0 - 0.4) = 0.2$
Employees Under Age 40, Terminated	5	$(0 - 0.5)(1 - 0.4) = -0.3$
Employees Age 40 and Older, Not Terminated	10	$(1 - 0.5)(0 - 0.4) = -0.2$
Employees Age 40 and Older, Terminated	15	$(1 - 0.5)(1 - 0.4) = 0.3$

Using the formula and data above, the covariance is:

$$Cov(X, Y) = \frac{1}{50}(20 \cdot 0.2 + 5 \cdot (-0.3) + 10 \cdot (-0.2) + 15 \cdot 0.3) = 0.1$$

See Also: Correlation coefficient, mean, variance.

Cox Proportional Hazards Model, *n.* a model that incorporates a time-dependent baseline hazard rate $h_o(t)$ and time independent explanatory variables X, and is written as follows:

$$h(t, X) = h_o(t)e^{\sum_i \beta_i X_i}$$

where $h_o(t)$ is the baseline hazard and X is the explanatory variables.

Discussion: In the Cox hazard model, the baseline hazard function is not specified, but is estimated using a kernel-smoothing methodology. The Cox proportional hazards model is used to estimate the length of time until failure. In an employment setting, this model is most appropriate for actions that are dispersed over a period of time. For instance, the Cox Proportional Hazards model could be used to study the time-to-promotion rates for men and women.

See Also: Model, odds ratio.

Critical Region, *n.* the region that leads to the rejection of the null hypothesis.

Discussion: In employment cases, the null hypothesis is that the company is not engaging in discriminatory behavior. When the deviation between the expected outcome and the observed outcome is sufficiently large, the test statistic falls into the critical region and the analyst must reject the null hypothesis.

Example: For a normal-distribution, two-tailed test, the critical region is $|z| \geq 1.96$ for significance at the 5% level and $|z| \geq 2.58$ at the 1% level.

See Also: Alternative hypothesis, critical value, hypothesis testing, normal distribution, null hypothesis.

Critical Value, *n.* the numerical border value between statistical significance and insignificance.

Discussion: If the absolute value of the test statistic is greater than the critical value, then the null hypothesis is rejected because the test statistic is statistically significant. If the absolute value of the test statistic is less than the critical value, then the null hypothesis cannot be rejected because the test statistic is statistically insignificant.

Example: For a normal-distribution, two-tailed test, the critical value at the 5% level is 1.96 and the critical value at the 1% level is 2.58.

See Also: Absolute value, alternative hypothesis, critical region, hypothesis testing, normal distribution, null hypothesis.

Cross-Section Analysis, *n.* an analysis of datasets that are taken from one point in time.

Discussion: Most analyses of hiring, promotion, and termination events are cross-sectional analyses. In these studies, the economist examines only the number of individuals in the relevant pool and the number of individuals selected.

See Also: Applicant flow data, data.

Cross Tabulations, *n.* tables that compare two aspects of a dataset.

Discussion: In employment cases, cross tabulations are frequently used to compare race and promotion rates, gender and termination rates, or age bands and hiring rates.

Example: This table presents the number of people promoted and not promoted by race.

	Race	
	White	African-American
Promoted	3	1
Not Promoted	7	8

The table shows that three white employees were promoted and seven white employees were not promoted. One African-American was promoted and eight African-Americans were not promoted. By summing across the rows, we can see that four people were promoted and fifteen people were not promoted. If we sum down the columns, we can see that ten whites were in the pool and nine African-Americans were in the pool.

See Also: Fisher Exact test, frequency.

Cumulative Frequency, *n.* a count of the number of data points that are less than or equal to a given value.

Discussion: The cumulative frequency is also referred to as a running total.

Example: A frequency and cumulative frequency table is presented below.

Salary	Frequency	Cumulative Frequency
$20,001–$30,000	5	5
$30,001–$40,000	7	12
$40,001–$50,000	15	27
$50,001–$60,000	12	39
$60,001–$70,000	4	43

The table shows that there are 15 individuals whose salary is between $40,001 and $50,000. However, there are 27 individuals whose salary is between $20,001 and $50,000.

See Also: Frequency.

D

Data, *n.* information collected from a survey, experiment, investigation, or records.

Discussion: Employment cases generally involve employer-specific data as well as labor-market-specific data. Employer-specific data includes applicant flow, hiring, and salary data.

See Also: Applicant flow data.

Database, *n.* a collection of a large amount of information, typically on a computer.

Discussion: This information is usually stored as multiple records or files with entries under headings or fields. Employment databases can take several forms.

In a relational database, each data table contains specific types of information concerning the employee's complete compensation history. In many of the most popular human resource software packages, there is usually a data table that records the complete salary history of an employee.

The different pieces of information in the data tables are commonly referred to as data fields. The data fields are columns within the data table that contain information on a certain characteristic such as employee salary, date of birth or the company's employee identification number.

A data record is a row of data field entries that is specific to a particular employee transaction. In each data table, a new compensation data record is created each time a new compensation transaction occurs in the employee's work history.

Job-related information for each employee is also usually included with the compensation data tables. The job-related tables have information concerning the individual's job title, the employee's supervisor, and similar types of information. The job-related tables are typically linked to the compensation tables by an employee identifier such as a company-provided identification number or the employee's social security number.

Job-related information is constructed in the same way as the compensation data, using data tables, data fields, and data records. In many tables, the job and occupational titles are numerically coded, so deciphering this information typically requires additional documents, such as a data dictionary.

Employment database files can also be organized in a 'flat file' format instead of a relational format. Flat database file formats are organized so that each row of the data file represents an employee's complete employment history record. For example, there are separate columns for the employee's salary in each and every year, with a separate column for the employee's 2003 and 2004 year-end salaries.

In contrast, a relational database has a separate row for each year's salary. Flat files tend to be associated with older mainframe human resources data systems. Even if the data is maintained in a relational database format, some HR database programs export the results of a salary query in a flat file format.

Flat files tend to allow the analyst to perform basic data manipulation, such as the construction of employee's annual percentage increase in salary, more easily. However, flat database files tend to become large and difficult to manage as the number of work-related transactions and data fields increases. Relational database formats are easier to manage, because different types of data are maintained in different data tables. However, data manipulation exercises are significantly more difficult with relational databases, because the data must be linked carefully across different tables.

See Also: Data, data dictionary.

Data Dictionary, *n.* document that contains the definition of each variable in a data table.

Discussion: Some variables contained in a data table are coded values that represent data values, such as a numerical code for location. In this situation, a data dictionary is needed to decipher the codes. For instance, a large retail chain may house personnel data in a system that codes the location of each store as a numerical value.

See Also: Applicant flow data, coded data, database.

Deciles, *n.* one of nine numbers that divide ordered data into ten equal groups.

Discussion: When data is ordered in value, the first decile represents the 10th percentile, or the lowest ten percent of the data.

Example: If a dataset consists of 300 observations, the 30 smallest observations fall into the first decile.

See Also: Descriptive statistics, median, quantile.

Decimal Places, *n.* the figures to the right of the decimal point that are needed to express a number to a specified degree of accuracy.

Example: 33.33333% rounded to two decimal places is 33.33%.

See Also: Percentage.

Decision Point, *n.* any stage in an employment decision process where some candidates are selected and others are rejected, or where benefits are allocated.

Discussion: An appropriate statistical analysis treats each decision point as a separate event.

Example: A hiring process may have multiple decision points. The first decision point may be selecting candidates based on resumes for phone interviews. After the phone interviews, the second decision point may determine which candidates are selected for an exam. The third decision point may be selecting those candidates who passed the applicant exam for an in-person interview. The final decision point is selecting applicants for hire based on the interview results.

See Also: Applicant flow data, pool.

Degrees of Freedom, *n.* the number of free variables in a system.

Discussion: Degrees of freedom are important for calculating the critical values in many statistical tests.

See Also: chi-squared test, critical value, F-test, statistical significance.

Demography, *n.* the science of population statistics.

See Also: Data, statistics.

Dependent Variable, *n.* a variable that is determined by another (independent) variable.

Discussion: In employment litigation, employment outcomes are generally the dependent variables.

Example: In an analysis of salaries, employee salary is the dependent variable. Salary may be determined by tenure, education, and (allegedly) race, age, nation of origin, or gender. It is not expected that salary determines tenure, education, or race or gender. Therefore, salary is the dependent variable.

See Also: Linear regression, independent variable.

Descriptive Statistics, *n.* statistics that display, arrange, or describe data.

Discussion: Descriptive statistics are useful for determining practical significance and describing an employer's workforce.

Example: The statement that 15% of a company's workforce is over the age of 50 is descriptive.

See Also: Data, graph, statistic, statistical significance.

Deterministic Model, *n.* a model in which all outcomes are the result of an initial cause.

See Also: Model.

Deviation, *n.* the difference between an observed value and the mean value for a distribution.

Discussion: In employment statistics, economists often discuss the deviation between the observed outcome and the expected outcome. Practical or economic significance focuses on how large the deviation is if the test statistics have been found to be statistically significant.

Example: Assume there are 20 similarly situated applicants for five job openings. The probability of any applicant being hired, all else equal, is five out of 20 or 25%. Only one of the ten African-Americans in the applicant group is hired.

What is the deviation between the number of African-Americans actually hired and the number of African-Americans that would be expected to be hired in a race-neutral hiring process? All else being equal, one would expect 25% of the African-American applicants, or 2.5 applicants, to be hired.

The deviation in this instance is the expected number of hires minus the actual number of hires, or 1.5 (2.5 – 1). Statistical tests would need to be performed to determine whether this deviation is statistically significant.

See Also: Distribution, economic significance, mean, standard deviation, statistical significance.

Discrete, *adj*. consisting of separate or distinct parts.

Discussion: A discrete variable takes only integer values. Salary grades are commonly used discrete variables in employment litigation.

See Also: Continuous variable.

Disparate Application, n. the application of a facially neutral rule in a manner that is at least partially sensitive to the group status of each candidate, with the result that members of the protected group are treated less favorably than similarly situated members of the non-protected group.

Discussion: Proof in these cases typically hinges on the plaintiff demonstrating that the rule was not enforced for members of the non-protected class.

Example: Consider a case in which a company has a policy against employees browsing the internet for personal use. The plaintiff was fired for excessive time spent on the internet. However, the plaintiff alleges that other employees regularly visited internet news sites during down times without being disciplined. If the employer did not discipline other employees for reading internet news sites, then the plaintiff's dismissal may be a disparate application of the rule against internet browsing.

See Also: Adverse impact, disparate impact, disparate treatment.

Disparate Impact, *n.* a case in which employers allegedly use an employment-related selection process that disproportionately affects protected group members.

Discussion: The disparate impact paradigm, which is derived from the landmark *Griggs v. Duke Power Co.*, 401 U.S. 424 (1971) decision for proving discrimination, makes it illegal to employ a selection procedure that disproportionately affects protected group members, even if the employer did not intend to discriminate. Proof in these types of discrimination cases typically hinges on the charging party demonstrating that the employment-related selection process produced a disparate impact on the protected group and that the selection process was not job-related.

See Also: Adverse impact, disparate application, disparate treatment.

Disparate Treatment, *n.* a case in which employers allegedly treat individuals less favorably because of their race, religion, sex, age or nation of origin.

Discussion: Proof in these types of discrimination cases typically hinges on the charging party, or plaintiff, showing that the employer's conduct was intentionally discriminatory.

See Also: Adverse impact, disparate application, disparate impact.

Dispersion, *n.* the spread of a distribution.

Discussion: The dispersion of data is measured by the distance from each data point to the mean of the distribution. Large standard deviations imply very dispersed data.

Example:

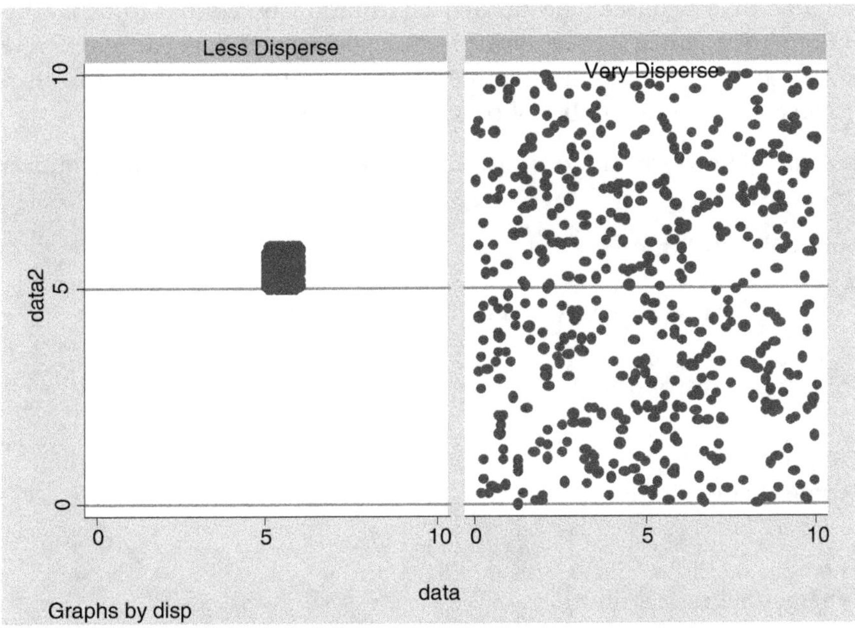

See Also: Standard deviation, variance.

Distribution, *n.* a set of frequencies or probabilities assigned to a set of events.

Example: The distribution of salary grades for employees at Company XYZ are shown in the table below:

Salary Grade	Number of Employees
Grade 11	22
Grade 12	5
Grade 13	10
Grade 14	17

See Also: Distribution function, frequency, probability, sampling distribution.

Distribution Function, n. a function that gives the cumulative frequency or probability function of a distribution.

Discussion: A probability distribution function is a mathematical equation that yields the probability or likelihood associated with a given outcome or range or outcomes. The normal distribution is referred to as a continuous probability distribution function because it is used to generate probabilities for random experiments that, unlike flipping a coin, can produce an infinite number of outcomes, such as salary.

Example: Below are the formulas for some commonly used distribution functions.

Binomial distribution:

$$\Pr(X = x) = \binom{n}{x} p^x (1 - p)^{n-x}$$

Chi-squared distribution:

$$\chi^2 = X_1^2 + X_2^2 + \ldots + X_n^2$$

Geometric distribution:

$$p(x) = p(1 - p)^{x-1}$$

Hypergeometric distribution:

$$f(x|A, B, n) = \frac{\binom{A}{x}\binom{B}{n-x}}{\binom{A+B}{n}}$$

Normal distribution:

$$f(x) = \left(\frac{1}{\sqrt{2\pi}\sigma}\right) \exp\left(-\frac{(x-\mu)^2}{2\sigma^2}\right)$$

Poisson distribution:

$$p(r) = e^{-\mu}\frac{(\mu)^r}{r!}$$

Uniform distribution:

$$f(x) = \frac{1}{b-a}$$

See Also: Binomial distribution, chi-squared distribution, geometric distribution, hypergeometric distribution, normal distribution, Poisson distribution, uniform distribution.

Dummy Variable, n. a variable that takes only two values, typically 0 or 1, with one value indicating the presence of a characteristic, attribute, or effect and the other value indicating its absence.

Discussion: A dummy variable is frequently referred to as an indicator variable. In simple linear regressions, the coefficient of a dummy variable is the average effect of having the characteristic compared to not having the characteristic.

Example: Assume the coefficient on a gender dummy variable is −2.5 in a regression where the natural log (ln) of salary is used as the independent variable. The gender dummy variable is coded 0 if an individual is male and 1 if an individual is female. All else being equal, a woman's salary is 2.5% less than that of a similarly situated man.

See Also: Binary event, continuous variable, discrete, linear regression.

E

Econometrics, *n.* the application of statistical and mathematical techniques to test economic theories.

See Also: Linear regression, statistics.

Economic Significance, *n.* a well established concept that considers the magnitude and implications of an alleged disparity in employment conditions.

Discussion: Economic significance is also referred to as 'practical significance'. In the context of an employment discrimination case, determining the economic significance of a particular analysis involves assessing the magnitude and scope of the alleged disparity in employment conditions between the protected and non-protected employee groups, as well as determining the congruence of the statistical analysis with the case facts. When used in conjunction with the traditional concept of statistical significance, inferences from a given statistical analysis can be quite probative and compelling. In recent years, courts have begun implicitly using both significance paradigms when dealing with statistical evidence in employment cases.

Example: Consider the alleged discrimination in a reduction-in-force suit. The analysis begins by examining whether the disparity in job terminations among groups is statistically significant. Statistical evidence of discrimination would arise where the observed number of terminations is statistically significantly greater than the expected number of terminations. If the statistical analysis shows disparity, then the courts will examine whether this disparity is economically significant. This entails looking at factors such as the magnitude of the statistically significant disparity, whether the disparity reflects permissible business practice, and whether ambient economic conditions may have created the disparity. In recent years, courts have found this two-pronged approach particularly suitable to the evidentiary framework established by McDonnell Douglas. See, e.g., *Smith v. Xerox Corp.*, 196 F. 3d 358, 364–65 (2d Cir. 1999).

See Also: Hypothesis testing, linear regression, statistical significance.

Efficient Estimator, *n.* an estimator of a population parameter, such as the mean, that has the smallest possible variance of two or more estimators.

See Also: Estimate, variance.

Equiprobable, *adj.* events having the same probability of occurring.

Example: The outcomes of rolling a six-sided die are equiprobable. It is equally likely that a 1, 2, 3, 4, 5, or 6 will turn up if the die is cast.

See Also: Probability.

Error, *n.* a measure of the magnitude of the inaccuracy when performing a statistical test; a mistake or inaccuracy.

Discussion: There are many different types of errors, from calculation errors to measurement errors. Type I and Type II errors are two possible errors in classical statistical hypothesis testing.

See Also: Hypothesis testing, sampling error, Type I and Type II error.

Estimate, *n.* an approximate calculation of a value unknown to the researcher.

See Also: Error.

Estimator, *n.* a random variable that is calculated based on sample data.

Discussion: A "good" estimator is consistent, unbiased, and efficient.

See Also: Consistent, efficient estimator, mean, unbiased, variance.

Event, *n.* something that may or may not occur.

Discussion: In employment cases, the event is often the subject of the lawsuits, such as hiring, promotion, or termination.

See Also: Exclusive, exhaustive, probability.

Exclusive, *adj.* two events that cannot both occur.

See Also: Event, Exhaustive.

Exhaustive, *adj*. two events such that at least one of the two events must occur.

Discussion: If event A and event B are exhaustive, then events A and B cover all possible outcomes. Many events in employment cases are exhaustive.

Example: When considering a promotion decision for any given day, an employee may either be promoted or not promoted. These two outcomes cover all possibilities and are exhaustive.

See Also: Event, exclusive.

Expectancy Theory, *n*. the average outcome of a probability analysis related to modeling workforce behavior.

Discussion: The purpose of statistical tests is to determine if a deviation is sufficiently large enough to conclude that a result has not occurred by chance. In real life, actual results deviate somewhat from expected results.

Example: Consider a group of 1,000 employees, half of whom are male and half of whom are female. Assuming that all these employees are equal in every relevant respect (e.g., qualifications, job held, skills brought to the workplace), if an economist, organizational psychologist or statistician studied 100 promotions from this group, he or she would expect to find promotions awarded to 50 male and 50 female employees. This would be the "expected" result.

See Also: Average, probability.

Experimental or Empirical Probability, *n*. a probability determined by data or observation rather than some underlying theory.

Example: In determining economic damages in employment cases, an economist might wish to use the probability that an individual would remain in the workforce to estimate the individual's remaining working life. These probabilities are usually calculated from labor-market data. Therefore, the probability someone will remain in the labor force is an empirical probability and subject to a certain amount of error.

See Also: Data, probability.

Explanatory Variable, *n*. a variable that helps explain the values and outcomes of another variable; explanatory variables are also independent variables.

Discussion: In a discrimination analysis, the protected group status of an employee is the explanatory variable of interest. Depending on the allegations and the employer's decision-making process, the employer's years of service, job-performance rating, education, and salary grade may also be included as explanatory variables.

See Also: Dependent variable, independent variable, linear regression.

F

F-Test, *n.* any statistical test based on the F-probability distribution function.

Discussion: The F-distribution is derived from the chi-square probability distribution function.

Example: F-tests are used to determine the validity of a regression as seen in the STATA example below. In a linear regression setting, the F-statistic is used to test the hypothesis that all the coefficients in the linear regression model are equal to zero. If all the coefficients in the linear regression model were statistically not different from zero, then the model would be invalid.

```
educ = Bachelors

      Source |       SS       df       MS              Number of obs =   15330
-------------+------------------------------           F(  7, 15322) =  317.29
       Model |  1255.96566     7  179.423666           Prob > F      =  0.0000
    Residual |  8664.28793 15322   .56548022           R-squared     =  0.1266
-------------+------------------------------           Adj R-squared =  0.1262
       Total |  9920.25359 15329  .647155952           Root MSE      =  .75198

------------------------------------------------------------------------------
         inc |      Coef.   Std. Err.      t    P>|t|     [95% Conf. Interval]
-------------+----------------------------------------------------------------
      female |  -.3518044   .0123054   -28.59   0.000    -.3759245   -.3276843
       black |  -.1205785   .0221088    -5.45   0.000    -.1639144   -.0772427
      indian |  -.0892178   .0850171    -1.05   0.294    -.2558615    .0774259
       asian |  -.0566266   .0247676    -2.29   0.022    -.1051741   -.0080791
    hispanic |  -.2051414   .0247628    -8.28   0.000    -.2536794   -.1566033
       exper |   .0550911   .0018359    30.01   0.000     .0514925    .0586896
      exper2 |  -.0010939   .0000448   -24.44   0.000    -.0011816   -.0010061
       _cons |   10.33805   .0183995   561.86   0.000     10.30198    10.37411
------------------------------------------------------------------------------
```

In the example above, the STATA output shows that the F-test is statistically significant and therefore that the regression is valid.

See Also: Hypothesis testing, linear regression, statistical significance.

Factorial, *n.* the product of all positive integers from 1 to the given number.

Discussion: Algebraically, a factorial is written as $n! = 1 \times 2 \times \ldots \times n$.

Example: The factorial of 5 equals 120. Using the formula above, the factorial of 5 is written as: $5! = 1 \times 2 \times 3 \times 4 \times 5 = 120$. Factorials are used in many different probability distribution functions.

See Also: Integer.

Fisher Exact Test, *n.* a statistical test used to determine whether there is a nonrandom association between two categorical variables.

Discussion: Fisher Exact tests are common in employment litigation related to hiring, promotion, and termination decisions. This test is an alternative to the chi-squared test. The Fisher Exact test is based on exact probabilities from the hypergeometric distribution and is more appropriate in cases with few observations. Many employment decisions involve fewer than five employees in the protected class being hired, promoted, or terminated on a given date or in a given time period. The Fisher Exact test is a useful tool in these settings.

Example: Consider the following hiring pattern:

	Not Hired	**Hired**
Male	7	8
Female	3	1

A Fisher Exact test can be performed to calculate the probability that the observed outcomes would have happened through random chance. The Fisher Exact test calculates the probability of obtaining the observed outcome or one that is even more stratified by the variable of interest (such as race or gender). The formula to calculate the Fisher Exact Test probability involves calculating multiple probabilities from the hypergeometric probability distribution function.

In the example above, the Fisher Exact test yields a 58.2% probability of observing this outcome or one with even larger gender disparities.

Note that the Fisher Exact test does not require a large sample size. This makes it an ideal test for cases that involve smaller hiring, promotion, or termination decisions, as well as for cases in which the protected class is relatively small.

The STATA output below presents the Fisher Exact test results for a gender-discrimination hiring case.

tab female hire, exact

	hire		
female	0	1	Total
0	18	5	23
1	7	0	7
Total	25	5	30

Fisher's exact =	0.304
1-sided Fisher's exact =	0.236

In this case, five male applicants and no female applicants were hired. The difference between the number of expected and actual female hires is not statistically significant. The two-sided Fisher Exact text result is 0.304. That is, there is a 30.4% chance that this outcome or one even more unequal would have occurred by random chance. The one-sided Fisher Exact test result is 0.236. That is, there is a 23.6% chance that this outcome or one even less favorable to females would have occurred.

See Also: Cross tabulation, hypothesis testing, non-parametric test of significance, statistical significance.

Frequency, *n.* the number of times a given outcome is observed.

Example: Assume that the following salary grades are observed on an employee roster: 8, 8, 7, 5, 9, 5, 5, 9, 5, 8, 8, 6, 8, 5, 5, 9.

The frequencies are as follows:

- Salary Grade 5: 6
- Salary Grade 6: 1
- Salary Grade 7: 1
- Salary Grade 8: 5
- Salary Grade 9: 3

In STATA output, the frequency appears in the first column, as seen in this tabulation for the level of education:

. tab educ

educ	Freq.	Percent	Cum.
Less than HS	31,149	19.99	19.99
HS	46,926	30.12	50.12
Some College	40,938	26.28	76.39
Bachelors	24,506	15.73	92.12
Post Grad	12,269	7.88	100.00
Total	155,788	100.00	

See Also: Cumulative frequency, frequency distribution.

Frequency Distribution, n. a tabular way to organize data.

Example: Salary data can be grouped into x-dollar intervals. The number of people in each salary group is summed to calculate the frequency of each salary group. A quick inspection of the data reveals the most common salary interval.

The table below is a salary frequency distribution for $20,000 intervals.

Salary Intervals	Frequency of Workers
$30,000–$49,999	30
$50,000–$69,999	57
$70,000–$89,999	12
$90,000–$109,999	3

See Also: Cumulative frequency, frequency.

Function, *n.* an equation that defines the relationship between one dependent variable and another independent variable or variables.

See Also: Dependent variable, independent variable.

G

Geometric Distribution, *n.* a probability distribution function that yields the probability of the first success in a series of Bernoulli Trials occurring in the xth attempt.

Discussion: Given that each trial has a probability p of success and probability (1 – p) of failure, the probability distribution is given by $p(x) = p(1 - p)^{x-1}$.

Example: Suppose a company states that hiring for its entry-level position occurred on a first-come, first-served basis. The company did not keep track of the order in which applications were received, but the percentage of applicants who were female, 35%, is known. On a given Tuesday, no females were hired, but three males were hired. The economist wants to determine the probability of this occurring if the order of application was determined solely by random chance.

In this case, the probability of a woman not being one of the first three people to apply is equal to one minus the probability of a woman being one of the first three people to apply. To calculate this probability, we need to know the probability a woman is the first to apply, the probability a woman is the second to apply, and the probability a woman is the third to apply. These probabilities are as follows.

Probability a woman is the first to apply: $p(1) = 0.35 \cdot (1 - 0.35)^{1-1} = 35\%$

Probability a woman is the second to apply:

$$p(2) = 0.35 \cdot (1 - 0.35)^{2-1} = 0.35 \cdot 0.65 = 22.75\%$$

Probability a woman is the third to apply:

$$p(3) = 0.35 \cdot (1 - 0.35)^{3-1} = 0.35 \cdot 0.65^2 = 14.79\%$$

Probability a woman is not one of the first three applicants:

$$1 - 0.35 - 0.2275 - 0.1479 = 27.46\%$$

This means that if random chance alone determined the order of the applicants, there is a 27% chance a woman would not be one of the first three people to apply. Most economists would not view this outcome as statistically significant.

See Also: Distribution, statistical significance.

Geometric Mean, *n.* a special way to calculate averages.

Discussion: Formally, the geometric mean is calculated as the nth root of the product, or $\bar{x} = \sqrt[n]{x_1 x_2 \cdots x_n}$.

Example: The geometric mean is often used to calculate averages when discussing interest rates, wage-growth rates, inflation, and other rates. U.S. inflation from 2000 to 2004 is shown below.

Year	Inflation
2000	3.44%
2001	1.55%
2002	2.43%
2003	1.87%
2004	3.35%

Using the formula for the geometric mean, the average inflation rate for this time period is:

$$\bar{x} = \sqrt[5]{3.44 \cdot 1.55 \cdot 2.43 \cdot 1.87 \cdot 3.35} = 2.41\%$$

See Also: Average, mean.

Goodness of Fit, *n.* how well a dataset fits a distribution, test or equation.

Discussion: In employment litigation, the chi-squared test is often used as a goodness-of-fit test. The r-squared value is a measure of goodness-of-fit that tells how much of the variation in the dependent variable (salary) is explained by the regression equation's independent employment variables such as time in grade.

See Also: Chi-squared test, r-square.

Grade, *n.* a position or degree in a scale; salary grade.

Discussion: In an employment context, salary grades refer to groups of job titles within a minimum-maximum salary band. Each salary grade defines the acceptable minimum, maximum, and/or median salary. Salary grades are most commonly used by the government and larger organizations.

See Also: Cardinal number, ordinal number, ordinal scale.

Graph, *n.* a way to describe data visually.

Discussion: Graphs help convey complex ideas simply, but they can also be misleading.

Example: Consider a promotion discrimination case. The plaintiff's expert offers a chart comparing the percentage of women in the department to the percentage of promoted individuals who were female. The graph she uses is shown below. Note that the left-hand side represents the percentage of women and that the scale starts at 48% instead of 0%. The plaintiff's expert shows this graph as clear proof of discrimination:

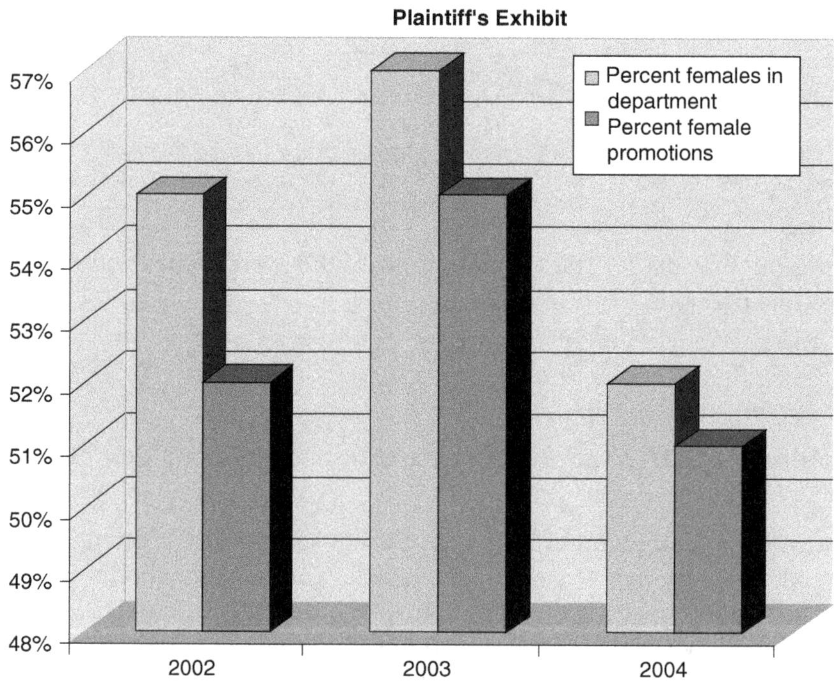

The defense expert, however, does not believe the differences are that large. She points out that in every year the differences are 3% or less.

The defense expert also wants to show this graphically. She presents the exhibit below, which is exactly the same as the plaintiff's exhibit, except that the scale on the left-hand side has been changed:

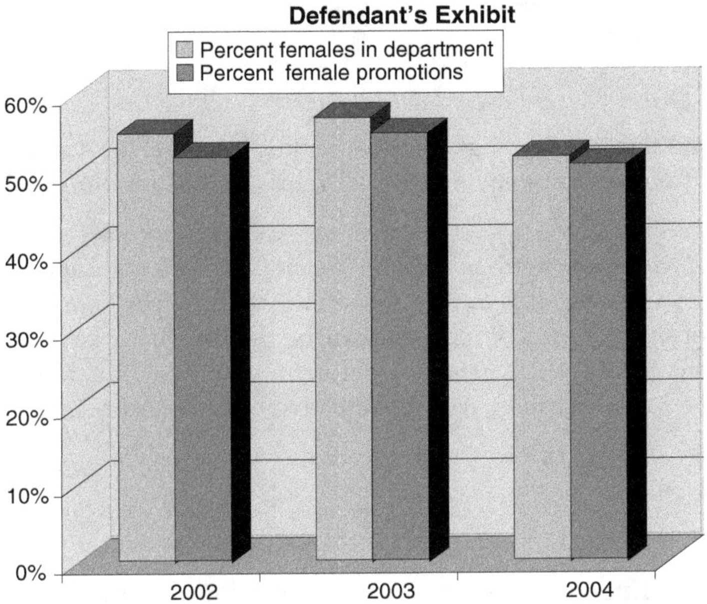

By starting the scale at 0% instead of 48%, the results look very different. Neither graph is wrong; each graph presents the same information. The reader must examine the details of the graph to determine how to interpret the data.

See Also: Bar chart, descriptive statistics, histogram, pictogram, pie chart.

H

Heteroscedastic, *adj.* a statistical condition where the variance of a random variable is not equal across all values of the random variable.

Discussion: If errors in a least squares regression are heteroscedastic, then the coefficients are neither efficient nor reliable. In some employment regression analyses, such as those involving salary, a mathematical transformation of the underlying data can be performed to ameliorate the condition. In salary regressions, a natural logarithmic transformation of employees' salaries can be performed to avoid the condition.

See Also: Correlation, error, homoscedastic, linear regression, regression analysis.

Histogram, *n.* a chart that displays the frequency of data.

Discussion: Histograms are extremely useful for displaying data in wage-and-hour cases.

Example: Assume a mid-sized manufacturing company is being sued for automatically deducting 30 minutes for lunch from employees' daily hours worked, even if they took less than 30 minutes for lunch. To address the issue, the employees are surveyed and asked how many minutes they took for lunch on average. Below is a histogram of the survey results.

See Also: Data, graph.

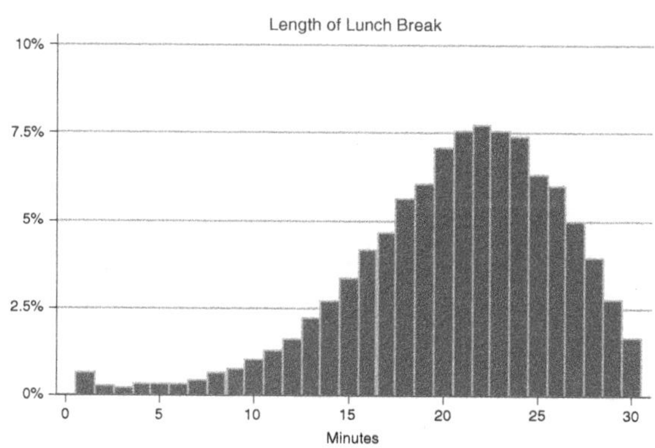

Homoscedastic, *adj*. a statistical condition where the variance of a random variable is equal across all values of the random variable.

Discussion: This is an underlying assumption of a linear regression. If the homoscedastic property is violated, the error is said to be heteroscedastic.

See Also: Correlation, error, heteroscedastic, linear regression, regression analysis.

Hypergeometric Distribution, n. a discrete probability distribution function that is the underlying distribution for many small-sample selection tests.

Distribution: The hypergeometric distribution function is given as:

$$f(x|A, B, n) = \frac{\binom{A}{x}\binom{b}{n-x}}{\binom{A+B}{n}}$$

Example: Let's consider a simple hiring example. Suppose six women (denoted A) and ten men (denoted B) are equally qualified for bank teller positions. The bank is opening a new branch and must hire multiple tellers. The total number of new hires is 11 (denoted n). The bank is concerned with the number of women being hired (denoted X).

The hypergeometric distribution contains several intuitive restrictions. First, the number of females hired (X) cannot be greater than the total number of new hires (n) or the total number of female applicants (A). Similarly, the number of females hired (X) cannot be less than zero and the number of female hires must be at least as large as the total number of new hires (n) less the number of male applicants (B). That is, if 11 tellers are hired, at least one of them must be female woman, because only ten men applied.

What is the probability of having three female new hires (X)? Plugging in the numbers from our example, we have:

$$f(3|6, 10, 11) = \frac{\binom{6}{3}\binom{10}{11-3}}{\binom{6+10}{11}} = \frac{\binom{6}{3}\binom{10}{8}}{\binom{16}{11}} = \frac{\frac{6!}{3!\cdot 3!} \times \frac{10!}{8!\cdot 2!}}{\frac{16!}{5!\cdot 11!}} = 20.6\%$$

If the hiring process was determined by sheer random chance, the probability that three females would be hired is 20.6%.

See Also: Distribution function, Fisher Exact test, hypothesis testing, non-parametric test of significance, statistical significance.

Hypothesis Testing, *n.* a generally accepted method of using data and statistical concepts to make inferences concerning a particular issue.

Discussion: For allegations of employment discrimination, hypothesis testing involves five main steps.

Step 1: State the null and alternative employment-discrimination hypothesis.

Step 2: Determine whether a one-sided or two-sided test is appropriate.

Step 3: Select and perform a statistical test.

Step 4: Determine the significance level.

Step 5: Make inferences.

See Also: Alternative hypothesis, null hypothesis, statistical significance.

I

Impossible, adj. having a zero probability of occurring.

See Also: Probability.

Increment, *n.* a small change in the value of a variable.

Discussion: In employment litigation, it is common to see estimates of remaining work-life expectancy based on an increment-decrement method. These work-life expectancy numbers differ from traditional methods of using a retirement age of 65 or the median number of years to retirement because they incorporate periods of labor-force inactivity.

Over the course of a lifetime, the average individual has periods of voluntary and/or involuntary absences from the labor force. These absences may include returning to school to pursue a degree or taking time off to care for children or other loved ones. The increment-decrement model looks at the probability a person will be in the labor force next year, given his or her current status in the labor force. A separate probability of labor-force activity is derived depending on whether an individual is currently active or inactive in the labor force. Using these probabilities, the economist can determine the expected number of years an individual would remain in the labor force excluding all voluntary and involuntary absences from the labor force.

See Also: Probability.

Independent Events, *n.* events that have no influence on each other.

Discussion: Mathematically, events are independent if:

$$p(A|B) = p(A|B') = p(A)$$

and

$$p(A \cap B) = p(A)p(B)$$

Example: Whether or not a person's favorite color is blue probably has no impact on the likelihood that he or she will be terminated as part of a department-wide layoff. If this is true, then some simple laws of probability hold, such as:

(1) Pr(terminated | favorite color blue) = Pr(terminated | favorite color red) = Pr(terminated)

(2) Pr(terminated and favorite color blue) = Pr(terminated) * Pr(favorite color blue).

Favorite colors are unlikely to be a source of contention in litigation. However, these laws can be extended to test the hypothesis that an employer was not discriminating against females, minorities, or individuals over the age of 40. In other words, an economist might test to determine whether terminations are independent of gender, race, or age.

See Also: Conditional probability, probability.

Independent Random Variables, *n.* variables such that the outcome of one variable does not affect the probability distribution of the other variable.

Discussion: If random variables are independent, then there is no relationship between the two variables and their covariance is zero.

Example: Gender and race are two independent random variables. A person's gender does not affect the probability that he or she is African-American. Hence, for independent random variables:

$$p(X = x \text{ and } Y = y) = p(X = x) \cdot p(Y = y)$$

or

$$p(\text{white female}) = p(white) \cdot p(female)$$

See Also: Covariance, random variable.

Independent Variable, *n.* a variable whose value does not depend on another variable.

Example: A person's race is an independent variable; therefore, a person's race does not depend on whether he or she is selected for termination. However, a person's selection for termination may or may not be dependent on the person's race and/or other factors. Hence, selection for termination is a dependent variable.

See Also: Dependent variable.

Index Number, *n.* the value of a quantity relative to some fixed baseline.

Discussion: In salary analyses, an economist might look at salaries across different locations. To compare salaries among cities, the economist may choose to consider the cost of living in each of those cities. One of the cities must be chosen as the baseline or index, or a comparison to the national average can be used. The salaries for other cities can then be scaled to adjust for the differences in the cost of living.

Example: Assume computer technicians in Manhattan earn $120,000 a year while computer technicians in Houston earn only $55,000 a year. Are these salaries comparable?

Compared to the national average, the cost-of-living index for Manhattan is 203.9. This means the cost of living in Manhattan is more than twice as high as the national average. The cost of living index for Houston is 88.7. This means the cost of living in Houston is only 88.7% of the national average.

To compare the salaries, divide each one by the cost-of-living index. The salary for Manhattan is now only $58,852, while the salary for Houston is $62,007. Hence, when the cost of living is accounted for, Houston technicians receive better financial compensation than Manhattan technicians do, even though their salaries are less than half of those of their counterparts in Manhattan.

See Also: Average.

Individual Selection Process, *n.* a process through which candidates for selection are separated into two groups, one containing individuals who were selected and the other containing individuals who were not selected.

Example: A firm is going through a reduction in force or a layoff. The managers must evaluate the employees based on a set of factors and determine which ones to terminate. Some employees are selected for termination; others are not selected and hence are retained. This is an individual selection process.

See Also: Adverse impact, applicant pool, disparate impact.

Inference, *n.* a statistical conclusion about data based on a sample of that data.

See Also: Hypothesis testing.

Infinite, *adj*. having no limits or boundaries.

Infinitesimal, *adj*. immeasurably small.

Integer, *n*. a whole number.

Example: −5, 0, and 16 are all integers.

See Also: Discrete, ordinal number.

Interaction, *n*. there is interaction in data when classifications are not independent.

Discussion: Interaction terms are sometimes used in regression analysis.

Example: Suppose an economist wanted to predict salary based on an individual's gender, race, work experience, and level of education. The economist also believes that the effect work experience has on salary varies by the level of education. The economist believes that individuals with a college degree will tend to earn larger annual salary increases over time than individuals who do not have a college degree. To test and account for this potential effect, the economist includes an interaction term. In linear regression, an interaction term is equal to level of education multiplied by the employee's number of years of work experience. In this way, the effect of work experience varies with education level.

See Also: Coefficient, linear regression, regression analysis.

Interpretive Statistics, *n*. statistics that allow conclusions to be drawn based on data.

See Also: Descriptive statistics, hypothesis testing, statistical significance.

Interquartile Range, *n*. a measure of the spread of the data observations that is equal to the difference between the 1st and 3rd quartiles.

Discussion: The interquartile range shows the range of values between which falls the middle 50% of the dataset.

See Also: Median, range, quartile.

Intersection, *n*. the elements common to both sets.

Example: The intersection of all female employees and all terminated employees is all female employees who were terminated. The intersection is written mathematically as $s(A \cap B)$, where A represents female employees and B represents terminated employees. Graphically, the intersection is shown as the area where circles A and B overlap.

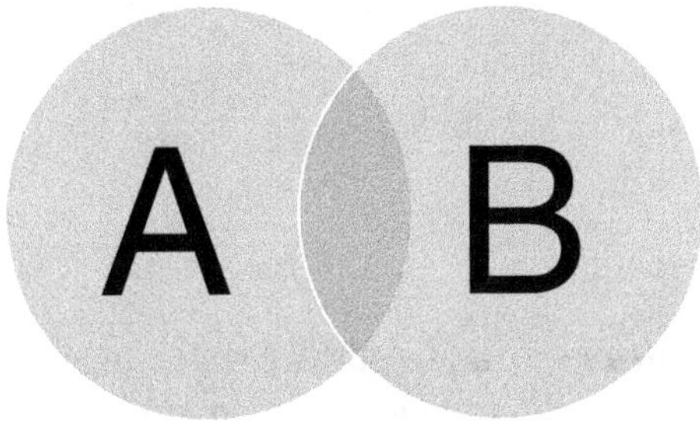

See Also: Union.

L

Law of Large Numbers, *n.* a law stating that the greater the amount of data included in the sample, the closer the estimated mean will be to the true mean.

Discussion: This law is an important basis for many statistical tests.

See Also: Mean, normal distribution, statistical significance.

Least Squares, Method of, *n.* a method of estimating the best-fit line through a series of points.

Discussion: The least-squares method estimates the best-fit line by minimizing the sum of the squared errors. Formally, the equation that describes the least-squares method is given by:

$$\min \sum_{i=1}^{n} [y_i - (\beta_0 + \beta_i x_i)]^2$$

In the equation, y is the dependant variable, the beta terms are mathematical coefficients, and x is the independent explanatory variable. As shown, the squares are determined by measuring the square of the distance from each data observation to the best-fit line. By squaring the distance, large differences from the y values are magnified. Conversely, small differences (those less than one) are minimized. Additionally, squaring the differences in the least-squares method causes positive and negative differences to be treated in the same way.

See Also: Linear regression, line of best fit.

Linear Estimator, *n.* an estimator that is derived from a linear function of the sample values.

See Also: Linear relationship, mean.

Linear Regression, *n.* a statistical method that is used to mathematically construct the best-fit linear relationship between two variables.

Discussion: In an employment setting, linear regression methods are used to model the effect of various explanatory factors such as race, gender, age, job performance, and years of service on employment-related outcomes. There are four basic steps in performing a linear regression.

Step 1: Find the line that best fits the data.

Step 2: Find and isolate the relationship between the employment variable of interest (usually race, gender or age) and salary.

Step 3: Check the statistical significance of the demographic effect estimate.

Step 4: Perform model diagnostics and fit tests.

See Also: Coefficient, coefficient of determination, method of least squares, line of best fit, slope, standard error.

Linear Relationship, *n.* a relationship between two variables that produces a straight line on a Cartesian graph.

Discussion: The relationship between variables x and y is linear if it can be described as $y = ax + b$, where a and b are scalars. In a linear regression, the factors or variables being examined are assumed to have a linear relationship.

Example: Assume an employee's salary is determined on a base level of $40,000 per year plus an additional $1,000 for each year the employee has worked with the company. Mathematically:

Salary = $40,000 + $1,000 x Years of Employee Tenure

This means there is a linear relationship between salary and employee tenure. Note that in the equation above, y is salary, x is employee tenure, a = $1,000, and b = $40,000. Hence, a new employee with zero years of job tenure would have an expected salary of $40,000. An employee with ten years of experience working for the employer would be expected to have a salary of $50,000.

See Also: Graph, scalar, variable.

Line of Best Fit, *n.* the line closest to all the data points in a scatter plot.

Discussion: Some of the data points will be above the line of best fit and others will be below it. The most common way to fit this line through the data is to find the line that produces the lowest sum of squares.

See Also: Least squares, method of, linear regression.

Logarithm, *n.* the power to which a base number, a, must be raised to obtain a given number, b.

Discussion: Mathematically, the logarithm is given by the equation $a^c = b$ and written as $c = \log_a b$.

Example: Natural logarithms, or logarithms with base e, are often used in salary regressions. The natural logarithm maps salary values to a new line. This new line slopes up steeply at first and then more slowly as salary increases.

The natural logarithm transformation of salary data generally results in a better fitting line in regression models. Using the natural logarithm does, however, change the interpretation of the coefficients in the regression. In the original model where the salary variable is not transformed, a one-unit change in an explanatory variable creates an average change equal to the coefficient in the dependent variable. For instance, if the coefficient on a years-of-service variable in a salary regression is equal to $10,768, then the salary model predicts that for each year of service with the employer, the employee will earn an additional $10,768.

When the salary values are transformed using the natural logarithm function, coefficients represent the average percentage change that is related to changes in the explanatory variable. For instance, in a transformed salary regression with tenure as an explanatory variable, a coefficient of 0.085 would mean that an increase in employee tenure by one year increases salary by 8.5% on average.

See Also: Coefficient, linear regression, variable.

Logistic Regression, *n.* a regression technique that is based on the logistic formula.

Discussion: In employment settings, the logistic-regression technique is used to estimate the effect of one or multiple independent variables on the 'success' likelihood associated with a dichotomous employment decision outcome, such as a promotion or termination event. A logistic regression assumes that there is a linear relationship between the likelihood of an employment-related success and the underlying factors that are related to the outcome variable. The underlying employment factors affect the likelihood of the employment outcome – not the actual probability.

In logistic-regression analyses, the log-odds ratio is commonly used to express the likelihood associated with the employment outcome. This likelihood is expressed as the ratio of the probability of being selected (p) divided by the probability of not being selected (1-p).

A logistic regression could be used in hiring, promotion, and termination cases. Based on demographic factors, a logistic regression can be used to predict the probability that an individual would be hired, promoted, or terminated. Logistic regressions are also used to determine work-life expectancy by calculating the probability that an individual will be in the work force from one year to the next.

Logistic regressions are preferred to linear regressions when estimating probabilities and likelihoods because all predicted values from logistic regressions must fall between 0 and 1. Linear regressions do not satisfy these restrictions and hence may return probability values that are negative or greater than 1.

See Also: Linear regression, linear relationship, probability.

Lottery Model, *n.* a model based on the premise that every element in the model is equal.

Discussion: In the selection process, each element has an equal chance of being selected.

Example: From a mathematical perspective, a nondiscriminatory termination process could be viewed as a lottery model. In this hypothetical lottery model, the decision-maker's process is similar to that of selecting balls from a bowl. That is, the decision-maker randomly selects one ball from the bowl, notes its color on a piece of paper, and then places it on the table outside of the bowl. This process continues until all the required balls (i.e., terminations) are selected from the bowl.

See Also: Probability.

M

Mantel-Haenszel Odds Ratio, *n.* a statistical test used to estimate the statistical significance associated with shortfalls across different data strata.

Discussion: Conceptually, the Mantel-Haenszel test estimates the collective statistical significance of having the hiring, promotion, or termination shortfalls in all of the different time periods in the analysis. In an employment analysis, the different data strata are typically job-related and include factors such as time periods, departments, and job locations.

The Mantel-Haenszel procedure requires that the data strata be independent and uniquely defined. If this basic assumption is invalid, it strongly calls into question the usefulness and reliability of the inferences that can be made from the test. Problems implementing this test occur primarily when applicants are included in multiple strata.

See Also: Hypothesis testing, statistical significance, strata.

Mann Whitney U-test, *n.* a non-parametric test of the null hypothesis that two samples are drawn from the same parent population.

Discussion: The Mann Whitney test does not depend on the assumption of a particular underlying distribution.

Markov Chain, *n.* a sequence of events where the probability of each event is dependent on the event immediately preceding it.

Discussion: Markov chains are sometimes used to compute work-life expectancies in employment cases. Markov chain estimates of work-life recognize that a person may have periods of labor-market inactivity. In this setting, work-life is calculated by using the probability that a person will be active in the labor force next year. This probability is dependent on the person's current labor-market status. That is, a person is more likely to be in the labor force next year if he or she is currently active in the labor force. By summing together these annual probabilities, the economist can arrive at an estimate of the remaining work-life expectancy based on whether the individual is currently active in the labor force.

Mean (arithmetic), *n.* the average value of a dataset.

Discussion: In the case of employment, the mean may tell us the salary of the average worker. By taking the mean salary for two groups of workers, one can observe any differences in salary for the average employee in each group. The mean, or average value, is calculated by summing the observations and dividing by the number of observations. Formally, the sample mean ($\bar{x}$) is calculated as:

$$\bar{x} = \frac{1}{n}\sum_{i=1}^{n} x_i$$

where n is the number of individuals in the sample and $\sum$ is the symbol for the summation. $\sum_{i=1}^{n} x_i$ is equal to $x_1 + x_2 + \ldots + x_n$. $\sum_{i=1}^{n} x_i$ means to take the first number, x_1, add it to the second number, x_2, add that to the third number, x_3, and continue doing that until we get to the last number, x_n.

Example: Below is a table of employees' salaries.

Name	Salary
Carol	$55,000
David	$90,000
Diane	$85,000
Erin	$25,000
Richard	$40,000

The mean salary is equal to the sum of the salaries divided by the number of employees. In this case, $n = 5$.

$$\bar{x} = \frac{55,000 + 90,000 + 85,000 + 25,000 + 40,000}{5} = \frac{295,000}{5} = \$59,000$$

Hence, the mean salary for this group of employees is $59,000.

See Also: Median, mode.

Median, *n.* the value of the middle observation of a dataset.

Discussion: In terms of salaries, half of the people in the dataset will have salaries above the median and half of the people will have salaries below the median.

The median is equal to the value of the dataset's middle observation. Half of the dataset's observations will be greater than or equal to the median. Half of the dataset's observations will be less than or equal to the median. Formally, the median is defined by two equations:

$$\Pr(X \leq m) \geq 1/2$$

$$\Pr(X \geq m) \geq 1/2$$

where X is any value in the dataset and m is the median of the dataset.

Although the mean and median both describe the center values of datasets, they are not necessarily the same value. The median is less sensitive than the mean to outliers in the dataset. If data is skewed toward the left or toward lower values, then the mean will be lower than the median. If data is skewed towards the right or towards higher values, then the mean will be higher than the median.

Example: In the salary table below, $45,000 is the median.

Salary	Frequency
$35,000	1
$40,000	2
$45,000	1
$50,000	3

There are 7 observations. This means that the median is the value of the 4th observation. That is, the first three observations are lower than the median and the last three observations are higher than the median.

See Also: Mean, mode.

Mode, *n.* the value of the variable that occurs most frequently.

Example: In the salary table below, $45,000 is the mode of the salary variable.

Salary	Frequency
$35,000	2
$40,000	5
$45,000	14
$50,000	13

See Also: Mean, median.

Model, *n.* a set of theoretical relationships that are intended to represent a real-life process, situation, or problem.

Discussion: Models tend to simplify reality to allow economists to quantify an issue. In employment cases, the choice of model is often as important as (or more important than) the statistical test used to analyze the data.

See Also: Statistical significance.

Moving Average, *n.* an average that has been adjusted to allow for seasonal or cyclical components.

Discussion: Unemployment rates vary over the course of any given year. Calculating a yearly average makes it difficult to see trends in the unemployment rate. A moving average, however, makes it easier to identify such trends over time.

See Also: Mean.

Multiple Regression, *n.* a technique for finding a best-fit line or an expression for dependent variables based on several other variables.

See Also: Linear regression, logistic regression, probit regression.

Multiplication Rule, *n.* a rule stating that for two events, A and B, the probability of both events occurring is given by:

$$p(A \cap B) = p(A|B) \cdot p(B)$$

or

$$p(A \cap B) = p(B|A) \cdot p(A)$$

Discussion: If the two events are independent, then the probability is simply:

$$p(A \cap B) = p(A) \cdot p(B)$$

Example: Consider an employment case in which two groups of petroleum analysts were recently eligible for raises at a large oil-and-gas employer. Fifty percent of the petroleum analysts received raises, whereas only 25% of the gas analysts received raises. There are ten petroleum analysts and five gas analysts. If one person is selected at random from the group, what is the probability that he or she will be a gas analyst who has received a raise? The probability of selecting a gas analyst is five out of 15 employees, or 33%. The probability that a gas analyst received a raise is

25%. Therefore, the probability of selecting a gas analyst who has received a raise is 33%*25%, or 8.3%.

If 50% of petroleum analysts and gas analysts receive raises, (i.e., the probability of receiving a raise was the same for both groups of employees), the two events are independent. The probability of selecting a gas analyst who recently received a raise is equal to the proportion of gas analysts in the two groups (33%) multiplied by the probability of receiving a raise (50%). Thus, the probability of selecting a gas analyst who has received a raise is 33%*50%, or 16.7%.

Mutually Exclusive, *adj.* such that no two events can occur at the same time in a group of three or more events.

N

Non-Parametric Test of Significance, *n.* a test of statistical significance that does not require assumptions concerning the underlying distribution of the data.

Discussion: These types of tests are most useful when sample sizes are small. Non-parametric tests include the Fisher Exact test, the Mann Whitney U-Test, and the Wilcoxen Matched-Pairs Signed-Rank test.

Normal Distribution, *n.* a bell-curve shaped continuous probability distribution function.

Discussion: A probability distribution function is a mathematical equation that yields the probability or likelihood associated with a given outcome or range or outcomes. The normal distribution is referred to as a continuous probability distribution function because it is used to generate probabilities for random experiments that, unlike flipping a coin, can produce an infinite number of outcomes, such as salary.

Intuitively, an employment factor that is normally distributed produces values that are close to the mean of the employment factor in most instances. The appearance of the normal curve is driven by two parameters: the mean and the variance. Conceptually, the normal curve for a normally distributed employment factor looks like a bell that is centered or balanced on the mean of the data. Values that are extremely large or extremely small compared to the mean of the data are not as likely for a normally distributed employment factor.

The width or girth of the conceptual bell curve is determined by a parameter called the standard deviation. The higher or greater the standard deviation parameter, the wider or more spread out the normal distribution curve will be. The dispersion of the data is measured by the distance from the mean of the data.

Null Hypothesis, *n.* in classical statistical models, the hypothesis or statement that is believed to be true prior to testing.

Discussion: In employment-discrimination cases, the null hypothesis is that the employment data at issue are consistent with unbiased and nondiscriminatory behavior by the employer. The alternative hypothesis is the statement we believe to be true if we reject the null hypothesis. In our setting, the alternative hypothesis is the statement concerning the employment data that we believe to be true if we reject the null hypothesis that the employer's data is not consistent with nondiscriminatory behavior by the employer.

If the employment data is consistent with the null hypothesis, we say that 'we accept the null hypothesis'. The employment data is inconsistent with the null hypothesis if there is a low probability that the result could have been generated by random chance. If the employment data is consistent with the alternative hypothesis we say that 'we reject the null hypothesis'.

O

Odds Ratio, n. the probability of being selected divided by the probability of not being selected.

Discussion: In employment cases, an odds ratio tells us how likely employees in a given group are to be selected versus the likelihood of that group not being selected. Mathematically, it is:

$$OR = \frac{p}{1 - p}$$

Where p is the probability of being selected and (1–p) is the probability of not being selected.

An odds ratio that is equal to 1 means that the group is equally likely to be selected or not selected. An odds ratio of less than 1 means the group of employees are less likely than not to be selected. An odds ratio greater than 1 means that the group is more likely than not to be selected.

Ordered Logit or Probit Regression, *n.* a mathematical model that estimates the effect of one or multiple independent variables on the 'success' likelihood associated with an ordered discrete outcome.

Example: Ordered probit and logit regressions are often used to predict educational attainment using data from the National Longitudinal Survey of Youth. In this data, educational attainment falls into discrete categories: less than high school, high school, some college, college degree, and postgraduate. These levels of education are clearly ordered, with less-than-high-school being the lowest level of educational attainment and postgraduate being the highest level of educational attainment. The ordered probit and logit regressions estimate the probabilities of each level of educational attainment based on demographic and other characteristics.

Ordinal Number, *n.* a number that denotes order, quality, or degree.

Ordinal Scale, *n.* a scale with classification and rank.

Outlier, *n.* an observation that is far removed from others in the set.

Discussion: An outlier may be from a different parent population, an error in the data, or a genuine result.

P

p Value, *n.* the probability value produced in a test of significance.

Discussion: The larger the p value, the more likely it is that the null hypothesis is true or that the outcome was produced by random chance. If the p value is less than 1% or 5%, then it is highly unlikely the outcome was produced by random chance and the result is generally said to be statistically significant.

Parameter, *n.* a value used to define a statistical model or a theoretical distribution.

Example: The normal distribution is defined by two parameters: mean and variance. A standard normal distribution assumes that these parameters are a mean of zero and a variance of one. A binomial distribution is also defined by two parameters: the number of trials and the probability of a successful trial.

Parametric Test of Significance, n. a test of significance that assumes the underlying population has a specific distribution.

Pascal's Distribution, *n.* the probability distribution for the number of Bernoulli trials needed to achieve a certain number of successes.

Discussion: Formally, this distribution is given by:

$$p(x) = {}^{x-1}C_{x-n}p^n(1 - p)^{x-n}$$

where $x>n$, $0<p<1$, x is the number of Bernoulli trials, p is the probability of a successful trial, and n is the number of successes.

Percentage, *n.* the proportion or rate per one hundred parts.

Percentage Frequency Distribution, *n.* a frequency distribution expressed as a percentage of the whole.

Example:

Salary Intervals	Frequency of Workers	% Frequency
$30,000–$49,999	30	29%
$50,000–$69,999	57	56%
$70,000–$89,999	12	12%
$90,000–$109,999	3	3%
Total	102	100%

Percentile, *n.* one of 99 values of a variable, dividing the distribution into 100 groups with equal frequencies.

Permutation, *n.* an ordered arrangement of numbers, letters, or other components of a set into specific groups.

Discussion: If all the objects are different, then the number of permutations for n different objects is n! The number of permutations of n elements selected r at a time is:

$$^{n}P_{r} = \frac{n!}{(n-r)!}$$

The number of permutations of n objects with p of one type, q of another type, r of a third type, etc., is given by:

$$\frac{n!}{p!q!r!}$$

Example: Assume an employer is restructuring due to budget concerns. Ten sales employees are affected by the restructuring and only five possible territory assignments remain. How many territory assignment permutations are there?

$$P_{5}^{10} = \frac{10!}{(10-5)!} = \frac{10!}{5!} = 30,240$$

There are more than 30,000 permutations.

Pictogram, *n.* a diagram that uses pictures to express frequency.

Discussion: Pictograms are straightforward ways to convey information.

Example: In an employment case, the following diagram might be used to show that there are 3 female employees and 5 male employees:

Pie Chart, *n.* a circular diagram divided into slices or sectors that are proportional to the frequencies or magnitude of the items being represented.

Example: The age composition a company's workforce is as follows:

Age	Number of Employees
20 – 29	20
30 – 39	57
40 – 49	62
50 and over	39

The pie chart representation of this data would be:

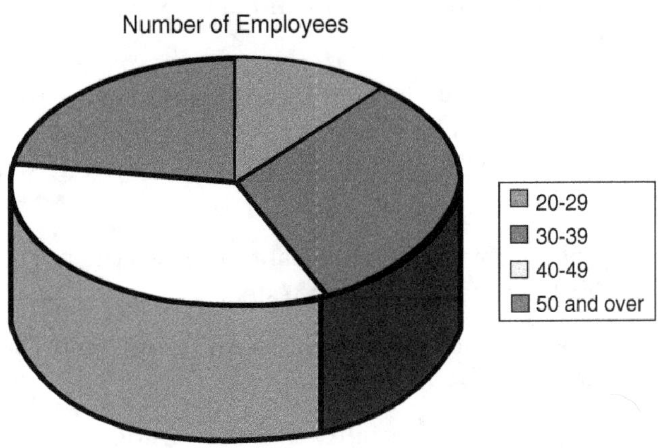

Pilot Survey, *n.* a survey carried out before a larger survey, generally on a smaller scale.

Discussion: Pilot surveys can be important because they give researchers a chance to test survey procedures and question designs. Pilot surveys may save additional time and expense by identifying survey questions with unclear wording or questions that have no appropriate answers.

Point Estimation, *n.* the estimation of a parameter as a single value.

Poisson Distribution, *n.* distribution of the probability of an event occurring a given number of times when the probability of the event occurring is small, but the number of times on which is could occur is large.

Discussion: Mathematically, the probability distribution is given as:

$$p(r) = e^{-\mu}\frac{(\mu)^r}{r!}$$

Where r is the number of event occurrences and μ is the mean. The mean is equal to the number of trials multiplied by the probability of the event occurring.

Pool, *n.* the group of individuals from which an employment selection is made.

Population, *n.* the entire collection of individuals or items from which a sample is drawn.

Post-Selection Pool, *n.* the pool of candidates selected in an employment selection process.

Potential Applicant Pool, *n.* the group of individuals that includes actual applicants for a decision process as well as individuals who did not apply due to either lack of interest or the fact that they were screened out as ineligible in a prior stage.

Power, *n.* the probability that a statistical test rejects the null hypothesis at a given value of the parameter being tested.

Pre-Selection Pool, *n.* the pool of individuals from which selections are made in an employment selection process.

Prior Probability, *n.* the probability that event A occurs when it is not known whether event B has occurred.

Discussion: Conversely, the posterior probability of event A is the probability that event A occurs given that it is known that event B has occurred. If the two events are independent, then the prior probability will be the same as the posterior probability.

Probability, *n.* the likelihood or occurrence of an event. Probability must be a value between 0 and 1.

Discussion: A probability of zero means there is no chance the event will occur. A probability of one means the event will occur with certainty.

Probability Density Function, *n.* a function of a random variable, X, such that the probability that the random variable is between two points, a and b, is defined by the equation:

$$\int_a^b f(x)dx$$

Discussion: The probability density function must satisfy two conditions. First, the total probability must be equal to one. Second, the probability must be non-negative for all values of x.

Probability Distribution, *n.* the distribution of probabilities of the different values of a discrete random variable X.

Discussion: The numbers on a pair of dice and the number of employees are both examples of discrete random variables. The probability distribution must satisfy two conditions. First, the sum of all the probabilities must be equal to one. Mathematically:

$$\sum_i p(x_i) = 1$$

Second, no probability can be negative. Mathematically $p(x_i) \geq 0$ for all i.

Probit Regression, *n.* a mathematical model that is based on the normal distribution that estimates the effect of one or more independent variables on the 'success' likelihood associated with a dichotomous employment decision outcome.

Discussion: The difference between a probit regression model and a logistic regression model is that a probit model relies on the standard normal density whereas a logit model uses the logistic probability density function.

See Also: Logistic regression.

Q

Qualitative Data, *n.* data classified by type, not by numerical values.

Example: Employee performance reviews are often qualitative, with managers ranking employees' skills as poor, fair, good, or excellent.

Quantile, *n.* values that divide a variable's distribution into equal groups.

Quantile Regression, n. a regression that estimates the median or other quantile value of the data.

Discussion: The median regression fits a line through the data by minimizing the sum of the absolute residuals.

Quantitative Data, *n.* data classified by numerical value, not by type.

Example: Employees' numerical test scores are quantitative data.

Quartile, *n.* one of two additional "medians" for the upper and lower halves of the data.

Discussion: Quartiles divide a dataset into four sections. First, note that the median divides the data into two halves. The first quartile is the value of the middle of the lower half created by the median. Twenty-five percent of the dataset has values lower than the first quartile, denoted Q1, and 75% of the dataset has values higher than Q1. The second quartile is the median itself. The third quartile is the value of the middle of the upper half created by the median. Seventy-five percent of the dataset has values lower than the third quartile, denoted Q3, and 25% of the dataset has values higher than Q3. In addition to providing information on the median, quartiles show the spread of the data. Quartiles give an upper and lower bound for 50% of the observed data.

Example: In the case of salary data, 50% of the observed salaries fall somewhere between the upper and lower quartiles.

Questionnaire, *n.* a set of questions on a form submitted to people to collect information.

R

Random, *adj.* such that it is governed by chance.

Random Numbers, *n.* numbers that are selected at random.

Discussion: Each number has an equal chance of being selected and each selection is independent of the number selected previously. Random numbers are typically used in choosing random sampling selections. They are also used in simulations.

Random Sampling, *n.* sampling in which every individual has a known probability of being selected.

Discussion: When it is infeasible to survey an entire group, random sampling is often used to select a representative group. Some surveys use random-number generators to select phone numbers from a telephone book in order to generate a random sample.

Random Selection, *n.* selection in which every item has a known probability of being selected.

Random Variable, *n.* a mathematical variable that produces a numerical representation of the possible outcomes of an employment process.

Example: The random variable describing an employee selection process could be described as a dichotomous mathematical variable that takes only one of two possible values, perhaps 1 if the person is hired and 0 if the person is not hired. A random variable could be set up to describe a person's salary or any employment process.

Range, *n.* the difference between the highest observation value and the lowest observation value in a dataset.

Discussion: Range, denoted Y, is equal to $x_n - x_1$ where x_n is the largest observed value and x_1 is the smallest observed value.

Rank, *n.* the position of a member within a set once the set is placed in order.

Ratio Scale, *n.* a measurement scale where equal differences between two numbers correspond to equal distances on the scale.

Regression Analysis, *n.* the use of a mathematical formula to express the influence of one or more independent variables, such as race, gender, or tenure, on the average level of a dependent variable, such as salary or hiring selection.

Regression Line, *n.* a line of best fit drawn through a set of points on a graph.

Discussion: The formula for the regression line is generated by the method of least squares. This method minimizes the sum of the squared distance from each point to the regression line.

See Also: Best fit line, linear regression.

Relative Frequency, *n.* the ratio of the frequency of the occurrence of a particular value of a variable to the sample size.

Residual, *n.* the distance from a point to a regression line.

S

Sample, *n.* a set of individuals or items drawn from a parent population.

Discussion: A sample is used to test hypotheses about the parent population and estimate parameters.

Sample Size, *n.* the number of individuals or items in a sample.

Sample Space, *n.* the parent population.

Sampling Distribution, *n.* the distribution of a statistic of a sample drawn from a parent population.

Discussion: In employment cases, a sampling distribution is the probability distribution function that describes all the possible mean salary samples that would have been generated by sheer randomness from a population of employees. The sampling distribution of a sample statistic simply tells us the probability associated with each possible theoretical set of employment outcomes.

Example: A sampling distribution that describes the possible mean salary outcomes for a group of employees could tell us the probability that an unbiased employment process will generate an average salary between $45,000 and $60,000.

Sampling Error, *n.* the difference between the true, typically unknown, value of a parameter of a parent population and the value estimated based on a sample from the parent population.

Discussion: The underlying population is most likely unknown, so there is some difference between the actual and estimated values of the parameter. To obtain the most precise and accurate estimate possible, we must minimize sampling error, if possible.

Scatter Diagram, *n.* a plot of dots on a Cartesian graph.

Discussion: The points are not connected or joined by lines. Scatter diagrams are often used to examine the correlation between two variables.

Example: The first scatter diagram below shows the relationship between age and salary. Scatter diagrams are also used to visually fit a regression line through points as shown in the second scatter diagram below. The second scatter diagram includes a best-fit line.

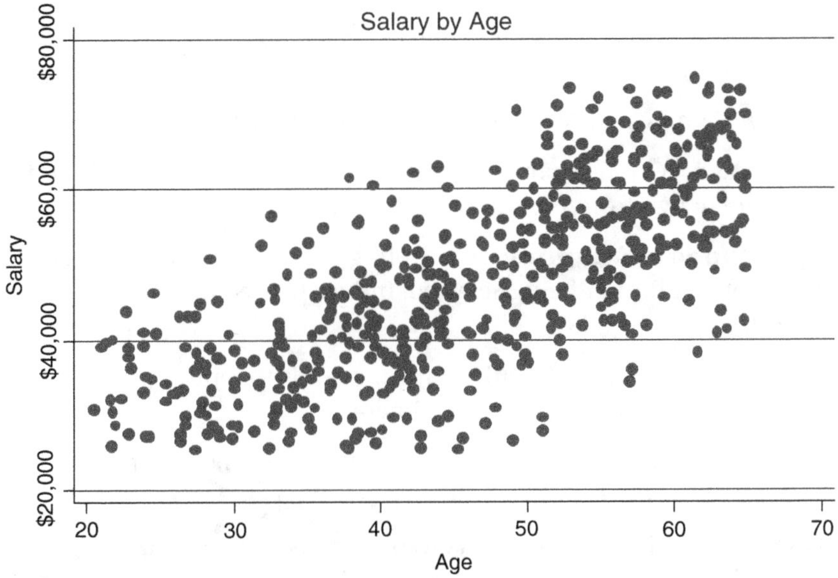

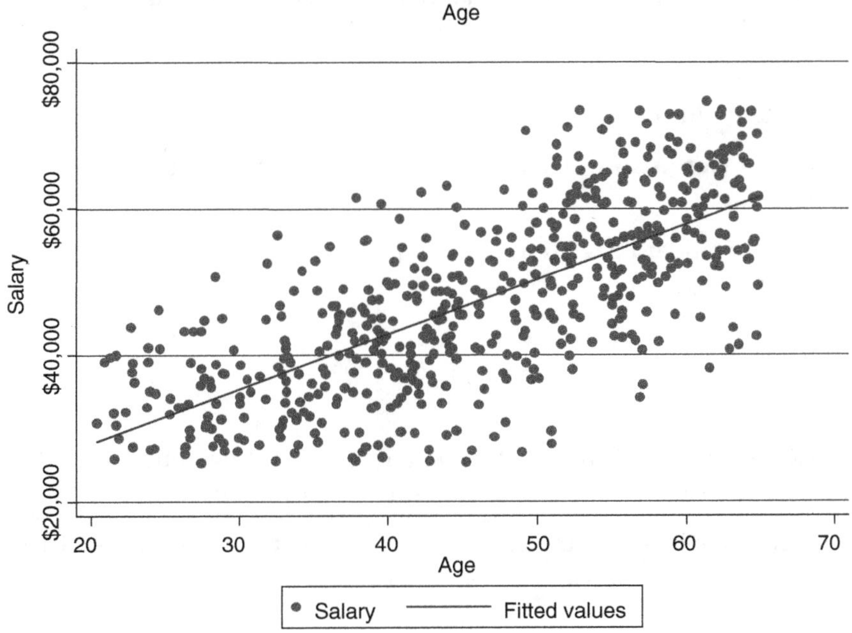

Seasonal Component, *n.* the component of a time series that is dependent on the time of the year.

Set, *n.* a collection of numbers or items that generally have at least one thing in common.

Shortfall, *n.* the difference between the actual and predicted outcomes.

Significance Level, *n.* the probability of rejecting a true null hypothesis in a statistical test.

Discussion: Significance levels are usually set to be small.

Sign Test, *n.* a non-parametric test of the null hypothesis that two samples are drawn from the same parent population.

Simple Random Sampling, *n.* sampling in which every individual has an equal probability of being selected and each selection is independent of the others.

Simulation, *n.* the use of mathematical models to reproduce a situation or process in order to carry out experiments.

Skew, *adj.* not equally distributed around the mean (i.e., the probabilities above and below the mean are not equal).

Discussion: If a distribution is skewed, the median and mean do not coincide.

Small Sample, *n.* a sample whose size is small, so results must be interpreted cautiously.

Standard Deviation, *n.* a measure of the dispersion of the data observations.

Discussion: Standard deviation is also equal to the square root of variance. Mathematically:

$$\sigma = \frac{1}{n}\sum_{i=1}^{n}(x_i - \bar{x})^2$$

Standard Error of Regression, *n.* a measure of how much the actual values differ from the projected values of a regression model.

Standardization, *n.* a transformation of the data such that the distribution has a mean of 0 with a standard deviation of 1.

Discussion: Standardization can be carried out using the following mathematical equation:

$$z = \frac{(x - \mu)}{\sigma}$$

Where μ is the mean, σ is the standard deviation, x is the original value, and z is the new value. Standardization allows tables to be used for certain distributions.

Stochastic Process, *n.* a random process.

Discussion: Usually a stochastic process involves a variable measure at different points in time or space that can be in one of a number of states.

Example: A Markov chain is a stochastic process where the present state depends on the history of previous states.

Stratified Sampling, *n.* a method of sampling that selects individuals from different strata within the sample space.

Discussion: Stratified sampling routines in employment analyses are commonly used to account for job-related variations across employees.

Subset, *n.* a set with all elements contained inside of another set.

Summation Notation, *n.* the use of $\sum$ to mean "the sum of" all the elements.

Discussion: Mathematically, the summation notation can be expressed as follows:

$$\sum_{n=1}^{n} x_n = x_1 + x_2 + \cdots + x_n$$

Sum of Squares, *n.* the summation of the squares of deviation from the mean.

Discussion: Mathematically, the sum of squares can be written as one of two equivalent expressions:

$$\sum_i (x_i - \bar{x})^2 = \sum_i x_i^2 - n\bar{x}^2$$

T

t-Distribution, *n.* a mathematical continuous probability density function that is similar in shape to the normal distribution.

Time Series, *n.* a set of values of a variable recorded over a period of time.

Time Series Analysis, *n.* a statistical analysis of data taken from a single source at different times.

Trimmed Mean, n. the average value of data excluding outliers.

Discussion: If the employment data contains extremely small or extremely large data observations, the arithmetic mean may not provide the best measure of the data's average value. Removing the largest and smallest or outlying data observations and then calculating the mean may produce a more accurate depiction of the average employment outcome.

t-Test, *n.* a statistical test based on the t-distribution probability distribution function.

Discussion: The t-test of the mean is used to examine differences in average scores.

Example:

<u>The One-Sample t-Test for a Population Mean</u>

This is used to test whether the mean of the data is equal to a specified value. For example, is the average salary of African-American software engineers at Company X equal to $50,000? To perform the test, we assume that the data was generated from a normal population or a large sample and that the standard deviation of the data is unknown. If the standard deviation of the data was known, we would use a z-test instead.

We test the null hypothesis that $H_0 : \mu = \mu_0$ or, as in our example, that average salary is equal to $50,000. The test statistic is computed as:

$$t = \frac{\bar{x} - \mu_0}{s/\sqrt{n}}$$

Where $\bar{x}$ is the sample mean, μ_0 is the value we are testing ($50,000), s is the sample standard deviation, and n is the number of observations. The null hypothesis is rejected if t is greater than the critical value with $n - 1$ degrees of freedom. These numbers are obtained from a table for the given significance level.

The Pooled t-Test for Two Population Means

This is used to test whether the mean of one population is equal to the mean of another population. For example, is the average salary of African-American software engineers at Company X equal to that of white software engineers? To perform the test, we assume independent samples, normal populations or large samples, and equal population standard deviations. Then we test the null hypothesis that $H_0 : \mu_1 = \mu_2$. The test statistic is computed as:

$$t = \frac{\bar{x}_1 - \bar{x}_2}{s_p\sqrt{(1/n_1) + (1/n_2)}}$$

where:

$$s_p = \sqrt{\frac{(n_1 - 1)s_1^2 + (n_2 - 1)s_2^2}{n_1 + n_2 - 2}}$$

and $\bar{x}$ is the population mean, s is the sample standard deviation, and n is the number of observations. The subscripts 1 and 2 denote the pool. The null hypothesis is rejected if t is greater than the critical value with $n_1 + n_2 - 2$ degrees of freedom. These numbers are obtained from a table for given significance level.

Two or Three Standard Deviation Rule, *n.* a rule stating that the difference between an observed and expected outcome is statistically significant if it is more than two or three times as large as its standard deviation.

Type 1 and Type 2 Errors, *n.* errors in hypothesis testing.

U

Uniform Distribution, *n.* a continuous distribution that is constant over a certain range of values and zero elsewhere.

Union, *n.* a set containing all the members of two sets.

Universal Set, *n.* the set of all elements from which the members of a particular set can be drawn.

V

Variable, *n.* any characteristic that may differ from one element or individual of a population to another.

Example: Gender, race, and employee tenure are all variables.

Variance, *n.* a measure of the spread of a dataset.

Discussion: Variance is the average of the squared standard deviation of each observation from the dataset's mean. Formally, variance, denoted σ_x^2, is:

$$\frac{1}{n}\sum_{i=1}^{n}(x_i - \bar{x})^2$$

where $\bar{x}$ is the mean of the dataset. Written out, the variance is:

$$\frac{1}{n}\left[(x_1 - \bar{x})^2 + (x_2 - \bar{x})^2 + \ldots + (x_n - \bar{x})^2\right]$$

To calculate variance, subtract the mean salary from each observed salary. Then square the differences. Divide the sum of the differences by the total number of observations.

W

Weight, *n.* a coefficient assigned to data to show relative importance or correct sampling errors.

See Also: Sampling error, weighted mean.

Weighted Mean, *n.* an average that is computed after assigning weights of relative importance to different values.

Discussion: Formally:

$$\bar{x} = \frac{w_1x_1 + w_2x_2 + \cdots + w_nx_n}{w_1 + w_2 + \cdots + w_n}$$

where w_i is the weight assigned to x_i.

Example: Assume an analyst wants to estimate economic damages for a minor child. Using an ordered probabilistic regression and factors concerning the child's family, the economist calculates the probability of different levels of educational attainment and the earnings loss for each level of education:

Education Level	**Probability of Achieving Education Level**	**Earnings Loss associated with Education Level**
Less than High School	0%	$400,000
High School	10%	$500,000
Some College, no degree	15%	$600,000
Bachelor's Degree	40%	$750,000
Postgraduate	35%	$1,250,000

The economist also wants to present the total expected earnings loss. He or she uses a weighted mean to calculate the total expected earnings loss. The weighted mean is calculated by multiplying the probability of achieving each education level by the associated earnings loss. That is:

$$\begin{aligned}\text{Expected Loss} &= 0 \times \$400,000 + 0.10 \times \$500,000 + 0.15 \times \$600,000 \\ &\quad + 0.40 \times \$750,000 + 0.35 \times \$1,250,000 \\ &= 0 + \$50,000 + \$90,000 + \$300,000 + \$437,500 \\ &= \$877,500\end{aligned}$$

See Also: Mean, probit regression, weight.

Wilcoxon Matched-Pairs Signed-Rank Test, *n.* a non-parametric test of the null hypothesis that two matched samples are drawn from the same parent population.

Z

z-Test, *n.* a commonly used statistical test for population means and proportions.

Discussion: The z-test assumes the data has a normal distribution and is most appropriate when the sample size is large or the data has a normal distribution.

Example:

The One-Sample z-Test for a Population Mean

This is used to test whether the mean of the data is equal to a specified value. For example, is the average salary of an African-American software engineer at Company X equal to $50,000? To perform the test, we assume a normal population or large sample and that the standard deviation of the data is known. If the standard deviation of the data were unknown (as is typically the case in employment litigation), we would use a t-test instead.

We test the null hypothesis that $H_0 : \mu = \mu_0$ or, as in our example, that average salary is equal to $50,000. The test statistic is computed as:

$$z = \frac{\bar{x} - \mu_0}{\sigma / \sqrt{n}}$$

where $\bar{x}$ is the sample mean, μ_0 is the value we are testing ($50,000), σ is the standard deviation of the data, and n is the number of observations. The null hypothesis is rejected if z is greater than the critical value elected for the normal distribution. For a two-tailed test, z values greater than 1.96 are significant at the 5% level and z values greater than 2.58 are significant at the 1% level.

The One-Sample z-Test for a Population Proportion

This is used to test whether a population proportion is equal to a specified value. For example, are half of all new hires female at Company X? To perform the test, we assume the population size is sufficiently large. Then we test that null hypothesis that $H_0 : p = p_0$ or, as in our example, that the proportion of new hires who are female is equal to $^1/_2$. The test statistic is computed as:

$$z = \frac{\hat{p} - p_0}{\sqrt{p_0(1 - p_0)/n}}$$

where $\hat{p}$ is the sample proportion, p_0 is the value we are testing ($^1/_2$ in the example), and n is the sample size. The null hypothesis is rejected if z is greater than the critical value selected for the normal distribution. For a two-tailed test, z values greater than 1.96 are significant at the 5% level and z values greater than 2.58 are significant at the 1% level.

The Two-Sample z-Test for Two Population Proportions

This is used to test whether two population proportions are equal to each other. For example, are employees over the age of 40 terminated at the same rate as younger employees at Company Y? To perform the test, we assume that the two samples are independent (i.e., no one belongs to both samples). We also assume the two samples are sufficiently large.

We test that null hypothesis that $H_0 : p_1 = p_2$ or, as in our example, that the proportion of employees over the age of 40 who are terminated is the same as the proportion of employees under the age of 40 who are terminated. The test statistic is computed as:

$$z = \frac{\hat{p}_1 - \hat{p}_2}{\sqrt{\hat{p}_p(1 - \hat{p}_p)}\sqrt{(1/n_1) + (1/n_2)}}$$

where $\hat{p}_1, \hat{p}_2$ are the sample proportions of samples 1 and 2, n_1, n_2 are the sample sizes, and $\hat{p}_p = (x_1 + x_2)/(n_1 + n_2)$. The null hypothesis is rejected if z is greater than the critical value elected for the normal distribution. For a two-tailed test, z values greater than 1.96 are significant at the 5% level and z values greater than 2.58 are significant at the 1% level.

See Also: Hypothesis testing, normal distribution, null hypothesis, probability, statistical significance.

Employment Datasets

American Time Use Survey

The American Time Use Survey (ATUS) is commonly used to estimate the amount of time spent on household services for valuing losses in personal injury and wrongful death cases. ATUS is sponsored by the U.S. Bureau of Labor Statistics and administered by the Census Bureau. It measures the amount of time people spend doing various activities, such as working for pay, caring for children, volunteering, commuting, and socializing.

The survey was given to 21,000 individuals in 2003 and 14,000 individuals in 2004. It asks participants to account for every hour between 4 a.m. the day before the interview and 4 a.m. the day of the interview. Using this data, it is possible to construct the average number of hours spent on household services based on demographic characteristics. The categories most often used to measure household services are time spent:

- Performing inside housework
- Cooking food and cleaning up after a meal
- Caring for pets, performing household maintenance, and maintaining vehicles
- Managing the household
- Shopping
- Obtaining services
- Traveling for household activities
- Caring for and helping household children
- Caring for and helping household adults
- Caring for and helping non-household members
- Traveling to care for and help household members
- Traveling to care for and help non-household members

For more information, refer to www.bls.gov/tus/home.htm

Census

Conducted every ten years, the Census is the largest survey in the United States. The 2000 Census gathered information on 281.4 million people across the United States. The 100% characteristics form was used with every person and housing unit in the United States. It includes information on sex, age, and race by geographic location. Census data is available at many geographic levels, including blocks, zip codes, county, and state.

The 2000 Census asked detailed questions that include information on educational attainment, marital status, labor-force status, and income. The Census is a very large database and hence has many uses ranging from racial profiling in police-stop baselines to wage data.

For more information, refer to www.census.gov.

Census of Fatal Occupational Injuries

The Census of Fatal Occupational Injuries, conducted by the Bureau of Labor Statistics, provides data on the number of fatal on-the-job injuries by type, occupation, industry, or worker characteristics. This data is sometimes used to statistically value a life. Dangerous jobs tend to offer a wage premium in exchange for additional risk of death on the job. Some economists have attempted to quantify the value of life based on the additional wages that must be paid for a worker to accept an increased chance of a fatal accident.

For more information, visit www.bls.gov/iif/oshcfoi1.htm.

Consumer Expenditure Survey

The Consumer Expenditure Survey (CEX) is conducted for the U.S. Census Bureau and the Bureau of Labor Statistics. It studies the expenditures, income, and household characteristics of American consumers. CEX is often used in wrongful death cases to estimate a personal consumption factor.

The personal consumption factor is the amount of income the decedent would have spent on personal expenditures and therefore would not have been used for household expenses or other members of the household. Personal consumption includes expenditures on food, clothing, alcohol, transportation, etc. This factor is generally estimated using the expenditure data from CEX and regression analysis.

For more information, refer to www.bls.gov/cex.

Consumer Price Index

The Consumer Price Index is monthly data released by the Bureau of Labor Statistics on the change in prices paid by urban consumers for a representative basket of goods and services. The CPI is available by region and consumer type. It is most often used to measure inflation. Inflation is an important concern when present-valuing economic damages in the future. Future damages must be discounted by the rate of inflation, because one dollar today is worth more than one dollar tomorrow.

Note: Even though CPIs differ by city, it is not appropriate to use CPI data to compare the cost of living between cities. The CPI does not measure price differentials between cities, but rather only over time. The representative basket of goods and services varies with geographic location.

For more information, refer to www.bls.gov/cpi.

Current Employment Statistics

The Current Employment Statistics program surveys approximately 160,000 businesses to provide detailed industry data on employment, hours, and earnings. This data is useful for determining the average amount of overtime worked in an industry.

For more information, refer to www.bls.gov/ces.

Current Population Survey

The Current Population Survey is a monthly survey of approximately 50,000 households conducted by the Bureau of Labor Statistics and the U.S. Census Bureau. The CPS collects a vast amount of data and is an excellent resource for information on labor-force characteristics.

The basic monthly CPS provides general demographic information as well as employment status, industry, and occupation. The monthly survey is often used to examine unemployment rates and the duration of unemployment. The Bureau of Labor Statistics publishes tables reporting the unemployment rate and the average and median duration of unemployment by gender and age, race, or marital status. These tables are generally referenced in wrongful termination cases to show the expected length of time it will take the plaintiff to find a new job.

In addition to the basic monthly survey, the CPS includes monthly supplements. These supplements include displaced workers, job tenure and mobility, and a demographic supplement (often referred to as the March supplement), just to name a few.

The job tenure supplement can be used to estimate the amount of time an individual would have likely remained at a job if the termination had not occurred. The demographic supplement is often used to determine average and median wages for particular education levels. Additionally, regression analysis can be used to estimate lifecycle earnings for individuals based on their age or years of experience, education, and other pertinent demographic factors.

For more information, refer to www.bls.census.gov/cps.

Equal Employment Opportunity Census

The Equal Employment Opportunity (EEO) Census is a tabulation created every ten years for the purpose of serving as an external benchmark for comparing the composition of a company's workforce to that of the external labor market within a specific geographic area and job category. The EEO Census provides worker counts based on race, ethnicity, gender, age, education level, industry, occupation, and geography. While the raw data is not readily available, 24 tables provide counts for varying cuts of the data.

The EEO Census is most often seen in Affirmative Action Plans and EEO Commission compliance reviews. It is also useful in the litigation setting to compare a defendant's workforce composition to that of comparable companies when there are allegations of discrimination.

For more information, refer to:
www.census.gov/hhes/www/eeoindex/eeoindex.html.

Job Openings and Labor Turnover Survey

The Job Openings and Labor Turnover Survey is a monthly survey conducted by the Bureau of Labor Statistics. JOLTS collects data on total employment, the number of job openings, the number of hires, and the number of separations including quits and layoffs. JOLTS can be used to measure the growth of a particular industry and to better understand labor-market opportunities.

For more information, refer to www.bls.gov/jlt.

Local Area Unemployment Statistics

Local Area Unemployment Statistics, available from the Bureau of Labor Statistics, offers data on employment and unemployment for 7,200 geographic areas. Unemployment rates are available monthly by county, MSA, and state level. These rates may be compared over time to examine changes in the labor market.

For more information, refer to www.bls.gov/lau.

National Longitudinal Survey of Youth

The National Longitudinal Survey of Youth (NLSY) is a longitudinal study by the Bureau of Labor Statistics that repeatedly surveys approximately 12,000 individuals every two years. These individuals, selected at the beginning of the survey, are followed over time and surveyed on factors such as the individual's educational and employment experiences.

Ordered probit regressions and the NLSY can be used to estimate the probability of different levels of educational attainment. The probability of an individual obtaining a high school or college degree can be calculated based on demographic characteristics, such as race and gender, and household characteristics, such as family structure or parental educational attainment levels.

For more information, refer to www.bls.gov/nls.

Occupational Employment Statistics

The Occupational Employment Statistics program, conducted by the Bureau of Labor Statistics, provides employment and wage information by occupation and geographic location. Hourly and annual mean and median wages are available for more than 800 different occupations at the national, regional, state, and MSA level.

For more information, refer to www.bls.gov/oes.

Occupational Information Network

The Occupational Information Network is a government database of worker attributes and job characteristics. It is the replacement for the Dictionary of Occupational Titles. The database contains information about knowledge, skills, and ability requirements for various occupations, as well as conditions of the work environment. The data can be mapped to other occupational databases, such as the Equal Employment Opportunity Census and Occupational Employment Statistics, to determine how occupational skill requirements, such as heavy lifting, affect workforce composition, such as the gender distribution.

For more information, refer to www.onetcenter.org.

Panel Study of Income Dynamics

The Panel Study of Income Dynamics is a longitudinal survey conducted by the University of Michigan. The PSID has been following families since 1968, collecting data on economic, health, and social behavior.

For more information, refer to psidonline.isr.umich.edu.

Employment Cases Using Statistical Analyses

U.S. Supreme Court Cases

Miller-El v. Cockrell, 537 U.S. 322 (2003)
National Railroad Passenger Corporation v. Morgan, 536 U.S. 101 (2002)
Kolstad v. American Dental Association, 527 U.S. 526 (1999)
O'Connor v. Consolidated Coin Caterers Corp., 517 U.S. 308, 134 L. Ed. 2d 433 (1996)
Ticor Title Ins. Co. v. Brown, 511 U.S. 117 (1994)
Daubert v. Merrell Dow Pharmaceuticals, 509 U.S. 579 (1993)
City of Richmond v. J.A. Croson Co., 488 U.S. 469 (1989)
Wards Cove Packing Company v. Antonio , 490 U.S. 642, 109 S.Ct. 2115, 493 U.S. 802 (1989)
Watson v. Fort Worth Bank & Trust, 487 U.S. 977, 108 S.Ct. 2777 (1988)
Bazemore v. Friday, 478 U.S. 385, 106 S. Ct.3000 (1986)
General Telephone Co. v. Falcon, 457 U.S. 395 (1982)
State of Connecticut v. Teal, 457 U.S. 440 (1982)
Upjohn Co. v. United States, 449 U.S. 383, 101 S.Ct. 677 (1981)
New York Transit Authority v. Beazer, 440 U.S. 568 (1979)
United Steelworkers v. Weber, 443 U.S. 193 (1979)
Coopers & Lybrand v. Livesay, 437 U.S. 463 (1978)
Furnco Construction Corp. v. Waters, 438 U.S. 567 (1978)
Castenada v. Partida, 430 U.S. 482, 97 S. Ct. 1272 (1977)
Dothard v. Rawlinson, 433 U.S. 321, 97 S.Ct. 2720 (1977)
Hazelwood School District v. United States, 433 U.S. 299; 97 S.Ct. 2742 (1977)
International Brotherhood of Teamsters v. United States, 431 U.S. 324, 97 S. Ct. 1843 (1977)
United Air Lines v. Evans, 431 U.S. 553 (1977)
Albemarle Paper Co. v. Moody, 422 U.S. 405, 95 S. Ct. 2362 (1975)
Eisen v. Carlisle & Jacquelin, 417 U.S. 156 (1974)
McDonnell Douglas Corp. v. Green, 411 U.S. 792, 93 S. Ct. (1973)
Teamsters v. United States, 431 U.S. 324 (1973)
Griggs v. Duke Power Company, 401 U.S. 424, 91 S.Ct. 849 (1971)

U.S. Appeals Court Cases

1st Circuit

Fudge v. Providence Fire Department, 766 F.2d 659 1st Cir. (1985)
LeBlanc v. Great American Ins. Co., 6 F.3d 836, 848 1st Cir. (1993)
LaPlace-Bayard v. Batlle , 295 F.3d 157 1st Cir. (2002)

2nd Circuit

Coser v. Moore, 739 F.2d 746, 750 2d Cir. (1984)
Zahorik v. Cornell Univ., 729 F.2d 85, 92–93 2d Cir. (1984)
Woodbury v. New York City Trans. Auth., 832 F.2d 764, 771 2d Cir. (1987)
Sobel v. Yeshiva Univ., 839 F.2d 18, 20–21 2d Cir. (1988)
Ottaviani v. State University of New York at New Paltz, 875 F. 2d 365, 371 2d Cir. (1989)
Waisome v. Port Auth., 948 F. 2d 1370, 1376 2nd Cir. (1991)
In Re Six Grand Jury Witnesses, 979 F.2d 939 2d Cir. (1992)
McCullock v. H.B. Fuller, 61 F.3d 1038 2d Cir. (1995)
EEOC v. Joint Apprenticeship Committee of Industry Board of Electrical Industry, 164 F. 3d 87, 96–97, 110 2nd Cir. (1998)
Hollander v. American Cynamid Co., 172 F.3d 192 2nd Cir. (1999)
Caridad v. Metro-North Commuter Railroad, 191 F.3d 283, 291–93 2d Cir. (1999)
EEOC v. Joint Apprenticeship Committee of Industry Board of Electrical Industry, 186 F.3d 110 2d Cir. (1999)
Joseph v. New York City Board of Education, 171 F.3d 87, 97 2d Cir. (1999)
Pietras v. Board of Fire Commissioners, 180 F.3d 468, 2d Cir. (1999)
Smith v. Xerox Corporation, 196 F.3d 358, 365 2d Cir. (1999)
Robinson v. Metro-North Comuter R.R., 267 F.3d 147, 160 2d. Cir. (2001)
Lavin-McEleney v. Marist College , 239 F.3d 476 2d Cir. (2001)
Amorgianos v. Amtrak, 303 F.3d 256, 268–69 2d Cir. (2002)
Malave v. Potter, 320 F.3d 321, 327 2d Cir. (2003)
Meacham v. Knolls Atomic Power Laboratory, 2004 U.S. App. LEXIS 17873, *46 2d Cir. (2004)

3rd Circuit

Mazus v. Dept. of Transp., 629 F.2d 870 3d Cir. (1980)
In Re Paoli R.R. Yard PCB Litigation, 35 F.3d 717 3d Cir. (1994)
Kannankeril v. Terminix International Inc., 128 F.3d 802, 806 3d Cir. (1996)
Lanning v. Southeastern Transportation Authority, 199 U.S. App. LEXIS 14607 3rd Cir. (1999)
Heller v. Shaw Industries, Inc., 167 F.3d 146, 153 3d Cir. (1999)
Elcock v. Kmart Corp., 233 F.3d 734 3rd Cir. (2000)
Oddi v. Ford Motor Co., 234 F.3d 136 3rd Cir. (2000)

Newton v. Merrill Lynch, Pierce, Fenner & Smith, Inc., 259 F.3d 154 3rd Cir. (2001)
Johnston v. HBO Film Mgmt., Inc., 265 F.3d 178 3d Cir. (2001)
Vulcan Pioneers v. New Jersey Dep't. of Civil Serv., 625 F. Supp. 527, aff'd 832 F.2d 811 3rd Cir. (1985, 1987)

4th Circuit

EEOC v.Radiator Specialty Co., 610 F.2d 178 4th Cir. (1979)
United States v. County of Fairfax, 629 F.2d 932 4th Cir. (1980)
EEOC v. Federal Reserve Bank of Richmond, 698 F.2d 633, 648–49 4th Cir. (1983)
United States v. Dorsey, 45 F.3d 809 4th Cir. (1995)
Smith v. Virginia Commonwealth University, 84 F.3d 672 4th Cir. (1996)
Lowery v. Circuit City Stores, 158 F.3d 742, 7861 4th Cir. (1998)
Oglesby v. GMC, 190 F.3d 244 4th Cir. (1999)
Bryant v. Aiken Regional Medical Centers Incorporated, 333 F.3d 536 4th Cir. (2003)

5th Circuit

Alabama v. United States, 304 F.2d 58, aff'd, 371 U.S. 37 3 5th Cir. (1962)
Rowe v. General Motors Corp., 457 F.2d 348 5th Cir. (1972)
Hester v. Southern Ry Co., 497 F.2d 1374, 1379 5th Cir. (1974)
Robinson v. Union Carbide, 538 F.2d 652, 658 5th Cir. (1976)
Williams v. Tallahassee Motors, Inc., 607 F.2d 689 5th Cir. (1979)
Fisher v. Proctor & Gamble Mfg. Co., 613 F.2d 527 5th Cir. (1980)
Pouncy v. Prudential Ins. Co., 668 F.2d 795 5th Cir. (1982)
Markey v. Tenneco Oil Co., 635 F.2d 497 5th Cir. (1982)
Rivera v. City of Wichita Falls, 665 F.2d 531 5th Cir. (1982)
Wheeler v. City of Columbus, Mo., 686 F.2d 1144, 1152 5th Cir. (1982)
Carrol v. Sears, Roebuck & Co., 708 F.2d 183, 191 5th Cir. (1983)
Plemer v. Parsons-Gilbane,, 713 F.2d 1127, 1136–7 5th Cir. (1983)
Page v. U.S. Industries, Inc., 726 F.2d 1038, 1054 5th Cir. (1984)
Bunch v. Bullard, 795 F.2d 284 5th Cir. (1986)
Rendon v. AT&T Technologies, 883 F.2d 388, 397–98 5th Cir. (1989)
Uffelman v. Lone Star Steel Company, 863 F.2d 404 5th Cir. (1989)
Johnson v. Uncle Ben's, Inc., 965 F.2d 1363 5th Cir. (1992)
Carroll v. Morgan, 17 F.3d 787 5th Cir. (1994)
Allison v. Citgo Petroleum Corp., 1998 U.S. App. LEXIS 9773 5th Cir. (1998)
Black v. Food Lion, Inc., 171 F.3d 308 5th Cir. (1999)
Munoz v. Orr, Secretary of US Department of the Air Force, 200 F.3d 291 5th Cir. (2000)
Pipitone v. Biomatrix, Inc., 288 F.3d 239 5th Cir. (2002)
Tyler v. Union Oil Co., 304 F.3d 279, 393 5th Cir. (2002)
James v. Stockham Valves and Fittings Co., 394 F. Supp. 434 5th Cir. (1975, 1977)

Trevino v. Holly Sugar Corp., 811 F.2d 896 5th Cir. (1987)
USM Corp. v. American Aerosols, Inc., 631 F.2d 420 6th Cir. (1980)

6th Circuit

EEOC v. Atlas Paper Box Co., 868 F.2d 1487 6th Cir. (1989)
Barnes v. Gencorp, Inc., 896 F.2d 1457, 1469 6th Cir. (1990)
United States v. Bonds, 12 F.3d 540 6th Cir. (1993)
Glaser v. Thompson Medical Co., Inc., 32 F.3d 969 6th Cir. (1994)
Kovacevich v. Kent State University, 224 F.3d 806 6th Cir. (2000)
Nelson v. Tennessee Gas Pipeline Co., 243 F.3d 244 6th Cir. (2001)
First Tennessee Bank Nat'l Ass'n. v. Barreto, 268 F.3d 319 6th Cir. (2001)
Hopson v. Daimler Chrysler Corp., 306 F.3d 427 6th Cir. (2003)
Hopson v. Daimler Chrysler Corp., 306 F.3d 427 6th Cir. (2003)
Van Aken v. Young, 541 F. Supp. 448, aff'd, 750 F.2d 43 6th Cir. (1982, 1984)

7th Circuit

Garcia v. Rush-Presbyterian-St. Luke's Medical Ctr., 660 F.2d 1217 7th Cir. (1981)
Craik v. Minnesota State University Board, 731 F.2d 465 7th Cir. (1984)
Coates v. Johnson & Johnson, 756 F. 2d 524, 536–48 7th Cir. (1985)
Shidaker v. Carlin, 782 F.2d 746 7th Cir. (1986)
Billish v. City of Chicago, 962 F.2d 1269, 1285 7th Cir. (1992)
Fisher v. Transco Services-Milwaukee, Inc., 979 F.2d 1239 7th Cir. (1992)
EEOC v. Francis W. Parker School, 41 F.3d 1073, 1076 7th Cir. (1994)
Melendez v. Illinois-Bell Telephone Co., 79 F.3d 661 7th Cir. (1995)
Hartley v. Wisconsin Bell, Inc., 124 D.3d 887 7th Cir. (1997)
Council 31, AFSCME v. Doherty, 169 F.3d 1068, 1071, n.1 7th Cir. (1999)
Huey v. United Parcel Service, Inc., 165 F.3d 1084 7th Cir. (1999)
Kidd v. Ill. State Police, 167 F.3d 1084 7th Cir. (1999)
NutraSweet Co. v. X-L Eng'g Co., 227 F.3d 776 7th Cir. (2000)
Smith v. Ford Motor Co., 215 F.3d 713 7th Cir. (2000)
Bell v. EPA, 232 F.3d 546 7th Cir. (2000)
Chavez v. Illinois State Police, 251 F.3d 612 7th Cir. (2001)
Guerro v. Ashcroft, 253 F.3d 309 7th Cir. (2001)
Kadas v. MCI Systemhouse, F. 3d 7th Cir. (2001)
Szabo v. Bridgeport Machs., Inc., 249 F.3d 672 7th Cir. (2001)
Adams v. Ameritech Services, Inc, 231 F.3d 414, 423 7th Cir. (2001)
Bennett v. Roberts, 295 F.3d 687 7th Cir. (2002)
United States v. City of Chicago, 411 F. Supp. 218, aff'd in relevant part, 549 F.2d 415 7th Cir. (1976, 1977)
EEOC v. Chicago Miniature Lamp Works, 622 F. Supp. 1281 7th Cir. (1985, 1991)
EEOC v. Sears Roebuck & Co., 628 F. Supp 1264 7th Cir. (1986, 1988)

8th Circuit

EEOC v. Rath Packing Co., 787 F.2d 318 8th Cir. (1985)
Catlett v. Missouri Highway & Transp. Comm'n, 828 F.2d 1260 8th Cir. (1987)
MacDissi v. Valmont Industries, Inc., 856 F.2d 1054, 1058 8th Cir. (1988)
Schultz v. McDonnell Douglas Corp., 105 F.3d 1258 8th Cir. (1997)
United States v. Molina, 172 F.3d 1048, 1056–57 8th Cir. (1999)
Thomas v. Caldera, 221 F.3d 1344 8th Cir. (2000)
Morgan v. UPS of America, Inc., 2994 U.S.App. LEXIS 18272, *12 8th Cir. (2004)

9th Circuit

Gay v. Waiters' & Dairy Lunchmen's Union, 694 F.2d 531, 551 9th Cir. (1982)
Clady v. County of Los Angeles, 770 F.2d 1421 9th Cir. (1985)
AFSCME v. Washington, 770 F.2d 1363 , 1401 9th Cir. (1985)
Diaz v. American Telephone & Telegraph, 752 F.2d 1356, 1363 9th Cir. (1985)
Palmer v. United States, 794 F.2d 534 9th Cir. (1986)
Sengupta v. Morrison-Knudsen Co. Inc., 804 F.2d 1072, 1076 9th Cir. (1986)
Eldredge v. Carpenter, 833 F.2d 1334 9th Cir. (1987)
Penk v. Oregon State Bd. Of Higher Educ., 816 F.2d 458, 464 9th Cir. (1987)
Rose v. Wells Fargo & Co., 962 F.2d 1417 9th Cir. (1990)
Associated General Contractors of Cal. v. Coalition, 950 F.2d 1401, 1415 9th Cir. (1991)
Bouman v. Block, 940 F.2d 1211 9th Cir. (1991)
Coral Construction Company v. King County, 941 F. 2d 910, 918–19 9th Cir. (1991)
Shutt v. Sandoz Crop Protection Corp., 944 F.2d 1431, 923 F.2d 722 9th Cir. (1991)
Antonio v. Wards Cove Packing Co., Inc., 10 F.3d 1485 9th Cir. (1993)
Nesbit v. Pepsico, Inc., 994 F.2d 703 9th Cir. (1993)
Cerrato v. San Francisco Community College Dist., 26 F.3d 968, 977 n.21 9th Cir. (1994)
Daubert v. Merrell Dow Pharmaceuticals, 43 F.3d 1311 9th Cir. (1995)
Mangold v. California Public Utilities Com'n, 67 F.3d 1470, 1477 9th Cir. (1995)
Warren v. City of Carlsbad, 58 F.3d 439 9th Cir. (1995)
United States v. Equivel, 88 F.3d 722 9th Cir. (1996)
United States v. Artero, 121 F.3d 1256 9th Cir. (1997)
Walker v. American Home Shield Long-Term Disability Plan, 180 F.3d 1065 9th Cir. (1999)
Association of Mexican-American Educators v. California, 231 F.3d 572 9th Cir. (2000)
Fox v. Bonneville Power Admin., 2000 US LEXIS 31914 9th Cir. (2000)
Gile v. Olsten Health Corp., 2000 U.S. App. LEXIS 31191 9th Cir. (2000)
Ford v. Long Beach Unified School Dist., 291 F.3d 1086 9th Cir. (2002)
Mukhtar v. California State University, No. 01–15565, 2002 WL 1799785, 89 FEP (BNA) 849 9th Cir. (2002)

Paige v. State of California, 291 F.3d 1141, modified 2002 U.S. App. LEXIS 14463 9th Cir. (2002)
Ruderbusch v. Hughes, 313 F.3d 506 9th Cir. (2002)
Stout v. Potter, 276 F.3d 1118 9th Cir. (2002)
Beck v. Boeing, 2003 U.S. App. LEXIS 3619 9th Cir. (2003)
Pottenger v. Potlach Corporation, 329 F.3d 740 9th Cir. (2003)

10th Circuit

Ortega v. Safeway Stores, Inc., 943 F. 2d 1230, 1242 10th Cir. (1991)
Fallis v. Kerr-McGee Corporation, 944 F.2d 743, 746 10th Cir. (1991)
Rea v. Martin-Marietta Corp., 29 F.3d 1450, 1454 10th Cir. (1994)
Corneveaux v. CUNA Mutual Insurance Group, 76 F.3d 1498 10th Cir. (1996)
Bullington v. United Air Lines, Inc., 186 F.3d 1301, 1313 10th Cir. (1999)
Walther v. Lonestar Gas Company, 977 F.2d 161, 162 10th Cir. (1999)
Baker v. Ogden Servs. Corp., 74 F.3d 1248 10th Cir. (2000)

11th Circuit

Eastland v. Tennessee Valley Authority, 704 F.2d 613 11th Cir. (1983)
Griffin v. Carlin, 755 F.2d 1516 11th Cir. (1985)
Maddox v. Claytor, 764 F.2d 1539 , 1550–1551 11th Cir. (1985)
Kilgo v. Bowman Transportation, Inc., 789 F.2d 859, 868 11th Cir. (1986)
Powers v. Alabama Dept. of Educ., 854 F.2d 1285 11th Cir. (1988)
Hamer v. City of Atlanta, 872 F.2d 1521 11th Cir. (1989)
MacPherson v. University of Montevallo, 922 F.2d 766, 770–73 11th Cir. (1991)
Fitzpatrick v. City of Atlanta, 2 F.3d 1112, 1118 11th Cir. (1993)
Armstrong v. Flowers Hospital, Inc., 33 F.3d 1308, 1314 11th Cir. (1994)
Forehand v. Florida State Hospital, 89 F.3d 1562, 1574 11th Cir. (1996)
Kumho Tire Co. v. Carmichael, 526 U.S. 137 11th Cir. (1999)
Alexander v. Fulton County, 207 F.3d 1303, 1327–28 11th Cir. (2000)
Alexander v. Fulton County, 207 F.3d 1303 11th Cir. (2000)
EEOC v. Joe's Stone Crab, Inc., 220 F. 3d 1263 11th Cir. (2000)
Denney v. City of Albany, 247 F.3d 1172, 1185–86 11th Cir. (2001)
Hipp v. Liberty National Life Insurance Company, 252 F.3d 1208 11th Cir. (2001)

U.S. District Court Cases

Alabama

Wright v. Circuit City Stores, Inc., 201 F.R.D. 526 N.D. Ala. (2001)
Reynolds v. Alabama Dept. of Transportation, 955 F. Supp. 1428 M.D. Ala. (1997)
Murry v. Griffin Wheel Co., 172 F.R.D. 459 N.D. Ala. (1997)

Arkansas

Richardson v. Sugg, 325 F. Supp. 2d 919, 935 E.D. Ark. (2004)

California

Dukes v. Wal-Mart Stores, Inc., 222 F.R.D. 137 N.D. Cal. (2004)
FMC Corp. v. Vendo Co., 196 F. Supp. 2d 1023 E.D. Cal. (2002)
Butler v. Home Depot, U.S. Dist. LEXIS 16296 N.D. Cal. (1997)
Stender v. Lucky Stores, 803 F.Supp. 250 N.D. Cal. (1992)
McCaugherty v. Sifferman, 132 F.R.D. 234 N.D. Cal. (1990)
Hewlett-Packard Co. v. Bausch & Lomb, Inc., 116 F.R.D. 533 N.D. Cal. (1987)
In Re Pizza Time Theatre Securities Litigation, 113 F.R.D. 94 N.D. Cal. (1986)
Adams v. Pinole Point Steel Co., 1994 WL 515347 N.D. Cal. (1994)

Colorado

Gerrits v. Brannen Banks of Florida, Inc., 138 F.R.D. 574 D. Colo. (1991)

Connecticut

Robertson v. Sikorsky Aircraft Corp., No. 397 Civ. 1216, 2000 WL 33381019 D. Conn. (2001)
Messier v. Southbury Training Sch., No. 3:94CV1706, 1998 WL 422858 D. Conn. (1998)
Ouadrini v. Sikorsky Aircraft Division, 74 F.R.D. 594 D. Conn. (1977)
Anderson v. Zubieta, 180 F.3d 329 D.C. Cir. D.C. (1999)
Berger v. Iron Workers Reinforced Rodmen, Local 201, 170 F.3d 1111, 1121–22 D.C. Cir. D.C. (1999)
Coward v. ADT Security Systems, Inc., 140 F.3d 271 D.C. Cir. D.C. (1998)
Csicseri v. Bowsher, 862 F. Supp. 547 D. D.C. (1994)
Nakajima v. General Motors Corp., 857 F. Supp. 100 D. D.C. (1994)
Green v. Kinney Shoe Corp., 715 F. Supp. 1122 D. D.C. (1989)
Segar v. Smith, 738 F.2d 1249 D. D.C. (1984)
Trout v. Lehman, 702 F.2d 1094 D. D.C. (1983)
Marine Petroleum Co. v. Champlin Petroleum Co., 641 F.2d 984 D. D.C. (1979)
EEOC v. DuPont, 445 F. Supp. 223 D. Del. (1977)
Dyer v. Publix Super Mkt., Inc., No. 97–2706, Civ. T25E, 2000 WL 33339613 M.D. Fla. (2000)
Vincent v. Wells Fargo Guard Services, Inc. of Florida, 3 F.Supp.2d 1405, 1415 S.D. Fla. (1998)
Shores v. Publix Super Markets, Inc., 69 Empl. Prac. Dec. (CCH) para. 44, 477 M.D. Fla. (1996)
Kane v. Freeman, 10 Fla. L. Weekly Fed., D648 M.D. Fla. (1994)
Haynes v. Shoneys, Inc., 803 F. Supp. 393 N.D. Fla. (1992)

Rhodes v. Cracker Barrel Old Country Store, Inc., 213 F.R.D. 619 N.D. Ga. (2003)
Reid v. Lockheed Martin Aeronautics Co., 205 F.R.D. 655 N.D. Ga. (2001)
Ward v. Gulfstream Aerospace Corp., Inc., 894 F.Supp 1573, 1580 S.D. Ga. (1995)
Spearman Indus. v. St. Paul Fire & Marine Ins. Co., 128 F. Supp. 2d 1148 N.D. Ill (2001)
Gibbs v. G.D. Searle Co., 2000 U.S. Dist. LEXIS 9651 N.D. Ill (2000)
Karn v. Ingersoll Rand, 168 F.R.D. 633 N.D. Ill (1996)
Stanczyk v. Black & Decker, Inc., 836 F. Supp. 565 N.D. Ill (1993)
Adams v. R.R. Donnelley & Sons, No. 98 Civ. 4025, 2001 WL 336830 N.D. Ill. (2001)
Betts v. Sundstrand Corp., No. 97 Civ. 50188, 1999 WL 436579 N.D. Ill. (1999)
Billion v. Metro. Pier & Exposition Auth., 163 F.R.D. 517 N.D. Ill. (1995)
Eliasen v. Hamilton, 111 F.R.D. 396 N.D. Ill. (1986)
Dominguez v. Syntex Laboratories, Inc., 149 F.R.D. 158 S.D. Ind. (1993)
EEOC v. Von Maur Stores, No. Civ. 3:04-CV-00159-RP-RAW ECF S.D. Iowa (2008)
Brown v. Ringstad, 142 F.R.D. 461 S.D. Iowa (1992)
Western Resources, Inc. v. Union Pacific Railroad Co., No. 00-2043-CM, 2002 WL 181494 D. Kan. (2002)
Johnson v. Gmeinder, 191 F.R.D. 638 D. Kan. (2000)
Simmons v. City of Kansas City, No. 88-2603-0, 1992 WL 403096, *4 D. Kan. (1992)
Coates v. AC & S, Inc., 133 F.R.D. 109 E.D. La (1990)
Hillstrom v. Best Western TLC Hotel, 2003 U.S. Dist. LEXIS 8854 D. Mass. (2003)
Suskind v. Home Depot Corp., No. 99-10575, 2001 WL 92183 D. Mass. (2001)
Carson v. Giant Food Inc., 187 F.Supp.2d 462, 47 n.8 D. Md. (2002)
Haworth, Inc. v. Miller, Inc., 162 F.R.D. 289 W.D. Mich. (1995)
Morgan v. UPS of America, Inc., 143 F.Supp.2d 1143 E.D. Mo. (2000)
Shoemaker by Embree v. General Motors Corp., 154 F.R.D. 235 W.D. Mo. (1994)
Heitmann v. Concrete Pipe Machinery, 98 F.R.D. 740 E.D. Mo. (1983)
Reap v. Cont'l Cas. Co., 199 F.R.D. 536, 544 D. N.J. (2001)
DeMarco v. Lehman Brothers, Inc., 2004 U.S. Dist. LEXIS 12438, *10, *11 S.D. N.Y. (2004)
Aniero Concrete Supply Co., Inc. v. New York City School Const. Auth., 94 Civ. 9111 S.D. N.Y. (2002)
EEOC v. Venator Group, Specialty, Inc., 2002 U.S. Dist LEXIS 1724 Southern District N.Y. (2002)
Herman v. Marine Midland Bank, 207 F.R.D. 26 W.D. N.Y. (2002)
Rodolico v. Unisys Corp, 199 F.R.D. 468, 475 E.D. N.Y. (2001)
Moore U.S.A., Inc. v. Standard Register Co., 206 F.R.D. 72 W.D. N.Y. (2001)
United States v. N.Y. City Bd. of Educ., 85 F. Supp. 2d 130 E.D. N.Y. (2000)
W.R. Grace & Co. v. Zotos Intl, Inc., No 98-CV-838S, 2000WL 1843258 W.D. N.Y. (2000)
Krueger v. N.Y. Tele. Co., 163 F.R.D. 433, S.D. N.Y. (1995)

United States Postal Service v. Phelps Dodge Refining Corp., 852 F. Supp 156 E.D. N.Y. (1994)

Grindell v. American Motors Corp., 108 F.R.D. 94 W.D. N.Y. (1985)

Caston v. Duke University, 34 F.E.P. 102, 108 N.D. ND (1983)

AFSCME v. County of Nassau, 609 F. Supp. 695 ED NY (1985, 1987)

United Black Firefighters Ass'n v. City of Akron, 66 Fair Empl. Prac. Cases (BNA) 1452 N.D. Ohio (1994)

Webb v. Merck & Co., Inc., 206 F.R.D. 399 E.D. Pa. (2002)

Walrath v. Veteran's Administration, No. Civ. 4:07-cv-03089 S.D. Texas (2008)

Winslow v. Harris County et al., No. Civ. H-07-00767 S.D. Texas (2008)

Davis-Morgan v. DART, No. Civ. 3:04cv-1412-M N.D. Texas (2005)

Deborah Osborn v. Computer Sciences Corporation, No. Civ. A04CA158LY W.D. Texas (2005)

Nika McLin vs. Police Chief Juan Rodriguez, Officer C. Lynch, and DART, No. Civ. 3:03cv-1464-N N.D. Texas (2005)

Thomas v. Deloitte Consulting LP, No. Civ. A. 3-02-CV-0343, 2004 WL 1960097, *5 N.D. Texas (2004)

EEOC v. Mercantile Thrift, No. Civ. 4:02-cv-01348 S.D. Texas (2003)

Webb et. al. v. Barnes Group Inc., No. Civ. H-99-4544 N.D. Texas (2002)

EEOC v. Greensheet Inc., No. Civ. H-99-4526 S.D. Texas (2001)

Coleman et. al. v. Exxon Chemical Company, No. Civ. H-99-4543 S.D. Texas (2001)

Smith et. al. v. Texaco et. al, No. 1:97-cv-00272-HC E.D. Texas (1996)

In Re Sinking of Barge "Ranger I" etc., 92 F.R.D. 486 S.D. Texas (1981)

Vuyanich v. Republic Bank, 505 F. Supp 224; 24 FEP 128 N.D. Texas (1980)

Cooper v. University of Texas, 482 F. Supp 187 N.D. Texas (1979)

Trigon Ins. Co. v. United States,, 204 F.R.D. 277 E.D. Va. (2001)

Crockett v. Virginia Folding Box Co., 61 F.R.D. 312 E.D. Va. (1974)

Abram v. UPS, 200 F.R.D. 424, 426 E.D. Wis. (2001)

Daubert related Employment Cases

Appellate Court Cases

1st Circuit

Case Caption: Currier vs. United Techs. Corp.
Citation: 393 F.3d 246; 94 Fair Empl. Prac. Cas. (BNA) 1735
Lexis: 2004 U.S. App. LEXIS 26798
Outcome: Plaintiff's statistical analysis is admissible.
Court: 1st Circuit **Court Level:** Appellate
Challenged Party: Plaintiff

2nd Circuit

Case Caption: Hollander vs. American Cyanamid Co.
Citation: 172 F.3d 192,75 Empl. Prac. Dec. (CCH) P45,898
Lexis: 1999 U.S. App. LEXIS 5447
Outcome: Appeals court finds that District court acted within its discretion in holding the statistical evidence presented by witness inadmissible because no reasonable jury could infer from it that defendant discriminated against plaintiff because of his age.
Court: 2nd Circuit **Court Level:** Appellate

4th Circuit

Case Caption: Smith vs. Virginia Commonwealth University
Citation: 84 F.3d 672; 70 Fair Empl. Prac. Cas. (BNA) 1248
Lexis: 1996 U.S. App. LEXIS 10919
Outcome: Court notes that Defense statistical analysis is incomplete but does not exclude evidence.
Court: 4th Circuit **Court Level:** Appellate
Challenged Party: Defense

5th Circuit

Case Caption: Ross vs. University of Texas

Citation: 139 F.3d 521; 79 Fair Empl. Prac. Cas. (BNA) 788; 73 Empl. Prac. Dec. (CCH) P45,351; 49 Fed. R. Evid. Serv. (Callaghan) 545
Lexis: 1998 U.S. App. LEXIS 8039
Outcome: Plaintiff's statistical analysis is inadmissible.
Court: 5th Circuit **Court Level:** Appellate
Challenged Party: Plaintiff

Case Caption: Munoz vs. Orr
Citation: 200 F.3d 291; 81 Fair Empl. Prac. Cas. (BNA) 1318; 77 Empl. Prac. Dec. (CCH) P46,297; 53 Fed. R. Evid. Serv. (Callaghan) 1131
Lexis: 2000 U.S. App. LEXIS 63
Outcome: Plaintiff's statistical analysis is inadmissible.
Court: 5th Circuit **Court Level:** Appellate
Challenged Party: Plaintiff

6th Circuit

Case Caption: Kovacevich vs. Kent State Univ.
Citation: 224 F.3d 806; 2000 FED App. 0281P (6th Cir.); 83 Fair Empl. Prac. Cas. (BNA) 1306; 79 Empl. Prac. Dec. (CCH) P40,387; 55 Fed. R. Evid. Serv. (Callaghan) 728 **Lexis:** 2000 U.S. App. LEXIS 21436
Outcome: Plaintiff's self-performed statistical study is excluded.
Court: 6th Circuit **Court Level:** Appellate
Challenged Party: Plaintiff

7th Circuit

Case Caption: Sheehan vs. Daily Racing Form
Citation: 104 F.3d 940; 72 Fair Empl. Prac. Cas. (BNA) 1390; 69 Empl. Prac. Dec. (CCH) P44,442 72 Fair Empl. Prac. Cas. (BNA) 1390; 69 Empl. Prac. Dec. (CCH) P44,442 **Lexis:** 1997 U.S. App. LEXIS 640
Outcome: Statistical analysis is inadmissible.
Court: 7th Circuit **Court Level:** Appellate

Case Caption: Chavez vs. Illinois State Police
Citation: 251 F.3d 612; 49 Fed. R. Serv. 3d (Callaghan) 1127
Lexis: 2001 U.S. App. LEXIS 10560
Outcome: Statistical analysis is deemed unreliable by Court.
Court: 7th Circuit **Court Level:** Appellate

8th Circuit

Case Caption: Morgan vs. UPS of America
Citation: 380 F.3d 459; 94 Fair Empl. Prac. Cas. (BNA) 591
Lexis: 2004 U.S. App. LEXIS 18272

Outcome: Court finds substance of statistical expert report is not sufficient to ward off summary judgement.
Court: 8th Circuit **Court Level:** Appellate
Challenged Party: Plaintiff

Case Caption: Morgan vs. UPS of America
Citation: 380 F.3d 459; 94 Fair Empl. Prac. Cas. (BNA) 591
Lexis: 2004 U.S. App. LEXIS 18272
Outcome: Court finds substance of statistical expert report is not sufficient to ward off summary judgement.
Court: 8th Circuit **Court Level:** Appellate
Challenged Party: Plaintiff

District Court Cases

California

Case Caption: Dukes vs. Wal-Mart Stores, Inc.
Citation: 93 Fair Empl. Prac. Cas. (BNA) 1629
Lexis: 2004 U.S. Dist. LEXIS 11297
Outcome: Plaintiffs' statistical expert's declaration has enough probative value to warrant class certification on the issue of commonality.
Court: California, Northern District **Court Level:** Trial Court
Challenged Party: Plaintiff

Case Caption: Dukes vs. Wal-Mart Stores, Inc.
Citation: 93 Fair Empl. Prac. Cas. (BNA) 1671
Lexis: 2004 U.S. Dist. LEXIS 11365
Outcome: Court strike's defendant's manager survey but allows testimony in other areas.
Court: California, Northern District **Court Level:** Trial Court
Challenged Party: Defense

Case Caption: Dukes vs. Wal-Mart Stores, Inc.
Citation: 93 Fair Empl. Prac. Cas. (BNA) 1671
Lexis: 2004 U.S. Dist. LEXIS 11365
Outcome: Defendant's motion to strike a small portion of declaration granted.
Court: California, Northern District **Court Level:** Trial Court
Challenged Party: Plaintiff

District of Columbia

Case Caption: Mcreynolds vs. Sodexho Marriott Servs.
Citation: 349 F. Supp. 2d 1 **Lexis:** 2004 U.S. Dist. LEXIS 25516

Outcome: Court denies defendant's Daubert motion to exclude statistical evidence.
Court: District of Columbia **Court Level:** Trial Court
Challenged Party: Plaintiff

Case Caption: Mcreynolds vs. Sodexho Marriott Servs.
Citation: 349 F. Supp. 2d 1 **Lexis:** 2004 U.S. Dist. LEXIS 25516
Outcome: Defendant's statistical evidence is deemed unreliable.
Court: District of Columbia **Court Level:** Trial Court
Challenged Party: Defense

Case Caption: McReynolds vs. Sodexho Marriott Servs.
Citation: **Lexis:** 2004 U.S. Dist. LEXIS 25488
Outcome: Plaintiff's statistical analysis is admissible.
Court: District of Columbia **Court Level:** Trial Court
Challenged Party: Plaintiff

Florida

Case Caption: Culley vs. Trak Microwave Corp.
Citation: 117 F. Supp. 2d 1317; 84 Fair Empl. Prac. Cas. (BNA) 847
Lexis: 2000 U.S. Dist. LEXIS 15668
Outcome: Statistical analysis is inadmissible.
Court: Florida, Middle District **Court Level:** Trial Court

Case Caption: Perry vs. Orange County
Citation: 341 F.Supp. 2d 1197 **Lexis:** 2004 U.S. Dist. LEXIS 21132
Outcome: Plaintiff's statistical analysis is inadmissible.
Court: Florida, Middle District **Court Level:** Trial Court
Challenged Party: Plaintiff

Case Caption: Perry vs. Orange County
Citation: Unpublished
Outcome: Plaintiff's statistical analysis is inadmissible.
Court: Florida, Middle District **Court Level:** Trial Court
Challenged Party: Plaintiff

Georgia

Case Caption: Webster vs. Fulton County
Citation: 85 F. Supp. 2d 1375 **Lexis:** 2000 U.S. Dist. LEXIS 3778
Outcome: Statistical analysis is inadmissible.
Court: Georgia, Northern District **Court Level:** Trial Court

Illinois

Case Caption: Gerlib vs. R.R. Donnelley & Sons Co.
Citation: 27 Employee Benefits Cas. (BNA) 1168
Lexis: 2001 U.S. Dist. LEXIS 17879
Outcome: Statistical analysis is admissible.
Court: Illinois, Northern District **Court Level:** Trial Court

Case Caption: Petit vs. City of Chicago
Citation: 82 Empl. Prac. Dec. (CCH) P40, 994 **Lexis:** 2002 U.S. Dist. LEXIS 38
Outcome: Plaintiff's objections to defense expert's qualification leads to exclusion of statistical report.
Court: Illinois, Northern District **Court Level:** Trial Court
Challenged Party: Defense

Case Caption: Kay vs. First Continental Trading
Citation: 976 F. Supp. 772; 48 Fed. R. Evid. Serv. (Callaghan) 76
Lexis: 1997 U.S. Dist. LEXIS 14908
Outcome: Statistical analysis is inadmissible.
Court: Illinois, Northern District **Court Level:** Trial Court
Challenged Party: Plaintiff

Case Caption: Mi-Jack Prods. vs. International Union of Operating Eng'rs, Local 150 **Lexis:** 1995 U.S. Dist. LEXIS 16930
Outcome: Court grants motion to exclude plaintiffs' statistical evidence.
Court: Illinois, Northern District **Court Level:** Trial Court
Challenged Party: Plaintiff

Case Caption: Kitchen vs. TTX Co. **Lexis:** 1999 U.S. Dist. LEXIS 9975
Outcome: Court grants motion to exclude statistical evidence.
Court: Illinois, Northern District **Court Level:** Trial Court

Case Caption: Reeves vs. FRB **Lexis:** 2004 U.S. Dist. LEXIS 5730
Outcome: Plaintiff's statistical analysis is deemed to be inadmissible.
Court: Illinois, Northern District **Court Level:** Trial Court
Challenged Party: Plaintiff

Case Caption: Gerlib vs. R.R. Donnelley & Sons Co.
Lexis: 2002 U.S. Dist. LEXIS 10023
Outcome: Statistical analysis is admissible.
Court: Illinois, Northern District **Court Level:** Trial Court

Case Caption: Roy vs. Austin Co. **Lexis:** 1998 U.S. Dist. LEXIS 13374
Outcome: Statistical analysis is admissible.
Court: Illinois, Northern District **Court Level:** Trial Court

Case Caption: Kitchen vs. TTX Co. **Lexis:** 1999 U.S. Dist. LEXIS 9975
Outcome: Statistical analysis is inadmissible.
Court: Illinois, Northern District **Court Level:** Trial Court

Case Caption: Janes vs. Chicago Board of Education
Lexis: 2002 U.S. Dist. LEXIS 22239
Outcome: Plaintiff's statistical analysis is inadmissible.
Court: Illinois, Northern District **Court Level:** Trial Court

Louisiana

Case Caption: Smith vs. Petroleum Helicopters, Inc.
Lexis: 1999 U.S. Dist. LEXIS 18080
Outcome: Defendant's statistical analysis is admissible.
Court: Louisiana, Eastern District **Court Level:** Trial Court
Challenged Party: Defense

Case Caption: Reid vs. Albemarle Corp.
Citation: 207 F. Supp. 2d 499; 89 Fair Empl. Prac. Cas. (BNA) 392
Lexis: 2001 U.S. Dist. LEXIS 24505
Outcome: Plaintiff's statistical analysis is deemed to be inadmissible.
Court: Louisiana, Middle District **Court Level:** Trial Court
Challenged Party: Plaintiff

Case Caption: Reid vs. Albemarle Corp.
Citation: 207 F. Supp. 2d 499; 89 Fair Empl. Prac. Cas. (BNA) 392
Lexis: 2001 U.S. Dist. LEXIS 24506
Outcome: Plaintiff's statistical analysis is deemed to be inadmissible.
Court: Louisiana, Middle District **Court Level:** Trial Court
Challenged Party: Plaintiff

Case Caption: Reid vs. Albemarle Corp.
Citation: 207 F. Supp. 2d 499; 89 Fair Empl. Prac. Cas. (BNA) 392
Lexis: 2001 U.S. Dist. LEXIS 24506
Outcome: Court appointed expert to assist in technical issues presented in motion to exclude plaintiff's expert testimony resulting in denial of plaintiff's expert testimony.
Court: Louisiana, Middle District **Court Level:** Trial Court
Challenged Party: Court

Maine

Case Caption: Currier vs. United Techs. Corp.
Citation: 93 Fair Empl. Prac. Cas. (BNA) 1517
Lexis: 2004 U.S. Dist. LEXIS 7424
Outcome: Plaintiff's statistical analysis is admissible.
Court: Maine **Court Level:** Trial Court
Challenged Party: Plaintiff

Case Caption: Currier vs. United Techs **Lexis:** 2003 U.S. Dist. LEXIS 3698
Outcome: Plaintiff's statistical analysis is admissible.
Court: Maine **Court Level:** Trial Court
Challenged Party: Plaintiff

Maryland

Case Caption: Buchanan vs. Consol. Stores Corp.
Lexis: 2003 U.S. Dist. LEXIS 13516
Outcome: Plaintiff's statistical analysis is admitted in part.
Court: Maryland **Court Level:** Trial Court
Challenged Party: Plaintiff

Massachusetts

Case Caption: Flebotte vs. Dow Jones & Co.
Lexis: 2000 U.S. Dist. LEXIS 19875
Outcome: Statistical analysis is admissible.
Court: Massachusetts **Court Level:** Trial Court
Challenged Party: Plaintiff

Michigan

Case Caption: Mims vs. Electronic Data Sys. Corp.
Citation: 975 F. Supp. 1010 **Lexis:** 1997 U.S. Dist. LEXIS 12668
Outcome: Statistical analysis is inadmissible.
Court: Michigan, Eastern District **Court Level:** Trial Court

Case Caption: Ballor vs. Alcona County Rd. Comm'n
Lexis: 1997 U.S. Dist. LEXIS 4337
Outcome: Statistical analysis is inadmissible.
Court: Michigan, Eastern District **Court Level:** Trial Court

Missouri

Case Caption: Morgan vs. UPS of America
Citation: 143 F. Supp. 2d 1143 **Lexis:** 2000 U.S. Dist. LEXIS 21327

Outcome: Court finds substance of statistical expert report is not sufficient to ward off summary judgement.
Court: Missouri, Eastern District **Court Level:** Trial Court
Challenged Party: Plaintiff

Case Caption: Morgan vs. UPS of America
Citation: 143 F. Supp. 2d 1143 **Lexis:** 2000 U.S. Dist. LEXIS 21327
Outcome: Court finds substance of statistical expert report is not sufficient to ward off summary judgement.
Court: Missouri, Eastern District **Court Level:** Trial Court
Challenged Party: Plaintiff

Case Caption: Yapp vs. Union Pac. R.R. Co.
Citation: 301 F. Supp. 2d 1030; 63 Fed. R. Evid. Serv. (Callaghan) 826
Lexis: 2004 U.S. Dist. LEXIS 1661
Outcome: Defendant's statistical analysis is inadmissible.
Court: Missouri, Eastern District **Court Level:** Trial Court
Challenged Party: Defense

New Jersey

Case Caption: Planned Parenthood of Central New Jersey vs. Vernier
Citation: 22 F. Supp. 2d 331; 50 Fed. R. Evid. Serv. (Callaghan) 1309
Lexis: 1998 U.S. Dist. LEXIS 14319
Outcome: Defendant's statistical analysis is admissible.
Court: New Jersey **Court Level:** Trial Court
Challenged Party: Defense

Case Caption: McKenna vs. Pacific Rail Serv.
Citation: 67 Fair Empl. Prac. Cas. (BNA) 735; 817 F. Supp. 498
Lexis: 1993 U.S. Dist. LEXIS 4104
Outcome: Plaintiff's statistical analysis is inadmissible.
Court: New Jersey **Court Level:** Trial Court
Challenged Party: Plaintiff

New York

Case Caption: Wyche vs. Marine Midland
Citation: 73 Fair Empl. Prac. Cas. (BNA) 1600
Lexis: 1997 U.S. Dist. LEXIS 2613
Outcome: Plaintiffs' motion to exclude statistical testimony denied except as regards testimony concerning proportional hazards model.
Court: New York, Southern District **Court Level:** Trial Court
Challenged Party: Defense

Case Caption: EEOC vs. Venator Group
Citation: 88 Fair Empl. Prac. Cas. (BNA) 157
Lexis: 2002 U.S. Dist. LEXIS 1724
Outcome: Statistical analysis is admissible.
Court: New York, Southern District **Court Level:** Trial Court

Case Caption: Ellis vs. Provident Life & Accident Ins. Co.
Citation: 926 F. Supp. 417; 71 Fair Empl. Prac. Cas. (BNA) 88
Lexis: 1996 U.S. Dist. LEXIS 6979
Outcome: Court finds that Plaintiffs' expert's flawed analyses and insufficient to establish violation of age discrimination law.
Court: New York, Southern District **Court Level:** Trial Court
Challenged Party: Plaintiff

Case Caption: EEOC vs. Morgan Stanley & Co.
Citation: Lexis: 2004 U.S. Dist. LEXIS 12673
Outcome: Plaintiff's statistical analysis is admissible.
Court: New York, Southern District **Court Level:** Trial Court
Challenged Party: Plaintiff

Case Caption: EEOC vs. Morgan Stanley & Co.
Citation: Lexis: 2004 U.S. Dist. LEXIS 12724
Outcome: Plaintiff's testimony is properly admitted.
Court: New York, Southern District **Court Level:** Trial Court
Challenged Party: Plaintiff

Case Caption: EEOC vs. Morgan Stanley & Co.
Citation: Lexis: 2004 U.S. Dist. LEXIS 12673
Outcome: Defendant's statistical analysis is admissible.
Court: New York, Southern District **Court Level:** Trial Court
Challenged Party: Defense

Case Caption: Wado vs. Xerox Corp.
Citation: 991 F. Supp. 174; 75 Fair Empl. Prac. Cas. (BNA) 1807
Lexis: 1998 U.S. Dist. LEXIS 681
Outcome: Statistical analysis is inadmissible.
Court: New York, Western District **Court Level:** Trial Court

Case Caption: Layaou vs. Xerox Corp.
Citation: 999 F. Supp. 426 **Lexis:** 1998 U.S. Dist. LEXIS 4456
Outcome: Motion to exclude Defendant's reduction in force analysis not ruled as case is dismissed.
Court: New York, Western District **Court Level:** Trial Court
Challenged Party: Defense

Case Caption: Layaou vs. Xerox Corp.
Citation: 999 F. Supp. 426 **Lexis:** 1998 U.S. Dist. LEXIS 4456
Outcome: Dismissal of ADEA claim renders moot the proposed expert testimony regarding reduction in force statistics.
Court: New York, Western District **Court Level:** Trial Court
Challenged Party: Plaintiff

Oklahoma

Case Caption: Anderson vs. Boeing Co.
Citation: Lexis: 2004 U.S. Dist. LEXIS 11671
Outcome: Plaintiff's statistical analysis is admissible.
Court: Oklahoma, Northern District **Court Level:** Trial Court
Challenged Party: Plaintiff

Pennsylvania

Case Caption: Kelly vs. Drexel Univ.
Citation: 907 F. Supp. 864; 69 Fair Empl. Prac. Cas. (BNA) 593; 5 Am. Disabilities Cas. (BNA) 1101 **Lexis:** 1995 U.S. Dist. LEXIS 16873
Outcome: Court finds substance of statistical expert report is not sufficient to ward off summary judgement.
Court: Pennsylvania, Eastern District **Court Level:** Trial Court
Challenged Party: Plaintiff

Case Caption: Dunn vs. Hercules
Citation: Lexis: 1995 U.S. Dist. LEXIS 1891
Outcome: Statistical analysis admitted in part.
Court: Pennsylvania, Eastern District **Court Level:** Trial Court

Texas

Case Caption: Vance vs. City of Nacogdoches
Citation: 198 F. Supp. 2d 858; 83 Empl. Prac. Dec. (CCH) P41, 140
Lexis: 2002 U.S. Dist. LEXIS 7813
Outcome: Plaintiffs' statistical testimony is deemed admissible by Court but insufficient to establish disparate impact.
Court: Texas, Eastern District **Court Level:** Trial Court
Challenged Party: Plaintiff

Case Caption: Metzler vs. Express 60-Minutes Delivery
Lexis: 1997 U.S. Dist. LEXIS 11217
Outcome: Statistical analysis is inadmissible.
Court: Texas, Northern District **Court Level:** Trial Court

West Virginia

Case Caption: Ramseur vs. Reich
Citation: Lexis: 1997 U.S. Dist. LEXIS 23635
Outcome: Statistical analysis is deemed unreliable by Court.
Court: West Virginia, Southern District **Court Level:** Trial Court

Bibliography

Aaron, Henry J. "The Economic Status of African-Americans." *Journal of Economic Perspectives* 4.4 (1990): 3–7.

Abram, Thomas G., and George R. Neumann. "Economic and Statistical Analysis of Discrimination in Terminations, Layoffs, and Reductions in Force." *Industrial Relations Research Association* Proceedings of the Thirty-Sixth Annual Meeting of the Industrial Relations Research Association.1 (1984): 22–33.

Aigner, Dennis J. *A statistical theory of discrimination in labor markets (Discussion papers - Institute for Research on Poverty; 228–74)*. Madison: University Of Wisconsin–Madison, 1974.

Albright, S. Christian, Wayne Winston, and Christopher Zappe. *Data Analysis and Decision Making with Microsoft Excel, (with CD-ROM and Decision Tools and Statistic Tools Suite), Revised*. Mason, OH: South-Western College Pub, 2008.

Albright, S. Christian, Wayne Winston, and Christopher Zappe. *Data Analysis and Decision Making with Microsoft Excel, (with CD-ROM and Decision Tools and Statistic Tools Suite), Revised*. Mason, OH: South-Western College Pub, 2008.

Anderson, David R., Dennis J. Sweeney, and Thomas A. Williams. *Statistics for Business and Economics, Revised (with Student CD-ROM)*. Mason, OH: South-Western College Pub, 2008.

Anderson, L. *Handbook on the economics of discrimination*. Northampton: Edward Elgar Publishing, 2006.

Anker, Richard. "Theories of Occupational Segregation by Sex." *International Labor Review* 136.3 (1997): unknown.

Ashenfelter, Orley. *Labor Economics: Worth Series in Outstanding Contributions*. New York: Worth Publishers, 1998.

Ashenfelter, Orley. *The economics of discrimination thirty years later: Economists enter the courtroom (Working paper / Industrial Relations Section, Princeton University)*. Washington D.C.: Industrial Relations Section, Princeton University, 1986.

Ashraf, J. "Is Gender Pay Discrimination on the Wane?: Evidence From Panel Data, 1968–1989." *Industrial and Labor Relations Review* 49.3 (1996): 537–46.

Austen-Smith, David, and Roland Fryer. "An Economic Analysis of "Acting White"." *The Quarterly Journal of Economics* 120.2 (2005): 551–583.

Baldus, David C. "Book Review: Quantitative Methods in Law: Studies in the Application of Mathematical Probability and Statistics to Legal Problems." *Yale Law Journal* 89 (1980): 601.

Baldus, David C. *Statistical proof of discrimination.* Dubuque: Shepherd's/Mcgraw-Hill, 1980.

Baldus, James W L Cole David C. *Statistical Proof of Discrimination.* New York: McGraw-Hill, 1980.

Baldus, James W L Cole David C. *Statistical Proof of Discrimination.* New York: McGraw-Hill, 1980.

Bayard, Kimberly. "New Evidence on Sex Segregation and Sex Differences in Wages from Matched Employee-Employer Data." *Journal of Labor Economics* 21.4 (2003): 887–922.

Becker, Gary S. *The Economics of Discrimination (Economic Research Studies).* Chicago: University Of Chicago Press, 1971.

Beeson Royalty, Anne. "Job to Job and Job to Nonemployment Turnover by Gender and Education Level." *Journal of Labor Economics* 16.2 (1998): 392–433.

Bellante, Don, and Mark Jackson. *Labor Economics: Choice in Labor Markets.* New York: Mcgraw-Hill (Tx), 1983.

Benson, P. George, James T. Mcclave, and Terry Sincich. *Statistics for Business & Economics (10th Edition).* Alexandria, VA: Prentice Hall, 2007.

Berenson, Mark L., Timothy C. Krehbiel, David M. Levine, and David Stephan. *Statistics for Managers Using Microsoft Excel, Fourth Edition.* Alexandria, VA: Prentice Hall, 2004.

Betts, Julian R. "The Impact of School Resources on Women's Earnings and Educational Attainment: Findings from the National Longitudinal Survey of Young Women." *Journal of Labor Economics* 19.3 (2001): 635–657.

Black, Dan, Natalia Kolesnikova, and Lowell Taylor. "Earnings Functions When Wages and Prices Vary by Location." *Journal of Labor Economics* 27.1 (2009): 21–47.

Blau, David M. "Labor Force Dynamics of Older Men." *Econometrica* 62.1 (1994): 117–156.

Blau, Francine D. "Changes in the Labor Supply Behavior of Married Women: 1980–2000." *Journal of Labor Economics* 25.3 (2007): 393–438.

Bloom, David E., and Mark R. Killingsworth. "Symposium: FEO Policies and Research." *Pay Discrimination Research and Litigation: The Use of Regression* 21. Symposium (1982): 318.

Boston, Thomas D. *Affirmative Action and Black Entrepreneurship (A Century Foundation Book).* New York: Routledge, 1998.

Bound, John. *What went wrong?: The erosion of relative earnings and employment among young black men in the 1980s (NBER working papers series).* New York: National Bureau Of Economic Research, 1991.

Brown, Charles. "Sex-Based Differences in School Content and the Male-Female Wage Gap." *Journal of Labor Economics* 15.3 (1997): 431–465.

Cain, Glen George. *The economic analysis of labor market discrimination: A survey (IRP reprint series)*. Wisconsin: University Of Wisconsin-Madison, Institute For Research On Poverty, 1986.

Carlson, William L., Paul Newbold, and Betty Thorne. *Statistics for Business and Economics and Student CD (6th Edition)*. Alexandria, VA: Prentice Hall, 2006.

Carlson, William L., and Betty Thorne. *Applied Statistical Methods: For Business, Economics, and the Social Sciences*. Alexandria, VA: Prentice Hall, 1996.

Carlson, William L., and Betty Thorne. *Applied Statistical Methods: For Business, Economics, and the Social Sciences*. Alexandria, VA: Prentice Hall, 1996.

Carrington, W.J., K. McCue, and B. Pierce. "Black/White Wage Convergence: The Role of Public Sector Wages and Employment." *Industrial Labor Relations Review* 49.3 (1996): 456–471.

Carrington, William J. *Interfirm segregation and the black/white wage gap (CES)*. Washington: Center For Economic Studies, U.S. Dept. Of Commerce, Bureau Of The Census, 1996.

Chan, Sewin. *Job loss and retirement behaviour of older men (NBER working paper series)*. New York: National Bureau Of Economic Research, 1999.

Chiswick, Barry R. "Racial Discrimination in the Labor Market - A Test of Alternative Hypotheses." *Patterns of Racial Discrimination* 1.1 (1974): 107–19.

Clayton, Gary E. *A Guide to Everyday Economic Statistics*. New York: Mcgraw-hill Companies, 1997.

Cleves, Mario, William Gould, Roberto Gutierrez, and Yulia Marchenko. *An Introduction to Survival Analysis Using Stata, Second Edition*. New York: Stata Press, 2008.

Cohn, Richard M. "On the Use of Statistics in Employment Discrimination Cases." *Indiana Law Journal* 55 (1980): 493.

Connolly, Michael, Walter B. Connolly, and David W. Peterson. *Use of Statistics in Equal Employment Opportunity Litigation*. New York: Law Journal Seminars Press, 1979.

Darity, William. "Evidence on Discrimination in Employment: Codes of Color, Codes of Gender." *Journal of Economic Perspectives* 12.2 (1998): 63–90.

David A. Freedman, David H. Kaye. "Reference Guide on Statistics, in Federal Judicial Center and The Carnegie Corporation of New York, ed.,." *Reference Manual on Scientific Evidence* Federal Judicial Center and The Carnegie Corporation of New York, ed.,. Federal Judicial Center and The Carnegie Corporation of New York, ed., (1994): 331–93.

Davis, Jules, and John P. Fernandez. *Race, Gender and Rhetoric: The True State of Race and Gender Relations in Corporate America*. New York: Mcgraw-hill Companies, 1998.

Degroot, Morris H., and Mark J. Schervish. *Probability and Statistics (3rd Edition)*. Toronto: Addison Wesley, 2001.

Degroot, Morris H. *Probability and Statistics (2nd Edition)*. Reading, Mass: Addison Wesley Publishing Company, 1986.

Dillman, Don A. *Mail and Internet Surveys: The Tailored Design Method 2007 Update with New Internet, Visual, and Mixed-Mode Guide*. New York, NY: Wiley, 2006.

Dunlop, Dorothy D., and Ajit C. Tamhane. *Statistics and Data Analysis: From Elementary to Intermediate*. Alexandria, VA: Prentice Hall, 1999.

Ehrenberg, Ronald G., and Robert S. Smith. *Modern Labor Economics: Theory and Policy (10th Edition)*. Toronto: Addison Wesley, 2008.

Fairlie, Robert. "The Absence of the African-American Owned Business: An Analysis of the Dynamics of Self-Employment." *Journal of Labor Economics* 17.1 (1999): 80–108.

Filer, Randall K. "Male-Female Wage Differences: The Importance of Compensating Differentials." *Industrial and Labor Relations Review* 38.3 (1985): 426–437.

Finkelstein, Michael 0. "Multiple Regression Models in Employment Discrimination Cases –The Problem of Imperfect Proxies." *Jurimetrics Journal of Law, Science and Technology* 31.1 (1990): 109.

Finkelstein, Michael O., and Bruce Levin. *Statistics for Lawyers (Springer Texts in Statistics)*. Berlin: Springer-Verlag Berlin And Heidelberg Gmbh & Co. K, 1990.

Fogel, Walter A. *Class pay discrimination and multiple regression proofs (University of California, Los Angeles, Institute of Industrial Relations)*. Nebraska: University Of California, Los Angeles, Institute Of Industrial Relations, 1986.

Fryer, G Roland, Levitt, D Steven, List, and A John. "Exploring the Impact of Financial Incentives on Stereotype Threat: Evidence from a Pilot Study." *The American Economic Review* 98.2 (2008): 370–375.

Fryer, Jr., Roland G. "An Economic Analysis of Color-Blind Affirmative Action." *Journal of Law, Economics, and Organization*. Abstract (2006): 1–44.

Fryer, R.G. *Belief flipping in a dynamic model of statistical discrimination [An article from: Journal of Public Economics]*. St. Louis : Elsevier, 2007.

Fryer, Roland G. *The causes and consequences of distinctively black names (NBER working paper series)*. New York: National Bureau Of Economic Research, 2003.

Fryer, Roland. "A Measure of Segregation Based on Social Interactions." *The Quarterly Journal of Economics* Vol. 122.2 (2007): 441–485.

Fryer, Ronald. "A Categorical Model of Cognition and Biased Decision-Making." *The B.E. Journal of Theoretical Economics:* Vol. 8 : Iss. 1 (2008): all.

Gilmartin, Kevin, and Srijati Ananda. "Inclusion of Potentially Tainted Variables in Regression Analysis for Employment Discrimination Cases." *Industrial Relations Law Journal* 13.1 (1991): 121–152.

Goldberger, Arthur. "Reverse Regression and Salary Discrimination." *The Journal of Human Resources* 19.3 (1984): 293–318.

Goldstein, Richard. "Two Types of Statistical Errors in Employment Discrimination Cases." *Jurimetrics Journal* 26.1 (1985): 32–47.

Gottschalk, Peter. "Changes in Job Instability and Insecurity Using Monthly Survey Data." *Journal of Labor Economics* 17.s4 (1999): S91–S126.

Greene, William H. "Reverse Regression: The Algebra of Discrimination." *Journal of Business and Economic Statistics* 2.2 (1984): 117–120.

Griffith, Rachel, and Andrew Neely. "Performance Pay and Managerial Experience in Multitask Teams: Evidence from within a Firm." *Journal of Labor Economics* 27.1 (2009): 49–82.

Grogger, J. "Does School Quality Explain the Recent Black/White Wage Trend?." *Journal of Labor Economics* 14.2 (1996): 231–53.

Heckman, James J. "Bias–Corrected Estimates of GED Returns." *Journal of Labor Economics* 24.3 (2006): 661–700.

Hellerstein, Judith, David Neumark, and Kenneth Troske. "Wages, Productivity, and Worker Characteristics: Evidence from Plant-Level Production Functions and Wage Equations." *Journal of Labor Economics* 17.3 (1999): 409–446.

Hirsch, Barry T. "Wages, Sorting on Skill, and the Racial Composition of Jobs." *Journal of Labor Economics* 22.1 (2004): 189–210.

Hollander, Myles, and Douglas A. Wolfe. *Nonparametric Statistical Methods, 2nd Edition.* New York: Wiley-Interscience, 1999.

Holzer, Harry. "Are Affirmative Action Hires Less Qualified? Evidence from Employer–Employee Data on New Hires." *Journal of Labor Economics* 17.3 (1999): 534–569.

Hosmer, Jr., Stanley Lemeshow, and David W. *Applied Logistic Regression (Wiley Series in Probability and Statistics - Applied Probability and Statistics Section).* New York: Wiley-Interscience, 2000.

Iarossi, Giuseppe. *The Power of Survey Design: A User's Guide for Managing Surveys, Interpreting Results, and Influencing Respondents.* New York: World Bank Publications, 2006.

Jacobsen, Joyce. *The Economics of Gender.* Malden, MA: Wiley-Blackwell, 2007.

Jerrell, Stephen B. "Declining Bias and Gender Wage Discrimination? A Meta-Regression Analysis." *Journal of Human Resources* 39.3 (2004): 828–838.

John S. Heywood, Dale Belman. "Sheepskin Effects in the Returns to Education: An Examination of Women and Minorities." *Review of Economics and Statistics* 73.4 (1991): 720–724.

John Ward, Robert Thornton. "The Economist in Tort Litigation." *Journal of Economic Perspectives* 13.2 (1999): 101–112.

Joseph, Michael E. "Evidence: Statistical Proof in Employment Discrimination Cases." *Oklahoma Law Review* 885.23 (1975): article.

Judge, George G., Douglas J. Miller, and Ron C. Mittelhammer. *Econometric Foundations Pack with CD-ROM.* New York: Cambridge University Press, 2000.

Kaye, David, and Hans Zeisel. *Prove It With Figures: Empirical Methods in Law and Litigation (Statistics for Social and Behavioral Sciences).* New York: Springer, 1997.

Kaye. *Statistical Methods in Discrimination Litigation (Statistics: a Series of Textbooks and Monogrphs).* Boca Raton: CRC, 1986.

Kaye. *Statistical Methods in Discrimination Litigation (Statistics: a Series of Textbooks and Monogrphs).* Boca Raton: CRC, 1986.

Keane, Michael P. "Eliminating Race Differences in School Attainment and Labor Market Success." *Journal of Labor Economics* 18.4 (2000): 614–652.

Keller, Gerald. *Statistics for Management and Economics*. New York: Duxbury Resource Center, 2002.

Keller, Gerald. *Statistics for Management and Economics*. New York: Duxbury Resource Center, 2002.

Kiefer, Nicholas M., and George R. Neumann. *Search Models and Applied Labor Economics*. New York: Cambridge University Press, 2006.

Klein, John P., and Melvin L. Moeschberger. *Survival Analysis*. New York: Springer, 2005.

Krueger, Anne. "The Economics of Discrimination." *Journal of Political Economy* 71.5 (1963): 481–486.

Kurzeja, Zoriana Dyschkant, and Edward Minieka. *Statistics for Business with Computer Applications*. New York City: South-Western Pub, 2000.

Lazear, Edward P. *Personnel Economics for Managers*. New York, NY: Wiley, 1998.

Le, Chap T. *Applied Categorical Data Analysis*. New York: Wiley-Interscience, 1998.

Leonard, Johnathan. "Women and Affirmative Action." *Journal of Economic Perspectives* 3.1 (1989): 61–75.

Leonard, Jonathan. "The Impact of Affirmative Action Regulation and Equal Employment Law on Black Employment." *Journal of Economic Perspectives* 4.4 (1990): 47–63.

Mann, Prem S. *Introductory Statistics*. New York, NY: Wiley, 2006.

McClave, James T. *Statistics*. london: Collier Macmillan, 1985.

Meier, Paul. "What Happened in Hazelwood: Statistics, Employment Discrimination, and the 80% Rule." *Journal of the American Bar Foundation* 9.1 (1986): 139–186.

Meyer, David Krueger Ruth. *Minitab Guide to Statistics, A*. Alexandria, VA: Prentice Hall, 1998.

Meyer, Paul L. *Introductory Probability and Statistical Applications*. Toronto: Addison Wesley, 1970.

Milkovich, George, and Jerry Newman. *Compensation*. New York: McGraw-Hill/Irwin, 2007.

Moss, Philip I. *Stories Employers Tell: Race, Skill, and Hiring in America*. New York: Russell Sage Foundation Publications, 2003.

Neal, D.A., and W.R. Johnson. "The Role of Premarket Factors in Black-White Wage Differences." *Journal of Political Economy* 104.5 (1996): 869–895.

Neumark, David. "Has Job Stability Declined Yet? New Evidence for the 1990s." *Journal of Labor Economics* 17.s4 (1999): S29–S64.

Neumark, David. *Sex discrimination in restaurant hiring: An audit study (NBER working paper series)*. New York: National Bureau Of Economic Research, 1995.

O'Neill, June. "The Role of Human Capital in Earnings Differences Between Black and White Men." *Journal of Economic Perspectives* 4.4 (1990): 25–45.

Oaxaca, Ronald. "On Discrimination and Decomposition of Wage Differentials." *Journal of Econometrics* 61.1 (1994): 5–21.

Olsen, R.N., and E.A. Sexton. "Gender Differences in the Returns to and the Acquisition of On-the-Job Training." *Industrial Relations* 35.1 (1996): 59–77.

Paetzold, Ramona L., and Steven L. Willborn. *The Statistics of Discrimination: Using Statistical Evidence in Discrimination Cases*. Colorado Springs: Shepards/Mcgraw-Hill, 1994.

Pascal, Anthony H. *Racial discrimination in economic life*. New York: Lexington Books, 1972.

Pergamit, Michael R., and Jonathan R. Veum. "What is a Promotion?" *Industrial and Labor Relations Review* 52.4 (1999): 581–601.

Peterson, unknown. "Binomial v. Hypergeometric Employee Selection Models." *720 F.2d 326 docket number No. 82–1831* Personnel Report. appeals from a judgment of the district court (1983): 1.

Phelps, Edmund S. "The Statistical Theory of Racism and Sexism." *American Economic Review* 62 (1972): 659–661.

Piette, Michael J., and Janet R. Thornton. "Cohort Analysis and the Determination of Economic Damages Resulting from Employment Discrimination." *Journal of Forensic Economics* 8.1 (1995): 69–80.

Piette, Michael J., and Paul F. White. "Approaches for Dealing with Small Sample Size in Employment Discrimination Litigation." *Journal of Forensic Economics* 12.1 (1999): 43–56.

Piette, Michael, and Douglas G. Sauer. "The Use of Multivariate Selection Models in Fair Employment Litigation." *Journal of Legal Economics* 2.3 (1992): 13–24.

Polacheck, Salomon W. "Earnings Over the Life Cycle: What do Human Capital Models Explain." *Scottish Journal of Political Economy* 42.3 (1995): 267–289.

Rodriguez, Daniel, and Madeline Zavodny. "Are Displaced Workers Now Finished at Age Forty?Federal Reserve Bank of Atlanta." *Economic Review* Second Qtr 2000 (2000): 1–47.

Rosén, Ǎsa. "Search, Bargaining, and Employer Discrimination." *Journal of Labor Economics* 21.4 (2003): 807–829.

S., Daniel, Rees, and Albert Hamermesh. *The Economics of Work and Pay*. New York: Harper & Row, 1984.

Sasaki, Masaru. "An Equilibrium Search Model with Coworker Discrimination." *Journal of Labor Economics* 17.2 (1999): 377–407.

Schuster, M., and C. S. Miller. "An Empirical Assessment of the Age Discrimination in Employment Act." *Labor Relations Review* 38.1 (1984): 64–74.

Shelton, Haskell. "Daubert v. Merrell Dow: Who Won?." *For The Defense* 35.11 (1993): 8–13.

Sheskin, David J. *Handbook of Parametric and Nonparametric Statistical Procedures, Fourth Edition*. Boca Raton: Chapman & Hall/CRC, 2007.

Sincich, James T., Terry; Benson, and P. George McClave. *A First Course in Business Statistics, 7th Edition*. Alexandria, VA: Prentice Hall, 1998.

Sincich, Terry L. *Business Statistics by Example (5th Edition) Part A and Part B*. Alexandria, VA: Prentice Hall, 1995.

Smith, James. "Affirmative Action and Labor Markets." *Journal of Labor Economics* 2.2 (1984): 269–298.

Van Ryzin, Robbins. *Introduction to statistics*. Chicago: Science Research Associates, 1975.

Welch, Finis R. "Black-White Differences in Returns to Schooling." *American Economic Review* 63.1 (1973): 893–907.

Zax, Jeffrey S. *Moving to the suburbs: Do relocating companies leave their black employees behind? (Discussion paper / Harvard Institute of Economic Research)*. Chicago: Harvard Institute Of Economic Research, Harvard University, 1991.

Ziliak, Stephen T. and Deirdre N. McCloskey. 2008. *The Cult of Statistical Significance: How the Standard Error Costs Us Jobs, Justice, and Lives* (Ann Arbor: University of Michigan Press).

Ziliak, Stephen T. and Deirdre N. McCloskey. "The Standard Error of Regressions." *Journal of Economic Literature* Vol. XXXIV (March 1996): 97–114.

Discrimination in Labor Markets. Princeton: Princeton Univ Pr, 1974.

Equal Employment Opportunity: Labor Market Discrimination and Public Policy (Sociology and Economics). New York: Aldine Transaction, 1994.

Fair lending analysis: A compendium of essays on the use of statistics. New York: American Bankers Association, 1995.

Labor Economics (International Library of Critical Writings in Economics). London: Edward Elgar Publishing, 1995.

Statistical Tables

The Standard Normal (z) Distribution Table

z	0	0.01	0.02	0.03	0.04	0.05	0.06	0.07	0.08	0.09
0.0	.0000	.0040	.0080	.0120	.0160	.0199	.0239	.0279	.0319	.0359
0.1	.0398	.0438	.0478	.0517	.0557	.0596	.0636	.0675	.0714	.0753
0.2	.0793	.0832	.0871	.0910	.0948	.0987	.1026	.1064	.1103	.1141
0.3	.1179	.1217	.1255	.1293	.1331	.1368	.1406	.1443	.1480	.1517
0.4	.1554	.1591	.1628	.1664	.1700	.1736	.1772	.1808	.1844	.1879
0.5	.1915	.1950	.1985	.2019	.2054	.2088	.2123	.2157	.2190	.2224
0.6	.2257	.2291	.2324	.2357	.2389	.2422	.2454	.2486	.2517	.2549
0.7	.2580	.2611	.2642	.2673	.2704	.2734	.2764	.2794	.2823	.2852
0.8	.2881	.2910	.2939	.2967	.2995	.3023	.3051	.3078	.3106	.3133
0.9	.3159	.3186	.3212	.3238	.3264	.3289	.3315	.3340	.3365	.3389
1.0	.3413	.3438	.3461	.3485	.3508	.3531	.3554	.3577	.3599	.3621
1.1	.3643	.3665	.3686	.3708	.3729	.3749	.3770	.3790	.3810	.3830
1.2	.3849	.3869	.3888	.3907	.3925	.3944	.3962	.3980	.3997	.4015
1.3	.4032	.4049	.4066	.4082	.4099	.4115	.4131	.4147	.4162	.4177
1.4	.4192	.4207	.4222	.4236	.4251	.4265	.4279	.4292	.4306	.4319
1.5	.4332	.4345	.4357	.4370	.4382	.4394	.4406	.4418	.4429	.4441
1.6	.4452	.4463	.4474	.4484	.4495	.4505	.4515	.4525	.4535	.4545
1.7	.4554	.4564	.4573	.4582	.4591	.4599	.4608	.4616	.4625	.4633
1.8	.4641	.4649	.4656	.4664	.4671	.4678	.4686	.4693	.4699	.4706
1.9	.4713	.4719	.4726	.4732	.4738	.4744	.4750	.4756	.4761	.4767
2.0	.4772	.4778	.4783	.4788	.4793	.4798	.4803	.4808	.4812	.4817
2.1	.4821	.4826	.4830	.4834	.4838	.4842	.4846	.4850	.4854	.4857
2.2	.4861	.4864	.4868	.4871	.4875	.4878	.4881	.4884	.4887	.4890
2.3	.4893	.4896	.4898	.4901	.4904	.4906	.4909	.4911	.4913	.4916
2.4	.4918	.4920	.4922	.4925	.4927	.4929	.4931	.4932	.4934	.4936
2.5	.4938	.4940	.4941	.4943	.4945	.4946	.4948	.4949	.4951	.4952
2.6	.4953	.4955	.4956	.4957	.4959	.4960	.4961	.4962	.4963	.4964
2.7	.4965	.4966	.4967	.4968	.4969	.4970	.4971	.4972	.4973	.4974
2.8	.4974	.4975	.4976	.4977	.4977	.4978	.4979	.4979	.4980	.4981
2.9	.4981	.4982	.4982	.4983	.4984	.4984	.4985	.4985	.4986	.4986
3.0	.4987	.4987	.4987	.4988	.4988	.4989	.4989	.4989	.4990	.4990

The figures in the table are the right-side probability of observing a z-statistic value as large as the one shown along the edges of the table. For example, the probability of a z-statistic of 2.05 is .4798. The number .4798 is found by the intersection of the 2.0 row and 0.05 column.

The t-Distribution Table

Degrees of Freedom	0.005	0.01	0.025	0.05	0.1	0.25
1	63.657	31.821	12.706	6.314	3.078	1.000
2	9.925	6.965	4.303	2.920	1.886	0.816
3	5.841	4.541	3.182	2.353	1.638	0.765
4	4.604	3.747	2.776	2.132	1.533	0.741
5	4.032	3.365	2.571	2.015	1.476	0.727
6	3.707	3.143	2.447	1.943	1.440	0.718
7	3.499	2.998	2.365	1.895	1.415	0.711
8	3.355	2.896	2.306	1.860	1.397	0.706
9	3.250	2.821	2.262	1.833	1.383	0.703
10	3.169	2.764	2.228	1.812	1.372	0.700
11	3.106	2.718	2.201	1.796	1.363	0.697
12	3.055	2.681	2.179	1.782	1.356	0.695
13	3.012	2.650	2.160	1.771	1.350	0.694
14	2.977	2.624	2.145	1.761	1.345	0.692
15	2.947	2.602	2.131	1.753	1.341	0.691
16	2.921	2.583	2.120	1.746	1.337	0.690
17	2.898	2.567	2.110	1.740	1.333	0.689
18	2.878	2.552	2.101	1.734	1.330	0.688
19	2.861	2.539	2.093	1.729	1.328	0.688
20	2.845	2.528	2.086	1.725	1.325	0.687
21	2.831	2.518	2.080	1.721	1.323	0.686
22	2.819	2.508	2.074	1.717	1.321	0.686
23	2.807	2.500	2.069	1.714	1.319	0.685
24	2.797	2.492	2.064	1.711	1.318	0.685
25	2.787	2.485	2.060	1.708	1.316	0.684
26	2.779	2.479	2.056	1.706	1.315	0.684
27	2.771	2.473	2.052	1.703	1.314	0.684
28	2.763	2.467	2.048	1.701	1.313	0.683
29	2.756	2.462	2.045	1.699	1.311	0.683
Large (.30) use z tables						

The table presents the critical values for the one-sided probability to the right of the figures shown at the top of the table. The probabilities are for a one-sided test. The table can be used for a two-sided statistical test by doubling the probabilities shown at the top of the table. For example, the one-sided 0.025 critical value or a 0.05 two-sided, for a t-distribution with 10 degrees of freedom is 2.228.

Chi-Square Distribution Table

Degrees of Freedom	0.99	0.95	0.9	0.1	0.05	0.025	0.01	0.005
1	0.000	0.004	0.016	2.706	3.841	5.024	6.635	7.879
2	0.020	0.103	0.211	4.605	5.991	7.378	9.210	10.597
3	0.115	0.352	0.584	6.251	7.815	9.348	11.345	12.838
4	0.297	0.711	1.064	7.779	9.488	11.143	13.277	14.860
5	0.554	1.145	1.610	9.236	11.070	12.833	15.086	16.750
6	0.872	1.635	2.204	10.645	12.592	14.449	16.812	18.548
7	1.239	2.167	2.833	12.017	14.067	16.013	18.475	20.278
8	1.646	2.733	3.490	13.362	15.507	17.535	20.090	21.955
9	2.088	3.325	4.168	14.684	16.919	19.023	21.666	23.589
10	2.558	3.940	4.865	15.987	18.307	20.483	23.209	25.188
11	3.053	4.575	5.578	17.275	19.675	21.920	24.725	26.757
12	3.571	5.226	6.304	18.549	21.026	23.337	26.217	28.300
13	4.107	5.892	7.042	19.812	22.362	24.736	27.688	29.819
14	4.660	6.571	7.790	21.064	23.685	26.119	29.141	31.319
15	5.229	7.261	8.547	22.307	24.996	27.488	30.578	32.801
16	5.812	7.962	9.312	23.542	26.296	28.845	32.000	34.267
17	6.408	8.672	10.085	24.769	27.587	30.191	33.409	35.718
18	7.015	9.390	10.865	25.989	28.869	31.526	34.805	37.156
19	7.633	10.117	11.651	27.204	30.144	32.852	36.191	38.582
20	8.260	10.851	12.443	28.412	31.410	34.170	37.566	39.997
21	8.897	11.591	13.240	29.615	32.671	35.479	38.932	41.401
22	9.542	12.338	14.041	30.813	33.924	36.781	40.289	42.796
23	10.196	13.091	14.848	32.007	35.172	38.076	41.638	44.181
24	10.856	13.848	15.659	33.196	36.415	39.364	42.980	45.559
25	11.524	14.611	16.473	34.382	37.652	40.646	44.314	46.928
26	12.198	15.379	17.292	35.563	38.885	41.923	45.642	48.290
27	12.879	16.151	18.114	36.741	40.113	43.195	46.963	49.645
28	13.565	16.928	18.939	37.916	41.337	44.461	48.278	50.993
29	14.256	17.708	19.768	39.087	42.557	45.722	49.588	52.336
30	14.953	18.493	20.599	40.256	43.773	46.979	50.892	53.672
40	22.164	26.509	29.051	51.805	55.758	59.342	63.691	66.766
50	29.707	34.764	37.689	63.167	67.505	71.420	76.154	79.490
60	37.485	43.188	46.459	74.397	79.082	83.298	88.379	91.952
70	45.442	51.739	55.329	85.527	90.531	95.023	100.425	104.215
80	53.540	60.391	64.278	96.578	101.879	106.629	112.329	116.321
90	61.754	69.126	73.291	107.565	113.145	118.136	124.116	128.299
100	70.065	77.929	82.358	118.498	124.342	129.561	135.807	140.169

The table presents the critical values for the probability to the right of the figures shown at the top of the table. For example, the 0.01 critical value for chi-square with 10 degrees of freedom is 23.209.

Binomial Probability Table

n	x	0.01	0.05	0.1	0.2	0.3	0.4	0.5	0.7	0.8	0.9
2	0	.9801	.9025	.8100	.6400	.4900	.3600	.2500	.0900	.0400	.0100
	1	.0198	.0950	.1800	.3200	.4200	.4800	.5000	.4200	.3200	.1800
	2	.0001	.0025	.0100	.0400	.0900	.1600	.2500	.4900	.6400	.8100
n	**x**	**0.01**	**0.05**	**0.1**	**0.2**	**0.3**	**0.4**	**0.5**	**0.7**	**0.8**	**0.9**
3	0	.9703	.8574	.7290	.5120	.3430	.2160	.1250	.0270	.0080	.0010
	1	.0294	.1354	.2430	.3840	.4410	.4320	.3750	.1890	.0960	.0270
	2	.0003	.0071	.0270	.0960	.1890	.2880	.3750	.4410	.3840	.2430
	3	.0000	.0001	.0010	.0080	.0270	.0640	.1250	.3430	.5120	.7290
n	**x**	**0.01**	**0.05**	**0.1**	**0.2**	**0.3**	**0.4**	**0.5**	**0.7**	**0.8**	**0.9**
4	0	.9606	.8145	.6561	.4096	.2401	.1296	.0625	.0081	.0016	.0001
	1	.0388	.1715	.2916	.4096	.4116	.3456	.2500	.0756	.0256	.0036
	2	.0006	.0135	.0486	.1536	.2646	.3456	.3750	.2646	.1536	.0486
	3	.0000	.0005	.0036	.0256	.0756	.1536	.2500	.4116	.4096	.2916
	4	.0000	.0000	.0001	.0016	.0081	.0256	.0625	.2401	.4096	.6561
n	**x**	**0.01**	**0.05**	**0.1**	**0.2**	**0.3**	**0.4**	**0.5**	**0.7**	**0.8**	**0.9**
5	0	.9510	.7738	.5905	.3277	.1681	.0778	.0313	.0024	.0003	.0000
	1	.0480	.2036	.3281	.4096	.3602	.2592	.1563	.0284	.0064	.0005
	2	.0010	.0214	.0729	.2048	.3087	.3456	.3125	.1323	.0512	.0081
	3	.0000	.0011	.0081	.0512	.1323	.2304	.3125	.3087	.2048	.0729
	4	.0000	.0000	.0005	.0064	.0284	.0768	.1563	.3602	.4096	.3281
	5	.0000	.0000	.0000	.0003	.0024	.0102	.0313	.1681	.3277	.5905
n	**x**	**0.01**	**0.05**	**0.1**	**0.2**	**0.3**	**0.4**	**0.5**	**0.7**	**0.8**	**0.9**
6	0	.9415	.7351	.5314	.2621	.1176	.0467	.0156	.0007	.0001	.0000
	1	.0571	.2321	.3543	.3932	.3025	.1866	.0938	.0102	.0015	.0001
	2	.0014	.0305	.0984	.2458	.3241	.3110	.2344	.0595	.0154	.0012
	3	.0000	.0021	.0146	.0819	.1852	.2765	.3125	.1852	.0819	.0146
	4	.0000	.0001	.0012	.0154	.0595	.1382	.2344	.3241	.2458	.0984
	5	.0000	.0000	.0001	.0015	.0102	.0369	.0938	.3025	.3932	.3543
	6	.0000	.0000	.0000	.0001	.0007	.0041	.0156	.1176	.2621	.5314
n	**x**	**0.01**	**0.05**	**0.1**	**0.2**	**0.3**	**0.4**	**0.5**	**0.7**	**0.8**	**0.9**
7	0	.9321	.6983	.4783	.2097	.0824	.0280	.0078	.0002	.0000	.0000
	1	.0659	.2573	.3720	.3670	.2471	.1306	.0547	.0036	.0004	.0000
	2	.0020	.0406	.1240	.2753	.3177	.2613	.1641	.0250	.0043	.0002
	3	.0000	.0036	.0230	.1147	.2269	.2903	.2734	.0972	.0287	.0026
	4	.0000	.0002	.0026	.0287	.0972	.1935	.2734	.2269	.1147	.0230
	5	.0000	.0000	.0002	.0043	.0250	.0774	.1641	.3177	.2753	.1240
	6	.0000	.0000	.0000	.0004	.0036	.0172	.0547	.2471	.3670	.3720
	7	.0000	.0000	.0000	.0000	.0002	.0016	.0078	.0824	.2097	.4783
n	**x**	**0.01**	**0.05**	**0.1**	**0.2**	**0.3**	**0.4**	**0.5**	**0.7**	**0.8**	**0.9**
8	0	.9227	.6634	.4305	.1678	.0576	.0168	.0039	.0001	.0000	.0000
	1	.0746	.2793	.3826	.3355	.1977	.0896	.0313	.0012	.0001	.0000
	2	.0026	.0515	.1488	.2936	.2965	.2090	.1094	.0100	.0011	.0000
	3	.0001	.0054	.0331	.1468	.2541	.2787	.2188	.0467	.0092	.0004
	4	.0000	.0004	.0046	.0459	.1361	.2322	.2734	.1361	.0459	.0046
	5	.0000	.0000	.0004	.0092	.0467	.1239	.2188	.2541	.1468	.0331
	6	.0000	.0000	.0000	.0011	.0100	.0413	.1094	.2965	.2936	.1488
	7	.0000	.0000	.0000	.0001	.0012	.0079	.0313	.1977	.3355	.3826
	8	.0000	.0000	.0000	.0000	.0001	.0007	.0039	.0576	.1678	.4305

n	x	0.01	0.05	0.1	0.2	0.3	0.4	0.5	0.7	0.8	0.9
9	0	.9135	.6302	.3874	.1342	.0404	.0101	.0020	.0000	.0000	.0000
	1	.0830	.2985	.3874	.3020	.1556	.0605	.0176	.0004	.0000	.0000
	2	.0034	.0629	.1722	.3020	.2668	.1612	.0703	.0039	.0003	.0000
	3	.0001	.0077	.0446	.1762	.2668	.2508	.1641	.0210	.0028	.0001
	4	.0000	.0006	.0074	.0661	.1715	.2508	.2461	.0735	.0165	.0008
	5	.0000	.0000	.0008	.0165	.0735	.1672	.2461	.1715	.0661	.0074
	6	.0000	.0000	.0001	.0028	.0210	.0743	.1641	.2668	.1762	.0446
	7	.0000	.0000	.0000	.0003	.0039	.0212	.0703	.2668	.3020	.1722
	8	.0000	.0000	.0000	.0000	.0004	.0035	.0176	.1556	.3020	.3874
	9	.0000	.0000	.0000	.0000	.0000	.0003	.0020	.0404	.1342	.3874

n	x	0.01	0.05	0.1	0.2	0.3	0.4	0.5	0.7	0.8	0.9
10	0	.9044	.5987	.3487	.1074	.0282	.0060	.0010	.0000	.0000	.0000
	1	.0914	.3151	.3874	.2684	.1211	.0403	.0098	.0001	.0000	.0000
	2	.0042	.0746	.1937	.3020	.2335	.1209	.0439	.0014	.0001	.0000
	3	.0001	.0105	.0574	.2013	.2668	.2150	.1172	.0090	.0008	.0000
	4	.0000	.0010	.0112	.0881	.2001	.2508	.2051	.0368	.0055	.0001
	5	.0000	.0001	.0015	.0264	.1029	.2007	.2461	.1029	.0264	.0015
	6	.0000	.0000	.0001	.0055	.0368	.1115	.2051	.2001	.0881	.0112
	7	.0000	.0000	.0000	.0008	.0090	.0425	.1172	.2668	.2013	.0574
	8	.0000	.0000	.0000	.0001	.0014	.0106	.0439	.2335	.3020	.1937
	9	.0000	.0000	.0000	.0000	.0001	.0016	.0098	.1211	.2684	.3874
	10	.0000	.0000	.0000	.0000	.0000	.0001	.0010	.0282	.1074	.3487

n	x	0.01	0.05	0.1	0.2	0.3	0.4	0.5	0.7	0.8	0.9
11	0	.8953	.5688	.3138	.0859	.0198	.0036	.0005	.0000	.0000	.0000
	1	.0995	.3293	.3835	.2362	.0932	.0266	.0054	.0000	.0000	.0000
	2	.0050	.0867	.2131	.2953	.1998	.0887	.0269	.0005	.0000	.0000
	3	.0002	.0137	.0710	.2215	.2568	.1774	.0806	.0037	.0002	.0000
	4	.0000	.0014	.0158	.1107	.2201	.2365	.1611	.0173	.0017	.0000
	5	.0000	.0001	.0025	.0388	.1321	.2207	.2256	.0566	.0097	.0003
	6	.0000	.0000	.0003	.0097	.0566	.1471	.2256	.1321	.0388	.0025
	7	.0000	.0000	.0000	.0017	.0173	.0701	.1611	.2201	.1107	.0158
	8	.0000	.0000	.0000	.0002	.0037	.0234	.0806	.2568	.2215	.0710
	9	.0000	.0000	.0000	.0000	.0005	.0052	.0269	.1998	.2953	.2131
	10	.0000	.0000	.0000	.0000	.0000	.0007	.0054	.0932	.2362	.3835
	11	.0000	.0000	.0000	.0000	.0000	.0000	.0005	.0198	.0859	.3138

n	x	0.01	0.05	0.1	0.2	0.3	0.4	0.5	0.7	0.8	0.9
12	0	.8864	.5404	.2824	.0687	.0138	.0022	.0002	.0000	.0000	.0000
	1	.1074	.3413	.3766	.2062	.0712	.0174	.0029	.0000	.0000	.0000
	2	.0060	.0988	.2301	.2835	.1678	.0639	.0161	.0002	.0000	.0000
	3	.0002	.0173	.0852	.2362	.2397	.1419	.0537	.0015	.0001	.0000
	4	.0000	.0021	.0213	.1329	.2311	.2128	.1208	.0078	.0005	.0000
	5	.0000	.0002	.0038	.0532	.1585	.2270	.1934	.0291	.0033	.0000
	6	.0000	.0000	.0005	.0155	.0792	.1766	.2256	.0792	.0155	.0005
	7	.0000	.0000	.0000	.0033	.0291	.1009	.1934	.1585	.0532	.0038
	8	.0000	.0000	.0000	.0005	.0078	.0420	.1208	.2311	.1329	.0213
	9	.0000	.0000	.0000	.0001	.0015	.0125	.0537	.2397	.2362	.0852
	10	.0000	.0000	.0000	.0000	.0002	.0025	.0161	.1678	.2835	.2301
	11	.0000	.0000	.0000	.0000	.0000	.0003	.0029	.0712	.2062	.3766
	12	.0000	.0000	.0000	.0000	.0000	.0000	.0002	.0138	.0687	.2824

Index